Robert Schumann's Leipzig Chamber Works

Robert Schumann's Leipzig Chamber Works

Music in the Great Stream of Time

JULIE HEDGES BROWN

OXFORD
UNIVERSITY PRESS

Oxford University Press is a department of the University of Oxford.
It furthers the University's objective of excellence in research, scholarship,
and education by publishing worldwide. Oxford is a registered trade mark of
Oxford University Press in the UK and in certain other countries.

Published in the United States of America by Oxford University Press
198 Madison Avenue, New York, NY 10016, United States of America.

© Oxford University Press 2024

All rights reserved. No part of this publication may be reproduced, stored in a retrieval system,
or transmitted, in any form or by any means, without the prior permission in writing of Oxford
University Press, or as expressly permitted by law, by license or under terms agreed with the
appropriate reprographics rights organization. Inquiries concerning reproduction outside the scope
of the above should be sent to the Rights Department, Oxford University Press, at the address above.

You must not circulate this work in any other form, and you must
impose this same condition on any acquirer.

Library of Congress Cataloging-in-Publication Data
Names: Brown, Julie Hedges, author.
Title: Robert Schumann's Leipzig chamber works / Julie Hedges Brown.
Description: New York : Oxford University Press, 2024. |
Includes bibliographical references and index. |
Identifiers: LCCN 2024026074 (print) | LCCN 2024026075 (ebook) |
ISBN 9780197749463 (hardback) | ISBN 9780197749487 (epub)
Subjects: LCSH: Schumann, Robert, 1810–1856. Chamber music. |
Schumann, Robert, 1810–1856—Criticism and interpretation. |
Chamber music—19th century—History and criticism.
Classification: LCC ML410.S4 B85 2024 (print) | LCC ML410.S4 (ebook) |
DDC 785.0092—dc23/eng/20240614
LC record available at https://lccn.loc.gov/2024026074
LC ebook record available at https://lccn.loc.gov/2024026075

DOI: 10.1093/9780197749494.001.0001

Printed by Integrated Books International, United States of America

For Steve and Maddie

Contents

List of Figures   ix
List of Musical Examples   xi
Acknowledgments   xiii
List of Abbreviations   xvii

1. Schumann in Time: Introduction   1
2. Competing Tonics   29
3. Nested Forms   69
4. Dancing to Schumann   106
5. Listening in London   142
6. Epilogue   183

Bibliography   189
Index   201

Figures

2.1. Formal overview of Schumann's String Quartet, Op. 41, No. 1   37

2.2. Formal overview of Beethoven's Cello Sonata in C Major, Op. 102, No. 1   48

2.3. Schumann, Piano Quintet in E-flat Major, Op. 44: formal overview of the finale, part I (mm. 1–220)   50

2.4. Schumann, String Quartet in A Major, Op. 41, No. 3: formal overview of the finale   53

2.5. Schumann, Piano Quintet in E-flat Major, Op. 44, finale: symmetrical pitch structures around G minor and E-flat major   54

2.6. Schumann, Piano Quintet in E-flat Major, Op. 44: formal overview of the finale, part II (doubly oriented coda)   56

3.1. Schumann, String Quartet in A Minor, Op. 41, No. 1: formal overview of the scherzo movement   88

3.2. Schumann, String Quartet in F Major, Op. 41, No. 2: formal overview of the slow movement   93

4.1. Hans van Manen rehearsing with Anthony Dowell in *Four Schumann Pieces*, 1975. Photograph by Anthony Crickmay. Image supplied by the Hans van Manen Foundation at the Dutch National Opera and Ballet. © Victoria and Albert Museum, London. Used with permission.   109

4.2. Anthony Dowell in front of the original backdrop designed by Jean-Paul Vroom for *Four Schumann Pieces* (pose beginning Piece 1). Photograph by Anthony Crickmay (cropped). Lillie F. Rosen, *Anthony Dowell*. Dance Horizons Spotlight Series. [Brooklyn]: Dance Horizons, 1976, 10–11. © Victoria and Albert Museum, London. Used with permission.   111

4.3. Schumann, String Quartet in A Major, Op. 41, No. 3: formal overview of the Adagio, showing placement of duets against main musical sections. Timings taken from the 1978 performance cited in the Note on Performance Sources at the end of the chapter.   122

4.4. Rudolf Nureyev (left) and Henny Jurriëns in a pose from the Adagio of *Four Schumann Pieces*. Performance by the Dutch National Ballet in 1976. Photograph by Jorge Fatauros and supplied by the Hans van Manen Foundation at the Dutch National Opera and Ballet. © Jorge Fatauros. Used with permission.   126

5.1. Front cover of *The Graphic*, April 16, 1887. "Presentation to Mr. Arthur Chappell, at St. James's Hall, after the Thousandth Popular Concert."   162

Music Examples

2.1. Comparison of Schumann's 1828 song "Hirtenknabe" with the fourth number from the *Intermezzi*, Op. 4
    (a) "Hirtenknabe"
    (b) Fourth number from the Op. 4 *Intermezzi*   31

2.2. Schumann, String Quartet in A Minor, Op. 41, No. 1: the slow introduction, link, and beginning of the F-major sonata form (mm. 1–37)   38

2.3. Schumann, String Quartet in A minor, Op. 41, No. 1, finale
    (a) Opening of the movement (mm. 1–28)
    (b) Transformation of the Neapolitan sixth in A minor into dominant harmony in C major (reduction)   42

2.4. Schumann, Piano Quintet in E-flat Major, Op. 44, finale: beginning of the opening theme (mm. 1–12)   51

2.5. Schumann, Piano Quintet in E-flat Major, Op. 44: comparison of themes in the slow movement
    (a) Opening of the funeral march theme (mm. 1–2)
    (b) Opening of the *Agitato* theme (mm. 92–93)   58

2.6. Schumann, Piano Quintet in E-flat Major, Op. 44: comparison of harmonic structure in E-flat major themes
    (a) First movement, opening theme (mm. 1–3; reduction)
    (b) Third movement, opening scherzo theme (mm. 1–8; reduction)
    (c) Last movement, idea "B" (mm. 22–25; piano part)   60

2.7. Schumann, Piano Quintet in E-flat Major, Op. 44: reincarnations of the first movement's main theme, with the subdominant inflection expunged
    (a) Abstracted transformation
    (b) First movement, varied return of the main theme (mm. 17–21; reduction)
    (c) Finale—climactic conclusion of the second fugato (mm. 355–71; reduction)   62

3.1. Comparison of themes by Marschner and Schumann
    (a) Heinrich Marschner, Piano Trio in G Minor, Op. 111: opening of the scherzo movement (piano part, mm. 1–24)
    (b) Schumann, String Quartet in A Minor, Op. 41, No. 1: opening of the scherzo movement (mm. 1–13)
    (c) Schumann, *Fünf Lieder und Gesänge*, Op. 127, Song 3 (mm. 3–6); originally Song 15 of *Dichterliebe*, Op. 48   72

3.2. Clara Schumann, *Quatre pièces caractéristiques*, Op. 5: the opening of
No. 1, "Impromptu. Le Sabbat" (mm. 1–14); also published independently
as "Hexentanz," Op. 5a 75

3.3. Felix Mendelssohn, Octet in E-flat Major, Op. 20, Scherzo: gallop motive in
the secondary theme (mm. 25–29) 80

3.4. Schumann, String Quartet in A Minor, Op. 41, No. 1, Scherzo: opening of
the Intermezzo (mm. 79–88) 81

3.5. Comparison of themes by Schumann and Beethoven
    (a) Schumann, String Quartet in F-Major, Op. 1, No. 2: opening of
        the slow movement (Theme 1, mm. 1–4)
    (b) Beethoven, String Quartet in E-flat Major, Op. 127: opening of the
        slow movement (mm. 1–4) 91

3.6. Schumann, String Quartet in F Major, Op. 41, No. 2, slow
movement: opening of Theme 2 (mm. 17–19) 94

3.7. Schumann, String Quartet in F Major, Op. 41, No. 2, slow
movement: opening of Theme 3, showing hemiola in an implied simple
meter (mm. 65–68) 95

3.8. Schumann, *Albumblätter*, Op. 124: opening of No. 13, Larghetto (mm. 1–4) 96

3.9. Schumann, String Quartet in F Major, Op. 41, No. 2: return of Theme 1
near end (mm. 89–91) 101

4.1. Schumann, String Quartet in A Major, Op. 41, No. 3: the opening theme of
the Adagio (mm. 1–19) 118

4.2. Schumann, String Quartet in A Major, Op. 41, No. 3: thematic similarity
between the Adagio's Coda and B materials
    (a) The coda (mm. 94–105)
    (b) The opening phrase of B^1 (mm. 19–24) 130

Acknowledgments

Academic research in the arts and humanities is often a solitary pursuit, more given to individual than collective authorship, and a pursuit to which I have committed innumerable happy hours. At the same time, I have had the pleasure of interacting with a variety of individuals who have aided my work in numerous ways. This book could not have arisen without their support, nor without the assistance of various organizations.

The idea for this book arose with dance-related research intended for a single article. The illuminating response of one choreographer to a string quartet by Robert Schumann—which eventually became the subject of Chapter 4—led me to think more about the influence of the composer and his music in different times, places, and disciplines. I would like to thank this choreographer for generously granting me an interview, and the Hans van Manen Foundation for facilitating access. Van Manen's feedback proved crucial in determining the subsequent direction of my chapter. Special thanks are due to Rachel Beaujean, the Associate Director of the Dutch National Opera and Ballet, and Henrik Lillin, the archivist for this organization; they provided invaluable help in obtaining relevant images and finding copyright holders of other images, including Jorge Fatauros, who allowed me to reproduce one of his photographs. At the Victoria and Albert Museum in London, Olivia Stroud generously allowed me to use sources from the Anthony Crickmay collection. My thanks also to staff at the New York Public Library–Jerome Robbins Dance Division, the National Ballet of Canada, the London Royal Ballet, and the BBC Written Archives, who provided materials or offered helpful feedback on other dance-related sources. I would also like to acknowledge the late Nando Schellen—former Managing Director and Associate General Director of Netherlands Opera, and an eventual colleague of mine—for sharing his own stories of Van Manen and the performing arts scene in Amsterdam during the 1970s and 1980s. Such exchanges were a happy coincidence with my own research.

Other individuals have provided materials to me or feedback on various portions of this book, including Janet Ritterman (who sent me a copy of her 1996 essay, an important resource for my work on Chapter 5);

Jonathan Bellman (who early on offered advice on material that found its way into Chapter 2); David Koerner and the late Tom Sheeley (for sharing their experiences of playing music in the Grand Canyon, the subject of the Epilogue); Andrew Smith (for permission to use the photograph on the book cover, taken during a shared and never-to-be-forgotten backpacking trip in the Grand Canyon); Cynthia Ahlers (for advice on choreographic matters in Chapter 4); Julie Pedneault-Deslauriers and Alexander Stefaniak (for graciously reading the entire book manuscript); Shannon Spark (who prepared all of the musical examples); and numerous conference-attending folks who offered feedback, ideas, and encouragement on a variety of papers presenting earlier stages of my work. I would especially like to thank the external reviewers of the book proposal, sample chapters, and subsequent manuscript. Their comments helped me to refine my arguments and analyses; any shortcomings in the final product are my own. Thanks also to Norm Hirschy, Laura Santo, and other staff at Oxford University Press, for guiding this book through the process of initial review to final production; I cannot overstate my appreciation for their support. I am also grateful to the University of California Press, and to Oxford University Press, for permission to provide updated versions of segments that appeared in two earlier publications. Finally, I offer heartfelt gratitude for a publication subvention from the John Daverio and General Fund of the American Musicological Society, supported in part by the National Endowment for the Humanities and the Andrew W. Mellon Foundation.

I have benefited greatly from scholars who have built impressive infrastructures to support music research, Schumann-related and otherwise. I would like to acknowledge those who maintain and continue to expand the invaluable online content of RIPM (*Répertoire international de la presse musicale*); when a hyperlink failed to work, or when a historical concert review or essay was unavailable or incorrectly indexed, their staff proved ever responsive. I would also like to express deep gratitude to the numerous scholars involved in producing the new edition of Schumann's complete works (under the general leadership of Akio Mayeda and Klaus Wolfgang Niemöller), accompanied by the excellent thematic catalogue by Margit L. McCorkle; the new edition of Robert and Clara Schumann's complete correspondence (overseen by Thomas Synofzik and Michael Heinemann); and earlier critical editions of Schumann's diaries and household books (compiled by Georg Eismann and Gerd Nauhaus). These sources are indispensable foundations on which to build new academic and interpretive work, and the people behind them are true Schumann lovers. So too are other scholars, both past and present, whose contributions have been similarly integral to my scholarship.

I remain ever indebted to the librarians at my home institution, Northern Arizona University; they have generously and patiently aided my work by facilitating access to a variety of sources, arcane and otherwise. I am also grateful to the Office of the Vice President for Research, which provided support for various summer research grants. I would also like to express appreciation to Todd Sullivan and Eric Lenz, past and present directors of the Kitt School of Music. They and other colleagues understand the difficulties of balancing teaching responsibilities with scholarly pursuits, and I thank them for their interest and confidence in my work.

I am grateful to my parents, Ann and Ward Hedges, who instilled within me the importance of education and hard work and who provided models for living an ethical life. To Maddie—my vibrant, intelligent, funny, sensitive, and beautiful daughter—I give thanks for generating moments of respite and laughter and for showing tolerance for a project that took longer than planned. Finally, I express deep gratitude to the beloved partner who has accompanied me through my academic and personal lives for many years. Steve and I met as doctoral students, and he witnessed the beginnings of my scholarly investment in all-things-Schumann. A fellow music academic, he has enriched my understanding of analytical and theoretical issues; served as a long-standing (and long-suffering) sounding board; and provided help with a multitude of other matters large and small. He inspires me with his intellect, musicianship, and sweetness of being.

Abbreviations

BNF
: Robert Schumann. *Robert Schumanns Briefe: Neue Folge*. 2nd ed. Edited by F. Gustav Jansen. Leipzig: Breitkopf & Härtel, 1904.

Briefedition
: Clara and Robert Schumann. *Schumann Briefedition*. Edited by the Robert-Schumann-Haus, Zwickau, the Institute für Musikwissenschaft der Hochschule für Musik Carl Marie von Weber, Dresden, and the Robert-Schumann-Forschungsstelle, Düsseldorf, with direction from Thomas Synofzik and Michael Heinemann. Cologne: Dohr, 2008–.

CC
: Clara and Robert Schumann. *The Complete Correspondence of Clara and Robert Schumann*. Edited by Eva Weissweiler with Susanna Ludwig, and translated by Hildegard Fritsch and Ronald L. Crawford. 3 vols. New York: Peter Lang, 1994–1996.

CS
: Berthold Litzmann. *Clara Schumann: Ein Künstlerleben nach Tagebüchern und Briefen*. 3 vols. Leipzig: Breitkopf & Härtel, 1902–1908.

GS
: Robert Schumann. *Gesammelte Schriften über Musik und Musiker*. 5th ed. Edited by Martin Kreisig. 2 vols. Leipzig: Breitkopf & Härtel, 1914.

Tb
: Robert Schuman. *Tagebücher*. Vol. 1. Edited by Georg Eismann Leipzig: VEB Deutscher Verlag für Musik, 1971.
Clara and Robert Schumann. *Tagebücher*. Vol. 2. Edited by Gerd Nauhaus. Leipzig: VEB Deutscher Verlag für Musik, 1987.
Robert Schuman. *Tagebücher*. Vol. 3 (*Haushaltbücher I* and *II*). Edited by Gerd Nauhaus. Leipzig: VEB Deutscher Verlag für Musik, 1982.

All translations are my own unless otherwise indicated.

1
Schumann in Time

Introduction

Robert Schumann (1810–1856) saw himself and his contemporaries as heirs of a venerable, largely Austro-German tradition whose value lay not just in the artworks of that past, but also in its ability to nurture present and future accomplishments. This outlook held true even for modern composers whose indebtedness to the past seemed less clear. As Schumann noted in 1838, "By no means did the new, so-called romantic school grow out of thin air; everything has its good foundation." More than a decade later, Schumann put it more baldly to Franz Liszt: "No one is *wholly original*," a telling response to a representative of the then budding "New" German School.[1] This perspective explains the importance that Schumann continually put on studying one's inherited musical traditions and the significant "individualities" who cultivated them. Nevertheless, mere imitation of past models, while helpful for training and study, risked one becoming "a mannerist and a Philistine." Thus Schumann always insisted that an artist "lead me a step further in the spiritual realm of art and provide poetic depth and novelty everywhere."[2]

Schumann's historical consciousness was in keeping with a larger cultural transformation in the nineteenth century, one that drew the past into various niches of the musical world. This period saw the development of various musical canons, with certain bodies of works and their composers assuming heightened cultural prestige for both contemporary musicians and audiences. Older esteemed works increasingly came to offer guideposts for younger composers, provide sources of programming for conductors and performers, and serve as touchstones of musical taste for people of various classes.[3] Canonic repertories evolved in various genres like song and opera, but first emerged in the sphere of instrumental music (solo, chamber, and symphonic), with concert series in Berlin, Vienna, and Leipzig leading the way in developing a culture of so-called serious music making, one centered initially on the "classical" works of Haydn, Mozart, and Beethoven, but eventually embracing more distant composers like J. S. Bach and others.[4]

Alongside concertizing practices, publications of various types helped to solidify the authority of the past: new biographies (Forkel on Bach, Carpani on Haydn, Niemetschek and Nissen on Mozart, among others); theoretical writings (e.g., *Formenlehre*-type discussions of Mozart and Beethoven's music by Momigny and A. B. Marx); pedagogical works (those by Czerny and Reicha, for instance, favored instrumental repertory from the Viennese classical tradition); and musical criticism (E. T. A. Hoffmann's 1813 essay "Beethoven's Instrumental Music," for example, proved influential in its elevation of instrumental genres over vocal ones).[5] The cultural impact of such writings, and of new approaches to programming, nevertheless took time to exert their force. As William Weber writes, "Endowing older works with canonic authority took two generations to accomplish."[6] Thus the canonic tradition only became an engrained, widespread reality in the second half of the nineteenth century. In the broader musical world of Schumann's time, the canonic tradition was still a developing concept, "neither monolithic nor static," as Alexander Stefaniak describes it, but rather "an evolving multifaceted part of the ... musical landscape."[7] In Schumann's own conception of the past, inherited artistic traditions were valuable contributions, but they served not merely as artifacts but as points of departure for new creative outcomes. "The future," he once quipped, "should be a higher echo of the past."[8]

As one who cofounded an innovative journal—the *Neue Zeitschrift für Musik*—and edited it for some ten years (1834–1844), Schumann had extensive opportunities for evaluating new works against his dynamic view of history. His reviews, however, make clear an open-mindedness about different pathways for compositional invention, what Edvard Grieg many years later called "one of the most beautiful memorials to Schumann."[9] Schumann briefly cited this receptive quality in his 1840 petition (quickly granted) for an honorary doctorate from the University of Jena. "I have sought to further the talents of the present time," he notes, "whether they are based on the past (like Mendelssohn to some extent) or have devised something unique and new (like Chopin, for instance)." This he did while remaining "conscious of my genuine veneration for the traditional, the old," a revealing statement from someone who had just spent a decade composing piano music known then and now for its experimentalism.[10] For Schumann, artists who built new monuments on historical roots, whether obvious or not, could achieve certain important goals. First, they assured a reinvigorated life for older models and principles, rather than a dusty preservation of them. As

Schumann noted in review of a sonata by F. A. Lecerf, which was "honest" but old-fashioned, "the sonata style of 1790 is not that of 1840; the demands on form and content have everywhere increased." Hence the importance of expressively reworking traditional models, which in turn could attain a second goal, longevity "in the great stream of time."[11] If the Lecerf sonata came up short in this regard (Schumann predicted that it would exist only "for a few moments" in this temporal stream), examples by Mendelssohn and Schubert, for instance, did not; they represented "the most beautiful things in the artistic genre of piano music since Beethoven, Weber, Hummel and Moscheles," blending "intellect and poetry" in a way that also justified their "resonating arc into the future."[12] In other words, significant artworks reveal a mutually interdependent relationship between the past, present, and future, an intertwining of time spans that Schumann hoped his own compositions would exemplify.

This book engages with things temporally "in the middle." First and foremost, it explores a repertory that stands centrally within Schumann's compositional career, namely, the multi-movement chamber works written during his time in Leipzig and representing some of his most well-known and most performed works in the medium. This repertory encompasses the three Op. 41 String Quartets (in A minor, F major, and A major, respectively), the Op. 44 Piano Quintet in E-flat Major, and the Op. 47 Piano Quartet in E-flat Major, all composed in the space of seven fruitful months in the year 1842.[13] In highlighting Schumann's "chamber music year" (as historians have dubbed it), this volume differs from a substantial portion of Schumannian scholarship, which has focused on the first and last parts of Schumann's compositional career. His early works—the piano music of the 1830s and the songs of 1840—have received an almost overwhelming amount of scholarly attention, likely because of their more overt musical experimentation, compelling literary and programmatic ties, and clearer biographical resonances. At the other end of the spectrum are Schumann's late works (especially those from the 1850s), which in the past decades have justly received increasing focus as scholars reassess them more on their own terms than in light of Schumann's later deteriorating mental condition.[14] Despite fine recent work done on various orchestral works, dramatic compositions, and other pieces, the music that falls in between the bookends of Schumann's career deserves more attention, including the Leipzig chamber repertory. For one, given its proximity to Schumann's earlier output, the 1842 repertory provides a window through which to understand its relationship to his youthful songs and piano music; indeed, unlike many appraisals, I will argue that Schumann's earlier music proved foundational for—rather than antithetical to—his efforts to successfully compose in the larger chamber genres. For another, the 1842 repertory illuminates Schumann's response to the mainly Austro-German past that loomed large in his consciousness and that of his contemporaries. By adopting genres, forms, and techniques from this past, Schumann not only positioned himself within this venerated tradition, he also affirmed its value for modern composers through what I will show was a compelling rethinking of its inherited models. If the 1842 works occupy a place "in the great stream of time" that puts them in dialogue with various pasts (including Schumann's own), they also elicited significant commentary from listeners in his day and beyond. Many saw this repertory and other adjacent works as signaling a break from his earlier compositional interests and tendencies, a framing that Schumann himself bemoaned. The Leipzig chamber works have also experienced colorful afterlives in different times and places, ones that provide new insights into whether this music represents a more conservative or progressive mindset for the composer. Sampling some of these afterlives will illuminate a telling array of values held around these works by different listeners, be they critics, audiences, performers, or even figures in disciplines outside of music. These values in turn reveal much about the cultural environments in which these works have been performed, the actors involved in facilitating—or sometimes hindering—their reproduction, and the aesthetic positions that underpin such activities. In all, the Leipzig chamber repertory brings with it a variety of reception stories from both composer- and listener-oriented perspectives that have yet to be told.

Compositional Aspirations

For Schumann himself, the 1842 chamber works held a special place in his progression as a composer. Earlier efforts in the medium had left mostly unfinished works. Although Schumann largely completed a piano quartet in C minor as a teenager, two other piano quartets begun around the same time remained incomplete, and an Allegro for solo instrument and piano was similarly abandoned. In the later 1830s, Schumann either began sketching, or considered writing, a piano quintet, a trio, and several string quartets, all of which came to nothing. Thus the 1842 repertory serves as a turning point because it comprises a series of completed works in the chamber medium.[15]

Schumann also valued chamber music because its sparer textures—so often performed "face to face" in private settings, as he noted in an 1842 review—offered little cover for weak writing. Hence, it was through "chamber music, with few instruments" that a "musician displays his real powers."[16] If Schumann's powers seemed lacking before, the Leipzig works indicate more confidence in the medium. Notable is the fairly rapid speed with which Schumann composed them. Each string quartet took about a week for sketching and about five days for scoring, with the A-minor and F-major quartets appearing in June 1842 and the A-major quartet in July. Further polishing of the quartets continued into the fall, even as Schumann composed the piano quintet from late September to mid-October, and the piano quartet from late October to late November. The Leipzig chamber repertory also brought Schumann considerable satisfaction, especially the string quartets, coming as they did from the hand of a pianist-composer. In offering their sale to Breitkopf & Härtel in October 1842, Schumann remarked: "It would not become me to say more about [them]. But rest assured that I have spared no effort to produce something quite decent, indeed, sometimes I think my best." Five years later, his opinion remained unchanged: "I still consider them the best work of my earlier period."[17] Schumann's confidence also manifested itself in his desire to get the Leipzig chamber repertory performed and published, in some cases in both parts and score form. Private performances of all five works occurred in 1842, and public to semi-public performances began with the A-minor string quartet and the piano quintet in January 1843. The parts of the string quartets and piano quintet were also published in time to be presented as birthday gifts to their respective dedicatees: Felix Mendelssohn in February 1843, and his spouse Clara Schumann (née Wieck) in September of the same year. (As a concert pianist, Clara was herself one of the most important members of Robert's professional circle.)[18] From the outset, Schumann wanted the string quartets to appear in score format as well, an edition that did not materialize until after Mendelssohn's untimely death in 1847. The event prompted Schumann to take up the issue once again, arguing the merits of score format from different perspectives. First, it presents "to the world" a cherished work "in its original form." Second, it facilitates understanding of the work since "it is rare to find four musicians who together, without a score, are able to understand the difficult combinations" found in quartet writing. Third, musical understanding will then allow players to "more easily do justice to the composer."[19] Schumann's request was successful, and the scores of all three quartets appeared in time to be presented as an 1848 Christmas gift to Ferdinand David, concertmaster of the Leipzig Gewandhaus orchestra and the person who led the first private and some of the first public performances of the quartets. The latter responded by expressing his hope for more such music; the Op. 41 set, however, remained Schumann's sole contribution to the genre.[20]

Schumann's Leipzig chamber repertory also proved important in his career for another reason. Together with the orchestral works of 1841 (the Symphony in B-flat Major, Op. 38, and the first version of the D-Minor Symphony, Op. 120, among other orchestral music), the multi-movement chamber works manifested a new stylistic orientation for Schumann, one that also expanded his reputation. In earlier years, he had concentrated his efforts in more intimate mediums: songs in 1840 (the year he married Clara), and in the previous decade numerous works for solo piano. As Anthony Newcomb has remarked, however, Schumann's piano output made him a "renegade as far as the market for piano music in the 1830s was concerned."[21] Instead of works for the dilettante, or showpieces based on new tunes or popular operatic melodies (rondos, variations, fantasies—the staples of piano concerts), Schumann wrote sets of miniatures, along with several sonatas. In the former, the pieces were often aphoristic, even fragmentary in nature, and both revealed bold experiments in form and tonal procedure. The musical surface seemed frequently disjointed, presenting rapid contrasts of character and sudden rhythmic or harmonic shifts. Moreover, evocative titles and cryptic mottos gave the appearance of secret programs. Such difficulties were routinely described by critics as bizarre, mystical, and eccentric.[22] Furthermore, as one contemporary noted, Schumann's music could be "extremely difficult [to play], not very rewarding [for the performer], and far removed from the trappings of virtuosity."[23] By turning in the early 1840s toward more traditional, large-scale genres, Schumann helped to popularize his music while also making his name more widely known. Indeed, it was works like the 1841 Symphony in B-flat, the 1842 Piano Quintet, and the 1843 oratorio *Das Paradies und die Peri* that especially solidified Schumann's reputation as a composer of consequence.

In Schumann's eyes, the shift toward larger genres with clearer historical roots also represented a progressive turn. He certainly acknowledged the value of small-scale composition, as his numerous reviews of songs and piano miniatures make clear. One could, for instance, "distinguish the higher artist from a middling one" by observing how even their "smallest works" are treated "with love and care."[24] Nevertheless, Schumann saw such works as only a "kind of preparatory study for the more important business of writing sonatas, concertos, and symphonies," as Leon Plantinga has remarked, and thus frequently "warn[ed] against a prolonged preoccupation with these small forms."[25] In 1837, for example, Schumann lamented that Chopin was not creating "any works at all of larger dimensions." By 1841 he feared that Chopin, while "always new and inventive, . . . won't ascend to a level higher than what he has already achieved" because "his effectiveness is limited to the smaller sphere of piano music."[26] Schumann expressed similar sentiments in reviews of music by other talented composers,[27] but he also took them to heart. Indeed, around the time of his earliest string quartet attempts (1838–1839), Schumann expressed growing frustration with the piano and its limits. In an 1838 letter to Clara, Robert indicated that "I myself am looking forward to the quartets; the piano is becoming too narrow for me" (a sentiment echoed by Clara). A year later, he wrote to Heinrich Dorn that "if only I could throw away my newspaper completely and live as an artist of music, . . . then there will be only my symphonies to publish and hear. Often I would like to crush the piano: it is becoming too limited for my thoughts."[28] By turning toward large-scale genres and forms in the early 1840s, Schumann found bigger canvases on which to work out his ideas. He also found a clearer way to express his relationship with the Austro-German tradition that he so admired.

It is significant that Schumann initiated his so-called chamber music year by composing a set of string quartets. In so doing, he overtly aligned himself with an instrumental tradition for which Haydn, Mozart, and Beethoven had set rigorous standards. (Of the string quartet, Schumann remarked in 1838 that "its rigor was its very beauty.")[29] This moment had come with much preparation. From 1836 on, Schumann had cultivated greater awareness of the genre. He regularly attended—even sponsored—rehearsals of a quartet led by Ferdinand David during 1836–1838. Along with contemporary music, the group played works by notable predecessors, including (unusually for the time) Beethoven's late string quartets. This experience seems to have prompted not only Schumann's first attempts in this genre, but also an 1838 series of essays ("Quartettmorgen" or Quartet Morning) evaluating recent contributions in this genre, both published and unpublished. He also began a prolonged study of Beethoven's late quartets, offering unusual praise for a repertory then considered strange and inaccessible.[30] Beginning in April 1842, Schumann again immersed himself in the study of string quartets by the Viennese triumvirate, building knowledge and confidence for when he began writing his own in early June.[31]

Schumann's composition of string quartets in 1842 is also striking because on certain fronts the genre appeared to have received less cultivation after Beethoven. Carl Dahlhaus has remarked that, unlike chamber music with piano, the nineteenth-century history of the string quartet—like that of the symphony and sonata—was "split by a rift, or perhaps we should say a gaping abyss" between its "role in reception history and in the history of composition." While Beethoven's symphonies and earlier quartets became concert staples, the subsequent development of such genres remained "checkered and disjoint," a testament to Beethoven's legacy, which for later composers seemed difficult to surmount.[32] Marie Sumner Lott has observed that the total number of string quartets from "canonic figures associated with Romantic instrumental music—Schumann, Mendelssohn, Brahms, and Dvořák—offers only twenty-six works over a seventy-year period," and that more than half (fourteen) came from the hand of Schumann's Czech successor.[33] Leon Plantinga has noted that during Schumann's ten-year career as a music critic (1834–1844), he reviewed only fourteen string quartets.[34] For Schumann, the composers of some of these works showed promise; for instance, in an 1842 review written just weeks before he began his own quartets, Schumann noted that Felix Mendelssohn's "aristocratic-poetic nature" seemed "particularly amenable to this genre." Nevertheless, Schumann worried that the string quartet had "come to a serious standstill." He continued:

> Who does not know the quartets of Haydn, Mozart and Beethoven, and who would wish to say anything against them? In fact it is the most telling testimony to the immortal freshness of their works that after a half-century they yet gladden the hearts of everyone; but it is no good sign that the later generation, after all this time, has not been able to produce anything comparable.... Thus we Germans are not poor [in quartets]; but only a few have known how to increase the capital.[35]

Such statements reveal a preoccupation about the development of the post-Beethovenian quartet, but they obscure a larger picture of string chamber music in the nineteenth century. As Marie Sumner Lott has extensively explored, this medium experienced a "flowering of social uses" in the first half of the century, with a healthy market of sheet music arising for a largely middle-class male audience, who played string quartets (among other string genres) not only for enjoyment, but also to enhance their cultural status and to strengthen social bonds.[36] Lott presents evidence for how string arrangements of folk songs and operatic pieces, like those published by Schlesinger in Berlin, were popular with consumers. Moreover, even if some catalogs showed a sharp decrease in wholly new chamber works for strings—as happened around 1840 in the catalogs of Schlesinger and the Leipzig-based publishers Hofmeister and Peters—the prevalence of reprinted works in this medium suggests its continued popularity within the marketplace. String quartets by the older Louis Spohr, for instance, or the younger Wenzel Heinrich (Václav Jindřich) Veit received multiple printings, becoming "best-sellers" for Peters and Hofmeister, respectively. From this repertory, Lott discerns traits of what she terms the "domestic string style": appealing melodies that undergo a fair amount of repetition; general adherence to standard forms and movement formats; and overall technical accessibility, among other traits.[37]

Schumann reviewed works associated with this style and target audience. In his 1838 series of "Quartettmorgen" articles, for example, he described the "cheerful and contented tone" of Veit's Op. 5 quartet; the "lively musical disposition" of Johannes Verhulst's Op. 6, No. 1 quartet; and the "animated rhythms" and "pleasant melodies" in Carl Reissiger's Op. 11 quartet, a work "for the entertainment of good amateurs." In response to one skeptical player, Schumann defended the seemingly easy finesse of Spohr's Op. 93 quartet, noting that "young artists... err in thinking they could do the same equally well." Nevertheless, while appreciative of composers' efforts in the genre, Schumann found many of them wanting. The string quartet by Veit, for instance, contained "no boldness nor novelty" in terms of its construction; for the Reissiger quartet, Schumann could not ascribe "great original value" to it, "nor promise it a long life"; and the Verhulst work prompted hopes for "more elevated and refined thought" in future works.[38] In 1842, the same quartet by Verhulst prompted further comments: it follows "older masters" in its "form and succession of movements," and its melodies show "no original character." A second quartet by Verhulst, while "more favorable" than the first, prompted Schumann to urge the composer to explore higher ground "where it is not easy to gain a foothold," and to "value inner gain above outward [presumably commercial] success."[39]

With its significant history of composition, the string quartet was for Schumann a genre that could not only accommodate, but deserved, continuing development and innovation. In a May 1842 review of a string quartet by Hermann Hirschbach, Schumann praised the composer's desire "to avoid stereotypical forms," a direction indicated by "Beethoven's last quartets," which for Schumann pointed to "the beginning of a new poetic era."[40] By offering new creative outcomes within his own string quartets, Schumann affirmed the value and possible rejuvenation of the genre. In a December 1847 letter, he not only asserted that "the genre is by no means exhausted, and new masters will come to glorify it," he also suggested that his own contributions illustrate "newer directions" in the medium.[41] This letter—written to urge Hermann Härtel to issue his Op. 41 quartets in score format—indicates both Schumann's satisfaction with his work and the significance he placed on the genre for study, not just for performance. Such study—which Schumann had already undertaken from the later 1830s onward—also suggests his investment in the larger project of canon formation for chamber music in the nineteenth century. In Schumann's eyes, this canonic tradition was ever evolving, with works by predecessors identified as not only foundational, but also capable of inspiring new expressive outcomes in the music of successors; to paraphrase the 1842 review quoted earlier, the "immortal freshness" of works by Haydn, Mozart, and Beethoven, for instance, could provide a basis on which to "increase the capital." As we shall see, Schumann's quartets, and his other 1842 chamber works, frequently reference works by important predecessors while reorienting them toward new artistic ends.[42]

Like the string quartet, chamber music with piano also had roots in the eighteenth century, and it too attracted various audiences who brought different expectations for the medium. On the one hand, chamber music with piano, especially piano trios, found a stronghold in the amateur marketplace. As Lott has shown, certain piano trios by Carl Reissiger, for instance, became "best-sellers" for both Peters and Hofmeister, receiving a strikingly high number of reprintings.[43] (Reissiger actually wrote more than two dozen trios, prompting Schumann to remark that the high number arose because the composer "makes it easy for himself. He does not contemplate new forms, turns, or modulations" and "his passages are entirely comprehensible. In short, he can have a trio ready in two to three days, and an ensemble can rehearse it in as many hours.")[44] On the other hand, chamber music with piano also appealed to professional musicians, partly because the medium could showcase contemporary advancements in the instrument and technique. As Alexander Stefaniak has remarked, even as piano trios by Haydn, Mozart, and Beethoven increasingly assumed canonic status, an accomplished pianist like Clara Schumann would have also understood the piano trio as a "virtuoso vehicle."[45] Yet, in the Schumanns' eyes, care was required for distinguishing between those works that forefronted pianism rather than accompanying it with more substantive musical treatment. A trio by Anton Bohrer, for instance, revealed for Robert a "hodge-podge" of a piano part, one that "could bend pretty fingers out of shape" in the work's overall "unruly" compositional style. Another by Johann Pixis, however, showed promise: while "brilliant and difficult," it was also "rewarding"—a "showpiece" that "demands more than mere skill" from the pianist, and more than "mere amusement for the listener."[46] Beginning in the 1830s, Clara began programming trios that fell more readily in the latter camp, including ones by Pixis, but also by Schubert, Mendelssohn, and Chopin.[47]

Of course, for his own 1842 chamber works with piano, Robert had in Clara a virtuoso ready to take on the challenging piano parts; in other words, a practical impulse lay partially behind the composition of the Op. 44 piano quintet and the Op. 47 piano quartet, two works that Clara subsequently began programming, especially the former. At the same time, both Clara and Robert would have recognized how pianistic accomplishment could interact with what Stefaniak calls the "hallmark[s] of serious chamber music," like "engagement with classical paradigms, and the quasi-conversational exchanges among players."[48] In the 1842 repertory, challenging piano parts help to serve larger formal arguments, ones that may evoke even more distant notable pasts. It is likely not a coincidence that the only two works from the 1842 repertory that each feature multiple fugatos are the two chamber works with piano. Contrapuntal rigor—with the pianist's hands contributing more than one line to the texture—thereby accompanies performative rigor. Moreover, these Bachian passages play crucial roles in generating new interpretations of sonata- and refrain-based forms in their respective finales.[49] In performing these works as a virtuoso pianist, Clara would have recognized how Robert tempered contemporary pianistic possibilities with various historicizing elements, a multifaceted approach that she subsequently adopted in her later Piano Trio in G Minor, Op. 17.[50]

Trends in Reception and New Perspectives

When Schumann composed his multi-movement chamber works on the heels of his 1841 orchestral music, critics took notice. While they disagreed about the success of Schumann's new orientation, virtually all acknowledged its distance from the music of his past. An 1844 review of the piano quintet, for example, commented that "the whole distinguishes itself mightily from the works of Schumann's earlier period through sureness and level-headed use of all means." Similarly, an 1845 review of the string quartets noted that, like other works of the early 1840s, "the musical ideas assume a clearer shape and lose themselves less readily in the mystical profundities and obscure reveries of earlier compositions." Likewise, an 1846 review of the piano quartet began by proclaiming: "How differently Schumann's more recent works appear from those he published ten years ago! Everything is clearer and milder, that which is eccentric has been restrained and instead blended into an independent style."[51] Perhaps not surprisingly, a variety of binary terms began surfacing in the discourse surrounding Schumann's youthful pieces and the large-scale works of the early 1840s: subjective-objective, private-public, and later, Romantic-Classical. Franz Brendel proved to be a particularly influential voice, especially with a lengthy 1845 article that assessed Schumann's compositional achievements thus far. Brendel had just assumed editorship of the *Neue Zeitschrift für Musik*, and during his tenure the journal eventually espoused the cause of the New German School, a term coined by Brendel. Writing in early 1845, however, Brendel was trying to evaluate his predecessor's contributions to the development of post-Beethovenian music. Where Schumann's earlier works continued the subjective threads of Beethoven's late style, allowing "fantasy" to dominate "intellect," the later, more traditional music attempted to "deflect" this subjectivity—a reorientation that Brendel suggests was influenced by Mendelssohn's presence "in classical Leipzig." Nevertheless, unlike the three positive reviews quoted earlier, Brendel asserted that "it seems as though [Schumann], from his subjective standpoint, is not entirely at home in the objective world and thus occasionally lapses into lack of clarity, even dryness." Brendel thus expressed hope for a third phase that "reconciles and unifies everything."[52] As Jürgen Thym has shown, Brendel's image of objectivity battling subjectivity, with hope for a more synthetic phase, influenced a variety of subsequent reviews of Schumann's music by both his supporters and detractors.[53] For his part, Wagner admired Schumann's early "genius" as both a composer and critic. In the 1869 version of his infamous essay "Das Judentum in der Musik [Judaism in Music]," Wagner asserted that the early Schumann represented "a mind [with which] I should have had to commune." But Schumann's early "noble freedom" supposedly became thwarted by composers like Mendelssohn, whose "Jewish influence" set Schumann—and the course of music itself—in the wrong direction by favoring pure instrumental forms and genres.[54]

Characterizations like the ones above suggest that Schumann's instrumental works of the early 1840s broke cleanly from the music of his past. And while overly simplistic (even contemporaries of Schumann noted aspects of his earlier style in the chamber and symphonic works), such descriptions crystallized to a degree that Schumann himself eventually lamented. In an 1854 letter to Richard Pohl—a previous supporter who had become a Wagnerite—Schumann complained that Pohl's manner of "venting" about him

> leads me to believe you do not understand me.... You speak of a lack of objectivity; have you considered this too? Are my four symphonies all alike? Or my trios? Or my songs? Are there really two kinds of creativity, one objective and the other subjective? Was Beethoven an objective [composer]? Let me tell you: these are secrets that cannot be revealed with such miserable words.[55]

Still, these and similar reductionist terms continued to inform discussions of Schumann's music, although writers increasingly favored the Romantic-Classical pairing, gave growing preference to the earlier works, and saw the influence of this youthful repertory as hindering Schumann's efforts within larger genres. In an 1897 publication, for instance, Felix Weingartner proclaimed that Schumann was the first and "the most peculiarly subjective of the romanticists," but that in his attempt "to be classical," Schumann's "own originality suffered severely without his being able to reach his model."[56] In a 1935 article, Mosco Carner noted that aspects of Schumann's earlier music, like "poetic-literary" images, "disconnected mood or character sketches," and "reposeful *Lied*-form" prevented Schumann from successfully composing sonata forms because such aspects proved "alien to its nature." As a result, Schumann's sonata forms signaled the dying life of the model.[57] In her 1967 biography, Joan Chissell asserted that most of the works composed in the 1840s fail to achieve "a happy balance between the romantic and classical elements in Schumann's makeup." The reason? "[T]oo frequently his mind—and often a tired mind—would labour to manipulate abstract sound-material in such a way as he thought befitted a would-be orthodox 'classical' composer, with the result that his most valuable attribute—his spontaneous imagination—was gradually smothered and destroyed."[58] In his 1980 entry on Schumann for the *New Grove Dictionary of Music and Musicians*, Gerald Abraham suggested that with "the great turning-point" in 1841, Schumann "did not cease to be a Romantic, but his Romantic conception of music first as a medium of self-expression was now modified by the older Classical view of musical composition as a craft to be practiced." According to Abraham, the craft was never mastered: Schumann's "playful aphorisms and lyrical melodies" explained his "inability to cover a large canvas." Moreover, "the inventiveness which seldom failed to produce new and interesting piano textures almost dried up when he had at his disposal a medium [like that of an orchestra] capable of figuration far richer but not shaped under his fingers."[59] The two criticisms that Abraham levels against Schumann's large-scale works—weak instrumental writing and the lack of sustained development arising from lyrical and epigrammatic impulses—surface in many twentieth-century writings on Schumann's instrumental music. In a 1957 publication, for instance, Percy Young asserted that Schumann's "technical miscalculations so frequently stand in the way of quick appreciation," and that "this is nowhere more apparent than in the chamber music." As a result, "the greater part of this music is virtually a closed book."[60] Even in the twenty-first century such sentiments have continued. After surveying the Leipzig chamber repertory in his 2001 biography, Eric Jensen suggests that although Schumann's "greater dependence on traditional models led those with more conservative taste to gain greater comprehension of his work," the change in style risked a loss in creativity: "The danger to Schumann lay in the degree to which he became dependent on musical tradition, with academicism replacing originality."[61]

Although highlighting Schumann's new compositional concerns of the early 1840s, the above descriptions are problematic in various ways. First, they discourage listeners from discerning ties between Schumann's earlier and later music and thus thwart full understanding of his stylistic development. Second, by emphasizing "classicism" and "academicism," such comments not only make it easier to fault Schumann's "technical miscalculations"—measured as they are against the output of his predecessors—they also hinder appreciation for how Schumann expressively reworked older forms in numerous ways. This study will offer a corrective by reconsidering the 1842 chamber repertory from both perspectives; in so doing, the book forms part of a larger revisionist effort in the past few decades to re-evaluate Schumann's work in the longer instrumental genres. New ways of understanding Schumann's instrumental writing—from matters of orchestration to thematic development—have been offered through in-depth studies. Jon Finson, for example, has suggested that the increasing size of orchestras in the nineteenth century and beyond (ones to which Weingartner, Abraham, and others would have been accustomed) may account for perceived problems of imbalance in Schumann's symphonies.[62] Markus Waldura has challenged Carner's organicist view of form; by thinking of concepts like "motivic-thematic working out" and "sonata form" in broader terms—the case in Schumann's day—Waldura argues that in many ways Schumann's instrumental forms continue, instead of undoing, the thematic processes of Beethoven while also anticipating those of Brahms.[63] More attention has also been paid to Schumann's rhythmic-metric innovations, ones more readily associated with Brahms but evident in works written throughout Schumann's career, as Harald Krebs has shown.[64] Scholars have also presented new frameworks for understanding admittedly idiosyncratic movements. John Daverio, for instance, has shown how a striking formal deviation may function not as a shortcoming, but rather as a self-conscious critique.[65] Drawing on structural studies of narrative, Anthony Newcomb has argued that a "defamiliarization" of a traditional form (compared to a "paradigmatic plot") may actually empower once again the form whose conventions it seems to "mock."[66] In an article on Schumann's sonata forms, Joel Lester shows how the continuous evolution of musical ideas helps to explain surprising departures from tonal norms and in ways that still produce satisfying— if alternative—results.[67] Schumann's music has also been reconsidered from the perspectives of Schenkerian theory and the new *Formenlehre*, with heretofore unacknowledged ties to tradition shown as successfully interacting with more novel elements in large-scale instrumental forms and genres.[68] Alexander Stefaniak has shown how even concerted showpieces by Schumann successfully blend elements of virtuosity with "strategies fundamental to the culture of serious music."[69] And Benedict Taylor has recently illustrated how notions of "subjectivity" might inform works beyond the early piano and song output.[70] Such scholarship belies reductionist views of Schumann's stylistic development while also challenging simplistic and less-than-flattering accounts of his relationship to the classical tradition overall.

In Schumann's own day, the argument that his larger instrumental genres—especially those of the early 1840s—represented a more "objective," classicizing turn came as much from his own supporters as his detractors, some of whom downplayed Schumann's innovations out of a sincere desire to promote them within an (often wary) public eye. In an 1843 article about the history of the string quartet, for instance, Hermann Hirschbach initially claimed that Schumann's recent quartets are "so unusual that I cannot compare them to anything else."[71] Yet to facilitate their public reception and to respond to criticism from a provincial quartet ensemble that the works were "rubbish," Hirschbach subsequently stressed their restraint and comprehensibility: Schumann's quartets "keep within traditional forms and are not at all revolutionary, but [rather] stand out by virtue of their particular quality of invention."[72]

A partial aim of this book is to uncover such unique "qualities of invention" within the 1842 repertory, ones that show how Schumann engaged dynamically with inherited models. Such recognition in turn enables fascinating new ways of hearing the Leipzig chamber repertory. Chapter 2, for instance, explores how Schumann reimagines rondo and sonata-form procedure through the lens of competing tonics that operate on either an intra-movement level (the finale of the piano quintet) or an inter-movement level (the first string quartet). Indeed, unambiguous tonal definition—something we take for granted in traditional paradigms—occurs only as an end-oriented event. Chapter 3 shows how Schumann reimagines the repetition concept in the two most predictable classical forms: scherzo-trio and theme-and-variations. In two movements based on these models (the scherzo of the first string quartet, and the slow movement of the second string quartet), passages that initially seem to reside within or outside the main form eventually assume the opposite function and in ways that yield unpredictable nested designs. Chapter 4 highlights a slow movement (that of the third string quartet) that challenges the concept of fixed identity on both thematic and formal levels, with Schumann successfully conflating seemingly contradictory structural principles. Viewed against conventional practices, the above movements may appear puzzling, perhaps even incoherent, as some critics have suggested. Yet surely they signal not compositional weakness (Schumann could write otherwise), but rather an effort to reinterpret old forms as a way of strengthening their rhetorical power. In this regard, the movements illustrate Schumann's notion that new artistic products should creatively develop—rather than imitate—traditional models to ensure their vitality for new generations of composers and listeners.

This dynamic relationship between past and present manifests itself in other ways. In a number of chamber movements, Schumann evokes specific works by predecessors and contemporaries, only to use them as a point of departure. Chapters 2 and 3 provide examples of movements that reference compositions by (among others) Beethoven, Schubert, and Mendelssohn, figures that Schumann greatly admired. In some cases, these references have been observed by others; elsewhere I am the first to perceive them. As the chapters show, equally important is how Schumann's music tends to distance itself from the very models that it conjures. Schumann's criticism sheds light on such allusions, for, as I have shown elsewhere, he observed a number of them in the work of his contemporaries, especially Beethovenian ones. (As Schumann once noted, "do we not all subsist on his treasures?")[73] However, some references prompted censure from Schumann, while others appeared acceptable. In his 1842 review of a string quartet by Johann Verhulst, for instance, Schumann observed: "The last movement begins, almost literally, like the last of the 'Eroica' Symphony. Did this elude the composer's notice? If not, why did he allow it to remain?" Similarly, after noting references to Mendelssohn, Spohr, Beethoven, Mozart, and Bach in a symphony by Carl Reissiger, Schumann wondered about the "ulterior motives" behind such "frequent and strong reminiscences," suggesting that "if one began removing them, half of the symphony would likely fall away."[74] In a review of a symphony by Christian Müller, however, Schumann was more favorably disposed: "those details that recall Beethoven's manner . . . work to the young composer's advantage" because "his own successful self is wholly and happily distinguished from the outside model he wanted to emulate." In other words, references should work in union with a composer's own creativity, even throwing the latter into relief. Thus, even though the first theme from Louis Hetsch's Grand Duo evokes "Beethoven's great E-flat Concerto, no harm is done because of [Hetsch's] warm treatment," with the movement offering "prominent curiosities, especially interesting and novel harmonic features." Likewise, if the first movement of Mendelssohn's Op. 6 Piano Sonata "recalls the thoughtful melancholy of Beethoven's last A-major Sonata, . . . this is not weak dependence but rather spiritual kinship."[75]

Schumann's 1842 chamber music illustrates his critical stance on references, Beethovenian and otherwise. Chapter 2, for instance, explores the remarkable way in which an inter-movement tonal dichotomy is introduced in the first string quartet, one that I argue was inspired by Beethoven's Cello Sonata, Op. 102, No. 1. Unlike his predecessor, however, Schumann sustains his split tonal focus far longer and resolves it wholly differently. Chapter 3 explores a scherzo movement that evokes a Mendelssohnian fairyland (among other intertextual references to the fantastic); indeed, Schumann's scherzo forefronts a rhythmic motive prominent in the analogous movement of Mendelssohn's Op. 20 Octet, the work in which this new fanciful scherzo style first fully expressed itself. Schumann, however, ends up juxtaposing this style with a quasi-religious counterpole that materializes in an unexpected place, and the negotiation of these contrasting sound worlds ultimately generates a scherzo movement unique in Schumann's instrumental output. Chapter 3 also discusses the Andante movement of the second quartet, which references the slow movement of Beethoven's Op. 127 String Quartet in various ways, including the superimposition of a larger form on a variation chain. But while Beethoven plays with a ternary concept, Schumann adopts a bait-and-switch approach, for the opening theme turns out not to be the source of internal variations. This surprising maneuver ends up yielding a highly unusual but remarkable nested structure in his "quasi-Variazioni" movement.

In the Leipzig chamber repertory, Schumann might imbue stylistic references with larger cultural echoes and in ways that yield creative adaptations of older forms. Chapter 2 explores Schumann's use of the *verbunkos* idiom—also called the *style hongrois*—in two finales (that of the piano quintet and the first string quartet, with some reference to the finale of the third quartet). Especially compelling is how this idiom and related cultural associations seem to have inspired Schumann's rethinking of sonata form and refrain-based form in these finales. For instance, by avoiding a stable tonal "home," the movements resonate with cultural stereotypes of the Hungarian-Gypsy wanderer as they were imagined in Schumann's day. Chapter 2 also considers Schubert's influence in this regard, especially the extra-musical qualities that Schumann perceived within Schubert's *Divertissement à l'Hongroise*, Op. 54, D. 818, and the points of departure they provided for his own engagement with this idiom.

The notion that Schumann's music of the early 1840s represents a conservative, "objective" turn proves problematic in yet another way, for it discourages listeners from perceiving how this music built upon Schumann's youthful output. As multiple chapters show, the Leipzig chamber works reveal a variety of traits typically associated with Schumann's earlier piano music and songs, among them aphoristic impulses, digressive passages, rhetorically unusual openings, "parallel" structures, hybrid forms, sustained tonal ambiguity, even competing tonics. Already mentioned above are chamber works that create split tonal foci on inter- and intra-movement levels. Chapter 2 also considers a finale (that of the third string quartet) that is rhetorically odd since it opens with a closing gesture, namely, a brief cadence in the home key. This aphoristic opening paradoxically serves not to confirm, but rather to confuse tonal focus, since the cadential gesture goes on to tonicize other keys just as strongly. Chapter 2 also surveys the "parallel" form of this finale, one that revisits strategies first introduced in Schumann's piano sonatas of the 1830s, and one that provides the point of departure for a much more ambitious design in the finale of the piano quintet. Chapter 3 considers the seemingly extraneous addition of a closed, lyrical number in the scherzo of the first quartet; this passage, like a similar lyrical digression in the sonata-form finale of the piano quartet, becomes the surprising means for yielding a new interpretation of the traditional form on which it is based. Chapter 4 explores the slow movement of the third string quartet, where structural seams become blurred by weakened and "misplaced" cadences, and by infiltration of materials from outside sections—traits that have precedents in Schumann's earlier piano music. Finally, Chapters 2, 3, and 4 each describe movements that hybridize formal principles in ways reminiscent of Schumann's earlier output and that yield chamber movements that are anything but "academic." Such hybridization may even challenge facets we take for granted in large-scale instrumental forms; for instance: what is the main theme? what material is principal versus secondary? and what is the overall form?

It is well known that the earlier songs and piano music by Schumann—the son of a bookseller and the editor of his own music journal—manifest a variety of literary influences. This book illustrates how literature yet continued to inform Schumann's compositional process within at least two chamber works, with Chapter 3 delving into the influence of Schumann's most admired authors, Jean Paul and Johann Wolfgang von Goethe. Schumann's manner of creating nested forms in two chamber movements via digressive maneuvers, with resulting confusion between *Hauptwerk* and *Beiwerk*, recall the narrative techniques of Jean Paul. The latter's output also illustrates how one might discern "witty" poetic links between seemingly disparate parts. Chapter 2 also explores the influence of Goethe, particularly two literary works that engage with the Walpurgisnacht legend: Part I of *Faust*, and the 1799 ballad "Die erste Walpurgisnacht." Both were known to Schumann, and both prompted musical settings by Felix Mendelssohn that Schumann also knew. The dream sequence from *Faust* famously inspired the elfin sound of Mendelssohn's new scherzo style, which Schumann evokes in the analogous movement of his first string quartet. As mentioned earlier, this movement also presents a quasi-religious counterpole in an unexpected passage, which in turn generates a seeming dichotomy whose reconciliation may well have been inspired by Goethe's 1799 ballad.

As the above suggests, the Leipzig chamber works reveal Schumann's creativity working more in harmony with, rather than battling against, the influences of his earlier output, be they literary or musical. That is, even while adopting forms and genres from the classical past, the 1842 chamber works illustrate how Schumann could affirm tradition not by rejecting his earlier experimentalism, but by reworking it toward new expressive ends.

While portions of this book emphasize composer-oriented viewpoints—highlighting Schumann's reception of his youthful past, of the classical past, of literary influences, even of a vernacular style with folk roots (the *verbunkos* idiom)—the book also favors listener perspectives, ones in Schumann's own day, but also ones that take us beyond Germanic regions and that feature more voices, including those in other spheres of artistic activity. Chapter 4 begins by surveying the numerous ways in which Schumann and his music have inspired creative figures in other disciplines, including art, film, theater, novelistic biography, and dance. Scholars are in the early stages of grappling with this repertory, and this chapter contributes to those efforts by exploring a 1975 ballet—*Four Schumann Pieces* by the Dutch choreographer Hans van Manen—that sets all four movements of Schumann's third string quartet. A devotee of Balanchine and his formalist creed to "make the music visible," yet someone also interested in human relationships, Van Manen produced a ballet that—in Balanchine's words—shows "a man who stands alone but who is surrounded by persons he would wish to know." The chapter zooms in on the Adagio, the most intimate of the four "pieces": here, Van Manen forges interactions between the dancers that articulate identity as multivalent and relational. I argue that this conceptual framework enables numerous insights into the music that have hitherto escaped notice: for instance, a "primary" theme that resists any fixed version of itself; a unique large-scale design that allows multiple formal principles to intersect; and a blurring of formal boundaries that helps to divulge ties between seemingly different materials. By bringing such aspects into view, *Four Schumann Pieces*—itself a classically based ballet—illuminates not only a continuing strain of experimentalism in Schumann's 1842 chamber music, but also the ability of such experimentalism to renew the expressive force of older, inherited genres and formal principles.

Chapter 5 creates a bookend by resuming the more expansive historical tone of this opening chapter. Now, however, it explores the reception of Schumann's Leipzig chamber works within a specific cultural context, namely, London in the second half of the nineteenth century. Here, questions about whether the 1842 chamber music represented a more conservative or progressive orientation for Schumann centered less on the music's relationship to his earlier works and more on its comparison with the output of Felix Mendelssohn. For conservative English critics, Schumann was Mendelssohn's opposite, the dubious modernist to Mendelssohn the classicist, with Schumann eventually linked with "Brother Wagner" and the "dangerous music of the future." Exploring this reception illuminates striking differences between mid-century English and Continental views of Schumann-the-figure, between conservative and progressive voices within London itself (including those of critics, directors, and performers), and between social classes, especially as the 1842 works moved from rarefied environments into newer, larger, and more affordable concert venues. Clara Schumann also figures prominently in this chapter, for as a widow she spent more time concertizing in London than in any other European capital, visiting nineteen times from 1856 to 1888. Her efforts to promote Robert's music—a focus of her widowhood and one facilitated in part by her performance of the piano quartet and piano quintet—played a substantial role in changing the English debate about the merits of her husband's music. In a sense, the efforts of Clara and other English "Schumannites" (performers, promoters, and more favorably disposed critics) resonate with my own desire in this book to offer a greater appreciation of the 1842 repertory.

As the above indicates, my discussion of the Leipzig chamber works will blend new critical and contextual frameworks that balance larger historical considerations with close analyses of selected movements revealing a broad range of forms. My aim, however, is not to provide a comprehensive analysis of every movement from every Leipzig chamber work. For that I refer the reader to Hans Kohlhase's landmark 1978 study, which sought to provide a systematic account of Schumann's entire chamber repertory.[76] Kohlhase discusses a wide range of musical topics, from Schumann's borrowing practices to his harmonic, motivic, and polyphonic techniques; in addition, Kohlhase offers chronological analyses of each movement from every chamber work, along with useful transcriptions of sketches containing rejected passages or incomplete projects. Kohlhase and other authors who have published either surveys of the chamber repertory or analyses of individual movements have provided many ideas on which my own work builds or (at times) plays against. Ultimately, my aim is to show that the Leipzig chamber repertory is anything but "a closed book," and that approaching it from new historical, cultural, biographical, literary, and analytical viewpoints will open tantalizing new ways of hearing the music.

In offering these diverse perspectives, I take a cue from Schumann himself. In an 1839 letter, he noted how "writings, surroundings, inner and outer experiences" had made their imprint on his work, "and now I sometimes ask myself where it could all end."[77] The 1842 chamber works indicate that such diverse influences had indeed not yet ended. A later anecdote connected to the Leipzig repertory also reveals the multifaceted understanding that Schumann advocated for his music. In an 1849 letter to Franz Liszt, he remarked: "If you were to take a closer look at my compositions, you would find quite a variety of views in them, as I have always sought to bring something new to light in each of my compositions, and not only in their form." Schumann's comment arose in response to a now well-known, but then awkward incident that occurred the previous year when Liszt remarked that the Op. 44 piano quintet was too "Leipzigerish." (The situation only worsened when Liszt began praising Meyerbeer over the recently deceased Mendelssohn; the latter had been a figurehead for Leipzig musical culture, which for two decades had nurtured reverence for past traditions alongside contemporary music.) A year later, when Liszt inquired about programming Schumann's *Szenen aus Goethes Faust* for an upcoming Weimar festival, Robert responded in a way that chided Liszt for his earlier dismissive remark:

> But, my dear friend, wouldn't the composition perhaps be too "Leipzigerish" to you? Or do you consider L[eipzig] a miniature Paris, where one might still accomplish something? In all seriousness, I would have expected something else from you—who knows so many of my compositions—than to have expressed such a sweeping judgment over an entire artist's life.

This perceived judgment then prompted Schumann's assertion about the "variety of views" and "new" aspects in his works that include, but are not limited to, matters of form.[78] These words, written in 1849, represent the defense of a composer whose music was coming under increasing skepticism from figures like Liszt, Brendel, and other Wagner supporters. Schumann's defense, however, relies not merely on his music as evidence, but on listeners who adopt a flexible mindset toward it. Schumann invited Liszt to undertake such an approach ("If you were to take a closer look"); indeed, he even suggests the common ground that might appear as a result, for Schumann concludes by noting that "the chief thing is the effort to advance."

Notes

1. *GS*, vol. 1, 330. Letter to Liszt of May 31, 1849, emphasis original; *Briefedition*, II/5, 147.
2. *GS*, vol. 1, 390 and 343.
3. Many scholars have explored this development of canon formation and its various facets. For more in-depth studies, see for instance William Weber, *The Great Transformation of Musical Taste: Concert Programming from Haydn to Brahms* (Cambridge and New York: Cambridge University Press, 2008); David Gramit, *Cultivating Music: The Aspirations, Interests, and Limits of German Musical Culture, 1770–1848* (Berkeley: University of California Press, 2002); and Lydia Goehr, *The Imaginary Museum of Musical Works: An Essay in the Philosophy of Music*, rev. ed. (Oxford and New York: Oxford University Press, 2007). For more succinct discussions, see for example Celia Applegate, "How German Is It? Nationalism and the Idea of Serious Music in the Early Nineteenth Century," *19th-Century Music* 21 (1998): 274–96; John Irving, "The Invention of Tradition," in *The Cambridge History of Nineteenth-Century Music*, ed. Jim Samson (Cambridge: Cambridge University Press, 2002), 178–212; Jim Samson, "The Great Composer," in *The Cambridge History of Nineteenth-Century Music*, ed. Jim Samson (Cambridge: Cambridge University Press, 2002), 259–84; and William Weber, "Musical Canons," in *The Oxford Handbook of Music and Intellectual Culture in the Nineteenth Century*, ed. Paul Watt, Sarah Collins, and Michael Allis (New York: Oxford University Press, 2020), 319–42.
4. In Berlin, for instance, Karl Möser initiated string quartet concerts in 1813—and soon thereafter symphonic concerts—that focused on works of "the classics," as an 1832 review described them; quoted in Irving, "The Invention of Tradition," 179. In Vienna, Ignaz Schuppanzigh founded a chamber series in 1823 that he asserted would comprise concerts "consisting of the quartets of the most famous masters," with those by Haydn, Mozart, and Beethoven filling the vast majority of programs; quoted in John M. Gingerich, *Schubert's Beethoven Project* (Cambridge: Cambridge University Press, 2014), 67. In Leipzig, Felix Mendelssohn's performances with the Gewandhaus orchestra included "historical" concerts that performed works by the Viennese triumvirate, but also ones by older composers like Bach and Handel, an orientation anticipated by Mendelssohn's successful 1829 Berlin performance of Bach's *St. Matthew Passion*.
5. For a summary of such writings, see Irving, "The Invention of Tradition," 180–84.
6. Weber, *The Great Transformation of Musical Taste*, 122.
7. Alexander Stefaniak, *Becoming Clara Schumann: Performance Strategies and Aesthetics in the Culture of the Musical Canon* (Bloomington: Indiana University Press, 2021), 5.
8. Entry of June 5–6, 1834. *Tb*, vol. 1, 304.
9. Edvard Grieg, "Robert Schumann (1893)," in *Edvard Grieg: Diaries, Articles, Speeches*, ed. and trans. Finn Benestad and William H. Halverson (Columbus, OH: Peer Gynt Press, 2001), 259. On Schumann's journal and facets of his writings, see Leon Plantinga, *Schumann as Critic* (New Haven, CT: Yale University Press, 1967), which yet remains the most substantial study of this topic.
10. Letter to Hofrath Reinhold of February 17, 1840; *BNF*, 182.
11. *GS*, vol. 2, 11.
12. Ibid., vol. 1, 123.
13. In the months that followed, Schumann also wrote a set of character pieces for trio ensemble later published as the *Phantasiestücke*, Op. 88, and the *Andante und Variationen* for two pianos,

two cellos, and horn, later arranged for two pianos and published as Op. 46. My focus, however, will be on the Leipzig chamber works composed as multi-movement works.

14. John Daverio's biography, *Robert Schumann: Herald of a "New Poetic Age"* (Oxford and New York: Oxford University Press, 1997) was important in this regard, and others have continued this revisionist work, including Laura Tunbridge in her book *Schumann's Late Style* (2007; reprint, Cambridge: Cambridge University Press, 2009). Based on new evidence, David Ferris has recently argued for the lack of any evidence for mental decline prior to February 1854; "Schumann and the Myth of Madness," *Nineteenth-Century Music Review* 18, no. 3 (2021): 389–426.

15. For transcriptions of these incomplete projects, see Hans Kohlhase, *Die Kammermusik Robert Schumanns: Stilistische Untersuchungen*, 3 vols. (PhD diss., University of Hamburg, 1978); published as no. 19 in the series Hamburger Beiträge zur Musikwissenschaft, ed. Constantin Floros (Hamburg: Verlag der Musikalienhandlung Wagner, 1979), vol. 3, 11–18; for a discussion of Schumann's early chamber-music efforts, see vol. 1, 6–17. See also John Daverio, "'Beautiful and Abstruse Conversations': The Chamber Music of Robert Schumann," in *Nineteenth-Century Chamber Music*, ed. Stephen E. Hefling (New York: Schirmer, 1998), 210–15.

16. *GS*, vol. 2, 89.

17. Letters to Raimund Härtel of October 15, 1842, and Hermann Härtel of December 3, 1847; *BNF*, 433 and 450.

18. The piano quartet took longer to appear in printed form. Schumann must not have expected this delay, for a letter to Carl Koßmaly dated May 5, 1843, indicates that it will "soon appear" (*BNF*, 226), although Whistling only published it in February 1845.

19. Letter to Hermann Härtel of December 14, 1847; *BNF*, 452. Marie Sumner Lott provides a larger cultural study of the likely audiences that played Schumann's quartets and those by his contemporaries, namely, "fellow composers, critics, and students of music." Lott, *The Social Worlds of Nineteenth-Century Chamber Music: Composers, Consumers, Communities* (Urbana: University of Illinois Press, 2015), 134.

20. Letters of December 24, 1848 (from Schumann), and December 27, 1848 (from David); *Briefedition* II/20, 298–99; also quoted in Werner Schwarz (who provides more context for this relationship), "Eine Musikerfreundschaft des 19. Jahrhunderts: Unveröffentlichte Briefe von Ferdinand David an Robert Schumann," in *Zum 70. Geburtstag von Joseph Müller-Blattau*, ed. Christoph-Hellmut Mahling (Kassel: Bärenreiter, 1966), 293–95. Years later, when Schumann took up the chamber medium again while living first in Dresden, then Düsseldorf (1847 on), he only cultivated genres with piano (trios and violin sonatas). For dates pertaining to the compositional origins, private and public premieres and related reviews, and first editions of the Leipzig chamber repertory, see Margit L. McCorkle's fine thematic catalog, *Robert Schumann: Thematisch-Bibliographisches Werkverzeichnis* (Munich: G. Henle Verlag, 2003), 177–84, 191–95, and 201–203. Hans Kohlhase provides excellent coverage and documentation of such facets in relation to the string quartets; see Kohlhase, "Kritische Bericht/Critical Report," in *Three Quartets for Two Violins, Viola and Violoncello op. 41*, ed. Hans Kohlhase; series II, group I, vol. 1 of *Robert Schumann: New Edition of the Complete Works* (Mainz: Schott, 2006), 137–83.

21. Anthony Newcomb, "Schumann and the Marketplace: From Butterflies to *Hausmusik*," in *Nineteenth-Century Piano Music*, ed. R. Larry Todd (New York: Schirmer, 1990), 265.

22. For instance, in an 1844 essay, Carl Koßmaly noted that the originality in Schumann's early piano output "does have a rather disturbing effect at times, when his intention always to be new and striking makes itself all too strongly felt. It annoys us even more, however, when this striving occasionally degenerates into the search for alienating, unheard-of-phrases and completely unenjoyable bizarreness." Koßmaly, "On Robert Schumann's Piano Compositions (1844)," trans. Susan Gillespie, in *Schumann and His World*, ed. R. Larry Todd (Princeton, NJ: Princeton University Press, 1994), 308. Writing in 1846, Eduard Hanslick praised the imagination and depth of feeling in the early piano works, but notes that they "were not free from bizarreness and eccentricity." Hanslick, "Dr. Robert Schumann," in *Sämtliche Schriften: Historisch-kritische Ausgabe*, ed. Dietmar Strauss (Vienna: Bohlau, 1993), vol. 1, no. 1, 106.

23. The comment comes from an 1845 essay by Franz Brendel, "Robert Schumann with Reference to Mendelssohn-Bartholdy and the Development of Modern Music in General (1845)," trans. Jürgen Thym, in *Schumann and His World*, ed. R. Larry Todd (Princeton, NJ: Princeton University Press, 1994), 326. In 1860, August Wilhelm Ambros also remarked that the early piano works were "too difficult to play and to understand for the common dilettante; for the

professional musician they were too eccentric and too far outside the habitual and the traditional rules of art." Ambros, "Die neu-romantische Musik," in *Culturhistorische Bilder aus dem Musikleben der Gegenwart*, 2nd ed. (Leipzig: H. Matthes, 1865), 60; translation from Newcomb, "Schumann and the Marketplace," 269.
24. *GS*, vol. 1, 417.
25. Plantinga, *Schumann as Critic*, 180–81.
26. *GS*, vol. 1, 255, and vol. 2, 31.
27. For more examples, see Plantinga, *Schumann as Critic*, 181. Even late in life Schumann expressed hope that Brahms too would turn to large-scale composition, as an 1855 letter to Joseph Joachim makes clear: "If only he, like you, honored friend, would go among the masses, the orchestra and chorus. That would be magnificent." Quoted and translated in Eduard Hanslick, "Robert Schumann in Endenich (1899)," trans. Susan Gillespie, in *Schumann and His World*, ed. R. Larry Todd (Princeton, NJ: Princeton University Press, 1994), 285.
28. Letter to Clara of mid-March 1838, *Briefedition* I/4, 266; cf. *CC*, vol. 1, 130. Letter to Dorn of April 14, 1839, *BNF*, 153.
29. *GS*, vol. 1, 336.
30. For instance, of Beethoven's Opp. 127 and 131 quartets, Schumann remarked that "they seem to me... the outermost limits yet achieved by human art and imagination." Ibid., vol. 1, 380. For more on this late 1830s activity, see Daverio, "'Beautiful and Abstruse Conversations,'" 213–15; and Lott, *The Social Worlds of Nineteenth-Century Chamber Music*, 126–29.
31. In Schumann's *Haushaltbuch*, see the entries for April 1, April 28, and May 6, 1842; *Tb*, vol. 3, 210 and 212–13. This study extended into June, with both Clara and Robert playing "from quartets by Haydn and Mozart"; entry of June 28, 1842; *Tb*, vol. 2, 229.
32. Carl Dahlhaus, *Nineteenth-Century Music*, trans. J. Bradford Robinson (Berkeley: University of California Press, 1989), 78. Friedhelm Krummacher similarly writes of the string quartet: "There is scarcely another genre in which the standards set by the Classical masterpieces were so domineering that the victims of later selection included even those works that had sought seriously to engage with the established canon." Krummacher, "Reception and Analysis: On the Brahms Quartets, Op. 51, Nos. 1 and 2," *19th-Century Music* 18 (1994): 26.
33. Lott, *The Social Worlds of Nineteenth-Century Chamber Music*, 4.
34. Plantinga, *Schumann as Critic*, 187–88.
35. *GS*, vol. 2, 71; partial translation from Plantinga, *Schumann as Critic*, 187.
36. Lott, *The Social Worlds of Nineteenth-Century Chamber Music*, 4–20; quotation from 6.
37. On the domestic string style, see ibid., chapter 3. For a survey of this "subgenre" of string chamber music from the perspectives of publisher production and consumer consumption, see ibid., chapter 1. Ibid., figure 1.1, charts the publication of new chamber string works by Hofmeister and Peters from 1800–1890, including precipitous declines therein.
38. *GS*, vol. 1, 341 (on Veit); 334 (on Verhulst); 338 (on Reissiger); and 335 (on Spohr).
39. Ibid., vol. 2, 75–76.
40. Ibid., vol. 2, 74.
41. Letter of December 14, 1847; *BNF*, 452.
42. On the role of string quartet concerts in the early development of canonic traditions, see Weber, *The Great Transformation of Musical Taste*, 122–40. For a discussion of nineteenth-century composers who held similarly "progressive" ideals in relation to their chamber output, see Lott, *The Social Worlds of Nineteenth-Century Chamber Music*, 107–43.
43. Lott, *The Social Worlds of Nineteenth-Century Chamber Music*, 30–31; Lott, however, keeps her focus on chamber music for strings only.
44. *GS*, vol. 1, 177.
45. Stefaniak, *Becoming Clara Schumann*, 174–75.
46. *GS*, vol. 1, 169–70 (on Bohrer) and 500 (on Pixis).
47. Stefaniak, *Becoming Clara Schumann*, 175; and Nicole Grimes, "Formal Innovation and Virtuosity in Clara Schumann's Piano Trio in G Minor, Op. 17," in *Clara Schumann Studies*, ed. Joe Davies (Cambridge: Cambridge University Press, 2022), 143.
48. Stefaniak, *Becoming Clara Schumann*, 175.
49. On the Op. 44 finale, see Chapter 2. On the Op. 47 finale, see my "Higher Echoes of the Past in the Finale of Schumann's 1842 Piano Quartet," *Journal of the American Musicological Society* 57 (2004): 511–64.
50. In the finale of her trio, for instance, bravura writing at the end of the sonata-form exposition gives way to a fugue, whose subject builds upon both intra- and inter-movement thematic

associations. For more on how this work "stage[s] multiple facets of [Clara's] 1840s persona," see Stefaniak, *Becoming Clara Schumann*, 174–86; quotation on 175. For an analysis of the work from the perspective of the new *Formenlehre*, see Grimes, "Formal Innovation and Virtuosity in Clara Schumann's Piano Trio in G Minor, Op. 17," 147–60.

51. Anonymous, "R. Schumann: Quintett für Pianoforte, zwei Violinen, Viola und Violoncelle, Op. 44," *Allgemeine musikalische Zeitung* (February 28, 1844): 149; Ernst Friedrich Richter, "Rob. Schumann: Drei Quartette für zwei Violinen, Viola und Violoncello, Op. 41," *Allgemeine musikalische Zeitung* (January 15, 1845): 38; and A[ugust] K[ahlert], "Robert Schumann: Quartett für Pianoforte, Violine, Viola und Violoncelle, Op. 47," *Allgemeine musikalische Zeitung* (July 15, 1846): 472.

52. Brendel, "Robert Schumann, with Reference to Mendelssohn-Bartholdy," 318–36; longer quotations from 331 and 335. Brendel was an avowed Hegelian; hence the principles of dialectical logic that he applied to Schumann's stylistic development.

53. Jürgen Thym, "Schumann in Brendel's *Neue Zeitschrift für Musik* from 1845–1856," in *Mendelssohn and Schumann: Essays on Their Music and Its Context*, ed. Jon W. Finson and R. Larry Todd (Durham, NC: Duke University Press, 1984), 21–36. Since Brendel eventually heralded Wagner as Beethoven's true successor, helping to precipitate the midcentury polemic about the development of contemporary music, reviews of Schumann's music in the journal should thus be seen against this backdrop.

54. Richard Wagner, "Judaism in Music [1869 version]," in *Richard Wagner's Prose Works*, trans. William Ashton Ellis, vol. 3, *The Theatre* (London: Routledge and Kegan Paul, 1894; reprint, New York: Broude Brothers, 1966), 117–18. Franz Liszt—another representative of the New German School—expressed his opinion of Schumann's continuing interest in instrumental music more diplomatically. "For my own part, I have a *very high opinion* of the talent of Schumann, who is an outstanding master of *musical* style and frequents the higher regions of art. However, I can best convey my impression by saying that I regard him as a kind of *Arius* in the little Church we are trying to build." Letter to Eduard Liszt of March 29, 1854; in *Franz Liszt: Selected Letters*, trans. and ed. Adrian Williams (Oxford: Clarendon Press, 1998), 355 (emphasis original).

55. Letter of February 6, 1854; *Briefedition* II/5, 409–10; translation from John Michael Cooper, with letter appended to his translation of an 1878 essay by Richard Pohl, "Reminiscences of Robert Schumann (1878)," in *Schumann and His World*, ed. R. Larry Todd (Princeton, NJ: Princeton University Press, 1994), 261. Even before composing his instrumental music of the early 1840s, Schumann seemed to recognize that his path would chart a unique course between overt experimentation and historically informed writing, as his 1840 petition to the University of Jena suggests. After describing his openness to works by composers as diverse as Mendelssohn and Chopin, Schumann stated that "as a composer I may well go down a path different from others." Letter to Hofrath Reinhold of February 17, 1840; *BNF*, 182–83.

56. Felix Weingartner, "On Schumann as Symphonist [1897; English translation from 1904]," in *Schumann and His World*, ed. R. Larry Todd (Princeton, NJ: Princeton University Press, 1994), 376–77. Like Brendel, Weingartner linked Schumann's change in orientation to Mendelssohn, a composer against whom Schumann's "individuality was diametrically opposed" (376).

57. Carner continues: Schumann's "finite lyrical ideas" hindered the organic "regeneration" of material in his sonata forms, and thus broke the dramatic thread that had previously sustained the form. Mosco Carner, "Some Observations on Schumann's Sonata Form," *Musical Times* 76 (1935): 884–86. This essay encapsulates conclusions reached in Carner's 1928 dissertation, "Studien zur Sonatenform bei Robert Schuman" (PhD diss., University of Vienna, 1928), see especially 1–15.

58. Joan Chissell, *Schumann*, 2nd ed. (London: Dent, 1967), 95–96.

59. Gerald Abraham, "Robert Schumann," *The New Grove's Dictionary of Music and Musicians*, ed. Stanley Sadie (London: Macmillan, 1980), vol. 16, 851–52.

60. Percy Young, *Tragic Muse: The Life and Works of Robert Schumann* (London: Hutchinson, 1957), 147. Felix Weingartner similarly complained that, while Schumann's treatment of the piano was "original," "he did not know how to handle the orchestra." Weingartner, "On Schumann as Symphonist," 376 and 378. According to Fanny Davies, the chamber music "betrays his want of practical familiarity with the strings." Davies, "Schumann, Robert Alexander," in *Cobbett's Cyclopedic Survey of Chamber Music*, ed. Walter Wilson Cobbett (London: Oxford University Press, 1930), 382. Like Carner, Carl Dahlhaus has remarked that by "substituting the motivic unity of the character piece for that of the Beethoven symphony, [Schumann] became embroiled

in contradictions between lyricism and monumentality, contradictions that led not so much to a productive dialectic as to mutual paralysis of its various components." Dahlhaus, *Nineteenth-Century Music*, 160. Donald Francis Tovey similarly asserted: "Schumann is a master of epigram ... [But] the creators of such *Einfälle* seldom show high constructive genius on a larger scale. ... Large forms imply the expansion of initial ideas by development; and development is the very thing than an epigram will not bear." Tovey, *Essays in Musical Analysis*, vol. 2: *Symphonies* (London: Oxford University Press, 1944), 46.

61. Eric Jensen, *Schumann*, The Master Musicians (Oxford and New York: Oxford University Press, 2001), 212.
62. Jon Finson, *Robert Schumann and the Study of Orchestral Composition: The Genesis of the First Symphony, Op. 38* (Oxford: Clarendon Press, 1989), 140–41.
63. Markus Waldura, *Monomotivik, Sequenz und Sonatenform im Werk Robert Schumanns* (Saarbrücken: Saarbrücker Druckerei und Verlag, 1990), 10–20.
64. Harald Krebs, *Fantasy Pieces: Metrical Dissonance in the Music of Robert Schumann* (New York and Oxford: Oxford University Press, 1999).
65. John Daverio, *Nineteenth-Century Music and the German Romantic Ideology* (New York: Macmillan, 1993), 19–47; Daverio considers the lyrical, self-contained "Im Legendenton" passage in the first movement of the Op. 17 *Fantasie*, which in his view interrupts the development section; in thereby opposing the modern character piece with an older model (sonata form), the *Fantasie* thus signifies "nothing less than the *impossibility* of writing sonatas after Beethoven" (21). For a different take on a similar formal problem, see my "Higher Echoes of the Past in the Finale of Schumann's 1842 Piano Quartet," 511–64.
66. Anthony Newcomb, "Schumann and Late Eighteenth-Century Strategies," *19th-Century Music* 11 (1987): 164–67 and 174; Newcomb considers the topsy-turvy treatment of rondo form in the finale of the third string quartet.
67. Joel Lester, "Robert Schumann and Sonata Forms," *19th-Century Music* 18 (1995): 189–210. In a positive assessment of sonata-form movements in Schumann's multi-movement piano works, Linda Correll Roesner has described unusual extensions that result in larger parallel structures, ones that find their justification in local-level details; "Schumann's 'Parallel' Forms," *19th-Century Music* 14 (1991): 265–78. For a discussion of chamber works that alter the tonal argument of sonata form by either compromising tonic identity at the outset, or by allowing the tonic key to monopolize the exposition (with recapitulations that provide compelling responses), see my "Study, Copy, and Conquer: Schumann's 1842 Chamber Music and the Recasting of Classical Sonata Form," *Journal of Musicology* 30 (2013): 369–423.
68. On the historical scarcity of Schenkerian readings for Schumann's large-scale instrumental works, see Peter Smith, "Harmonies Heard from Afar: Tonal Pairing, Formal Design, and Cyclical Integration in Schumann's A-minor Violin Sonata, op. 105," *Theory and Practice* 34 (2009): 47. For a Schenkerian reading of the Third Symphony, first movement, see Lauri Suurpää, "The Undivided *Ursatz* and the Omission of the Tonic *Stufe* at the Beginning of the Recapitulation," *Journal of Schenkerian Studies* 1 (2005): 70–77. For a discussion of one facet of the new *Formenlehre* in relation to Schumann, see Peter Smith, "Schumann's Continuous Expositions and the Classical Tradition," *Journal of Music Theory* 58 (2014): 25–56.
69. Alexander Stefaniak, *Schumann's Virtuosity: Criticism, Composition, and Performance in Nineteenth-Century Germany* (Bloomington: Indiana University Press, 2016), 197.
70. Benedict Taylor, *Music, Subjectivity, and Schumann* (Cambridge and New York: Cambridge University Press, 2022). While highlighting songs and piano works from Schumann's earlier years, Taylor considers other diverse mediums, from partsongs and large-scale dramatic works, to symphonic and chamber pieces.
71. Hirschbach, "Zur Geschichtes des Quartetts," *Neue Zeitschrift für Musik* (March 20, 1843); translation from Kohlhase, "Kritischer Bericht/Critical Report," 159. Hirschbach did not elaborate on what precisely made these works unusual, probably because Schumann—as a scrupulous editor—likely discouraged him from saying more.
72. Hermann Hirshbach, "Musikzustände der Gegenwart," *Repertorium für Musik* (June 1844); translated in Kohlhase, "Kritischer Bericht/Critical Report," 161. After hearing a private performance of the string quartets in September 1842, Moritz Hauptmann responded similarly. Noting that Schumann's earlier piano pieces had been "so aphoristic and fragmentary, with a mere complacent eccentricity," he observed that in the quartets "there is no lack of unusual features as regards form and content, but they are intelligently conceived and held together, and

a great deal of the music is very beautiful." Letter of October 2, 1842, translated in Kohlhase, "Kritischer Bericht/Critical Report," 154–55.
73. Brown, "Study, Copy, and Conquer," 383–87. *GS*, vol. 1, 330.
74. *GS*, vol. 1, 76 and 428. Excessive reminiscences constitute a recurring topic in Schumann's reviews of Reissiger; for more examples, see *GS*, vol. 1, 177 and 338. Elsewhere, Schumann decried the practice in even stronger terms: "people who search their music cabinets to seek resemblances and reminiscences are disagreeable and uncultured." *GS*, vol. 1, 94.
75. *GS*, vol. 1, 67 (on Müller); vol. 2, 153 (on Hetsch); and vol. 1, 124 (on Mendelssohn). Schumann urged originality even in arrangements. For instance, in one of the few published reviews of his own works, Schumann admitted that in his Op. 3 *Etudes after Paganini's Caprices* he "copied the original, perhaps to its detriment, nearly note for note, only elaborating harmonically." For the Op. 10 *Concert Etudes after Paganini's Caprices*, however, he sought to "give the impression of an independent piano composition," one that seemed to "forget" its "violin origin" but "without forfeiting the poetic idea" of the original work. *GS*, vol. 1, 212. Schumann also acknowledged that reminiscences could be accidental, something he termed "inverse imitation"; in such cases, "a composer, with all his diligence, seeks to avoid that which he resembles until, in an unguarded moment, he falls entirely into its arms." *GS*, vol. 1, 305.
76. Kohlhase, *Die Kammermusik Robert Schumanns*. This study—Kohlhase's doctoral dissertation—was published the following year.
77. Letter to Eduard Krüger of June 14, 1839; *BNF*, 157.
78. Letter to Liszt of May 31, 1849; *Briefedition* II/5, 147. For more on the previous year's incident, see Litzmann, *CS*, vol. 2, 120–23.

2
Competing Tonics

As a young man, Schumann displayed open-mindedness about music that challenged the notion of a single controlling tonic key, whether in his own output or that of others. In an 1836 review of piano variations by Carl Maher, for instance, Schumann observed a procedure that would "irritate pedants" but that he found acceptable, namely, a set of variations in F major that opened with an introduction in D-flat major. Schumann continued: "One may begin and end a piece in different keys and still compose very beautifully. It should remain an exception, but not a prohibition."[1] As is well known, Schumann experimented with split tonal foci in his own music, a feature appearing as early as the Op. 2 *Papillons* (1829–1833) and Op. 4 *Intermezzi* (1832), and continuing throughout the decade in works like the Op. 9 *Carnaval* (1834–1835), Op. 6 *Davidsbündlertänze* (1837), Op. 12 *Fantasiestücke* (1837), Op. 16 *Kreisleriana* (1838), and beyond. Tonal ambiguity in these works might arise in several ways: for instance, by beginning a piece in one key but ending in another—the strategy identified by Schumann in his 1836 review (e.g., the seventh number of *Papillons*, or the twelfth piece of *Davidsbündlertänze*); by framing a piece in one key yet presenting its core material in another key (e.g., the ninth number of *Papillons*, the fourth piece of the *Intermezzi*, or the fifteenth number of *Davidsbündlertänze*); or by balancing two keys throughout a piece (e.g., "Aveu" from *Carnaval*, "Aufschwung" from *Fantasiestücke*, or the fourth number of *Kreisleriana*). Intra-piece examples, like those above, are well known, though Schumann explored inter-piece relationships as well. The numbers in *Fantasiestücke*, for instance, mainly use D-flat major or F minor/major, and *Kreisleriana* holds the keys of B-flat major and G minor mostly in balance between its respective numbers.[2]

Writers have noted that Schumann's pairings generally favor relative keys,[3] though his piano music also reveals other relationships: for example, the major-third-related keys in *Fantasiestücke* cited above, or fourth relationships found in the twelfth and fifteenth numbers of *Davidsbündlertänze* (in B minor and E minor/major, and B-flat and E-flat major, respectively). Schumann also enjoyed inverting tonal relationships: a passage that emphasizes one key as tonic might stress the other of the pair as subordinate, with the relationship reversed in a subsequent context. In *Carnaval*, for instance, the F-minor-based "Paganini" treats A-flat major as an interior tonicized key; but "Paganini" is framed by statements of the "Valse Allemande" in A-flat major, which itself briefly tonicizes F minor. Schumann even played with such fluid hierarchies across separate but related works, something well illustrated in the fourth number of the Op. 4 *Intermezzi* and the 1828 lied on which its core material is based, "Hirtenknabe" (about a shepherd boy and his hunting horn). As Example 2.1a shows, the original song is strophic, with the vocalist's melody framed by a cadential phrase in A minor that serves as an instrumental prelude and postlude for each verse (mm. 1–4 and 21–24). The vocal melody begins by tonicizing C major (mm. 5–6), a tonal shading that the third phrase reinforces (mm. 13–16). But given the A-minor prelude and postlude, and given the V^7-i resolutions in A minor that end the other phrases (mm. 7–8, 11–12, and 19–20), the lied makes clear the subordinate role of C as III of A minor. However, in the 1832 Intermezzo (Example 2.1b), Schumann recolors this tonal relationship, partly by expanding the original song into a rounded form (the original vocal theme—(a)—appears in mm. 2–5 and returns in mm. 11–14 after a contrasting (b) section, mm. 7–10) and partly by adding a new refrain idea. This refrain takes the place of the original prelude and postlude of the song and now emphasizes C major instead of A minor, presenting a brief fanfare (the boy's horn?) that comprises cadential closure in C major (mm. 1, 6, and 15). As a result, the opening phrase of the original song (m. 2) now sounds like a progression in C: I–vi. (The same is true of the second statement since the preceding material (b) ends with a dominant arrival in C major, m. 10.) As the song theme continues, it still strongly implies A minor, but where V^7-i resolutions confirmed this key in the original lied, the Intermezzo consistently thwarts such closure by sustaining a bass E (the root of the dominant) under A-minor harmony (mm. 2, 3, and 5; in the second statement, mm. 11, 12, and 14). Thus, while still orienting itself toward A minor, the song material lacks the unambiguous cadential definition it held within the original lied. A *diminuendo* further emphasizes the receding influence of A minor: where the first statement of the vocal theme begins *forte* and ends *piano*, the second statement begins *piano* and ends *pianissimo*. On the flip side, the three statements of the refrain grow progressively louder: *mezzo forte, forte*, then *fortissimo*. In other

COMPETING TONICS 31

Example 2.1. Comparison of Schumann's 1828 song "Hirtenknabe" with the fourth number from the *Intermezzi*, Op. 4.

(a) "Hirtenknabe."

Example 2.1. Continued

(b) Fourth number from the Op. 4 *Intermezzi*.

Example 2.1. Continued

words, the boy's newly created C-major fanfare now challenges his formerly secure A-minor vocal utterances.

 Dualistic treatments like those described above are typically associated with Schumann's early music. This chapter, however, shows that such practices yet informed the 1842 chamber works and in ways that facilitated Schumann's rethinking of older models. Two examples will illustrate, one offering an inter-movement example of competing tonics, the other an intra-movement one, and both exploring third-related keys outside of the relative-key relationship. The first of the Op. 41 string quartets opens by generating an unusual split focus between A minor (the ostensible key of the quartet) and F major, a dichotomy sustained throughout the work; indeed, the sonata-form finale—where we expect tonal clarity to finally emerge—instead begins by compromising the tonic identity of A minor. Though surprising, this strategy allows Schumann to reimagine the recapitulation in a way that responds to the unusual exposition while also resolving the larger a/F interaction of the work. The Op. 44 piano quintet is a work in E-flat major, the key of its first-movement sonata form, third-movement scherzo, and the key in which the quintet ends. The finale, however, begins by establishing G minor, a key confirmed by other structurally significant passages but one that must ultimately yield to E-flat major. The process of bringing about this tonal capitulation results in a wholly new finale form, one that reinvents both rondo and fugal principles.[4]

The ways in which tonal ambiguity arises in these works conjure larger meanings. In the case of the string quartet, I argue that a Beethovenian precedent may well have inspired the astonishing manner through which Schumann sets his competing tonics into play. Of course, commentators have described a number of Beethovenian allusions in Schumann's output, thematic and otherwise, and the chapter summarizes those that have been offered in relation to the first string quartet. I suggest a new understanding of the quartet's dualism, however, by arguing that Schumann borrowed a formal strategy from one of Beethoven's cello sonatas. Even more compelling, though, is how the quartet underscores Schumann's creative distance from his predecessor, for the work sustains its split tonal focus far longer while also resolving it differently.

The finales of the string quartet and piano quintet share a separate but significant aspect with wider cultural resonances, namely, stylized references to Hungarian-Roma music. Termed the *style hongrois* by Jonathan Bellman, and the *verbunkos* idiom by Shay Loya, this type of reference found a regular place in Western European music from the later eighteenth century onward, often in lighter-weight contexts like divertimentos, dance-type pieces for amateurs, or rondo finales of keyboard sonatas.[5] Bellman has also suggested that even as the *style hongrois* continued to retain its vernacular appeal, nineteenth-century composers sometimes imbued the idiom "with powerful extra-musical associations," ones that might resonate with nineteenth-century stereotypes of the Roma: their supposed unrestrained energy, for instance, or what Europeans saw as their greater freedom of movement, willingness to transgress, and innate musicality.[6] (After hearing a Hungarian-Roma band while on tour in Budapest in 1856, Clara Schumann noted how "extraordinarily moving" it was to hear these "children of nature perform," a remark that reflects a common but problematic perception of the Roma as primitive and untutored.)[7] Sometimes these extra-musical associations could evoke particularly negative concepts, like deceitfulness, thievery, and the demonic. For example, Bellman suggests that Caspar's revelry number in Weber's *Der Freischütz*, "Hier im ird'schen Jammerthal," intimates Caspar's hollow friendship with Max by referencing the *style hongrois*. Although Gypsy characters do not appear in the opera, the reference would have prompted Weber's audiences to think of negative stereotypes associated with them, such as falseness of character and links with the diabolical.[8] Bellman also brings attention to the pronounced presence of the *style hongrois* in Schubert's late works (from 1823 on), suggesting that perhaps in these difficult years Schubert identified with Hungarian Roma, "whose mistreatment, ostracism, defiance, and reputed reliance upon music as the expression of their sorrows had resonances in his own life."[9]

Schumann's engagement with the *style hongrois* suggests that he understood its multifaceted nature. He clearly recognized its vernacular appeal, using it in the 1840s for various works meant clearly for the amateur marketplace.[10] Schumann also recognized the idiom's usage in more substantial works by his predecessors and peers, especially those of Schubert.[11] Indeed, the latter's 1824 *Divertissement à l'hongroise*, Op. 54, D. 818—Schubert's most famous essay in the *style hongrois*—prompted a multivalent listening experience from Schumann, who described the work as "the loveliest of vulgarities" (*die schönsten Grobheiten*). He continued:

> If I might put it into words, I could probably say: I comported myself appropriately at a traditional Hungarian wedding and stamped my feet much; but spare me, Florestan, from having to somehow convey the yearning, the melancholy of this song and all the lovely forms flying by as if in a dance. Eusebius thought that the pedal point at the end is like the blessings of the priest—and then they pull away, with tambourines sounding noisily on and on into the far-off distance, further and further away.[12]

The music, Schumann suggests, could function on different levels. On the one hand, it evoked outward aspects of a particular folk culture, eliciting certain responses within specific settings. (In reminiscences of Mendelssohn, Schumann also remembered the former "stamping his feet at the Schubert divertissement.")[13] On the other hand, Schubert's music seemed to simultaneously reference deeper, ineffable emotional states, ones evoking the melancholy and mystery that Europeans attached to so-called Gypsy life.

In this inexpressible quality, the *verbunkos* idiom—especially in the hands of someone like Schubert—could embody romantic yearning and distance, sounding eternally into the infinite expanse. In other words, the *style hongrois* seemed capable of surpassing public, collective experience—in the form of a wedding rite, for example—by offering access to the solitary world and emotional states of the romantic wanderer, a wayfarer whose song (Schumann implies) could be that of the imagined Gypsy.[14]

In the finales of the piano quintet and first string quartet, Schumann injects the *verbunkos* idiom with similar and other expressive qualities. In both movements, he aligns the idiom with striking formal experimentation that also withholds a true sense of a tonal "home." In so doing, these finales resonate with contemporary perceptions of Roma communities as distant from sociocultural norms, exploring the unknown through their peripatetic lifestyle. An entry in the 1837 edition of the *Austrian National Encyclopedia* asserted, for instance, that Gypsies are "unfamiliar with all the benefits of civilization" and that "they do not like to settle down; most of them follow their overpowering partiality to the wandering life, and roam with their tents through the land, where they prefer to seek out unbeaten paths and gloomy mountain ravines."[15] Such an image could be doubly spun. For the state, the Gypsy figure often appeared threatening and uncontrollable, a violator of boundaries; but for certain late eighteenth- and nineteenth-century artists, this same figure became idealized, a model for artistic freedom and innovation. (The latter notion helps to explain the double meaning that one French term for Gypsy, *Bohémien*, subsequently assumed.)[16] Schumann—himself perceived as a frequent transgressor of boundaries by his contemporaries—seems to have supported the latter perspective. In the finales cited above, the irregular forms and ambiguous tonality suggest that Schumann saw within the *style hongrois* a pathway for experimentation, a musical style offering a degree of latitude in the treatment of more traditional forms.[17]

Competing Tonics on an Inter-Movement Level: The String Quartet, Op. 41, No. 1

The first of Schumann's string quartets generates a split focus between A minor (the presumed tonic key) and F major in a most unusual way. The opening movement establishes A minor in the slow introduction (Andante espressivo) but F major in the following sonata form (Allegro), an extraordinarily surprising design that assigns F great weight. The following movements maintain the dual tonic focus: the Scherzo confirms A minor, the Adagio F major, and not until the end of the finale is A minor solidified as the tonic key. (For a formal overview of the work, see Figure 2.1.) An 1850 reviewer, who heard the first movement as "indubitably in F major," nevertheless found the sonata form as "characterized . . . by a certain monotony, so that one is left without any satisfactory overall impression."[18] It is true that Schumann minimizes internal contrast within the sonata form. For one thing, the thematic character remains largely uniform, and a continuous exposition means that a contrasting second theme does not appear. (Although a dominant arrival in C major occurs early on, m. 95, extended to m. 100, it functions not as a medial caesura that leads to a second theme, but instead initiates further modulation and thematic development.)[19] For another, true arrival and closure in C major occur within the first ending only. Indeed, in the second ending, an augmented-sixth chord embellishes C, suggesting its possible function as V of F—the home key of the sonata form (though resolution to A-flat occurs instead, m. 133 of the second ending). The tonal goal of the exposition thereby becomes unfixed and ambiguous, undermining any sense of C as a stable, independent key area. While these tonal and thematic elements likely explain the "monotony" heard by the 1850 reviewer, I would argue that such uniformity was intentional. By minimizing contrast within the sonata form, Schumann keeps the focus on the larger tension between A minor and F major.

From the beginning, Schumann considered his work a "Quartett in A moll." Yet significantly he composed the slow introduction to the first movement only after he had sketched and made a fair copy of all four movements.[20] Thus it seems that he initially conceived of a directional tonal scheme, with F major opening the work and A minor attained by its end. In later adding the slow Andante, Schumann altered the tonal argument, pairing two keys that compete for tonic identity from the outset. In fact, to make clear that A serves not a contingent but an independent role in relation to F (and hence

Figure 2.1 Formal overview of Schumann's String Quartet, Op. 41, No. 1.

to sharpen our sense of the tonal dichotomy), Schumann subverts another formal norm: the opening Andante is not left tonally open—for example, by having it end on V of A minor or V of F major—but instead concludes with full closure in A minor (m. 25, followed by a four-measure coda; see Example 2.2). Thus the Andante comprises a closed, self-contained structure. Indeed, its formal integrity even led one 1849 reviewer to view it as a separate

Example 2.2. Schumann, String Quartet in A Minor, Op. 41, No. 1: the slow introduction, link, and beginning of the F-major sonata form (mm. 1–37).

Example 2.2. Continued

Example 2.2. Continued

movement, although Schumann's heading, "Introduzione," suggests that we should hear its key in relation to the following F-major sonata form.[21] In all, Schumann's arrangement presents a radical reversal of formal functions: a typically ancillary passage—the slow introduction—assumes great weight by establishing and closing within the true tonic key, and the first-movement sonata form—though structurally complete in itself—ultimately represents a large-scale dissonance to which the quartet must respond.

While writers have acknowledged the a/F dichotomy of the quartet, they have not emphasized how the finale's sonata form ultimately resolves this split tonal focus. The process begins with an unexpected opening gambit: instead of solidifying A minor, the finale begins by quickly relinquishing its tonal control, for while the primary theme begins in A minor, it ultimately becomes subsumed into its relative key, C major. As a result, the unequivocal control of A minor emerges only as an end-oriented event, a situation that echoes what is true of the entire quartet.

The obscuring of tonic identity arises through the formal design of the finale's opening theme. As Example 2.3a shows, the theme comprises two parts: a statement in A minor (mm. 1–16), followed by a thematic extension in C major (mm. 17–23). Both parts end with full cadences, yet in a surprising move the theme dramatizes closure not in A minor but C major. Although the cadential progression in A minor occurs twice (mm. 13–14, ♭II^6–V^7–I, repeated in mm. 15–16), the cadence is rhythmically weak: tonic harmony falls on the second beat, and the root appears in the bass only on the offbeat. These syncopated treatments of the root each follow two previous bass-note syncopations, and together they throw into relief the downbeat harmonies that subsequently appear (♭II^6 in m. 15, and V^6 of C major in m. 17). In other words, the A-minor tonic acts less as a stable point of arrival than as a springboard into subsequent harmonies. Indeed, using metric and dynamic stress, Schumann seems to emphasize the larger transformation of the Neapolitan sixth in A minor into V$^4_3$ of C major (see Example 2.3b): both chords emphasize D in the bass and share two common tones, and—unlike the tonic—both occur on downbeats with *sforzando* accents. Enhancing the smooth transition into C-major territory, Schumann maintains the theme's overall surface rhythms, texture, and character. Ultimately the theme stresses as its goal closure in C major, punctuating this latter cadence with metrically stable half-note chords plus a series of *forte* accents (mm. 21–23). Thus the theme as a whole undercuts tonic identity, subsuming A into C as a submediant upbeat.

The theme's tonal procedure has significant ramifications, for C major ultimately serves as the secondary key. In other words, the primary theme ends by stressing the key in which the exposition will end, a maneuver that forces us to re-evaluate the function of subsequent sections. For instance, although the passage that follows sounds transitional—emphasizing model-sequence patterns, circle-of-fifths motion, and increased dynamic intensity (mm. 23–62)—it does not modulate but rather returns to the key in which the passage began. As a result, the subsequent passage (beginning in m. 63) represents not an arrival in a new key but a continuation of C major. Reinforcing our sense of key continuity, this passage restates material that arose with the earlier C-major cadence—broken third figuration accompanied by a drone (compare mm. 63–70 with mm. 23–26)—while also overlaying a melody clearly derived from the main theme's head motive. Given that transitional materials drive toward this C-major passage, the music constitutes a continuous exposition, and, accordingly, the

Example 2.3 Schumann, String Quartet in A minor, Op. 41, No. 1, finale.
(a) Opening of the movement (mm. 1–28).

COMPETING TONICS 43

Example 2.3 Continued

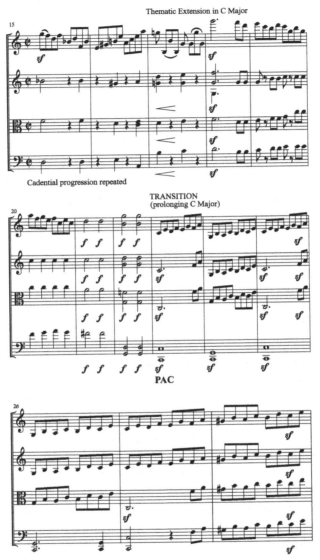

(b) Transformation of the Neapolitan sixth in A minor into dominant harmony in C major (reduction).

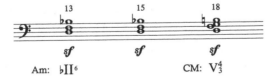

passage serves a closing function. (It prolongs C major via tonic-dominant alternations over a C drone.) Nevertheless, in Schumann's exposition, this closing material does not solidify a new key (as tradition would have it) but instead reconfirms a tonal goal achieved nearer the beginning of the movement.

The primary theme's closure in C major thus results in an anomalous reworking of sonata-form procedure: the secondary key dominates the exposition and does so at the expense of A-minor. If tonal contrast is lacking, so is thematic variety. Virtually all materials derive from the opening theme, borrowing either its rising-fifth head motive or its broken third figuration. Moreover, a rustic character and persistent eighth-note motion remain constant throughout, a *perpetuum mobile* that heightens the uniformity wrought by the saturation of C major. I would argue that the specific character of Schumann's music helps to illuminate its formal irregularities; in particular, that his challenging of formal norms receives additional meaning through his reference to the *verbunkos* idiom. This style saturates Schumann's movement, illustrated by the following traits: fiery Hungarian anapest rhythms (short-short-long), first stated in the theme's rising-fifth head motive and permeating the finale; pronounced syncopations, including the stomping *alla zoppa* rhythms of mm. 11–12 (short-long-short) and the off-beat accents accompanying the A-minor cadence (mm. 13–14, repeated in 15–16) and closing theme (mm. 73–74); frequent drones (e.g., beginning of the transition and all of the closing theme); detached articulations produced by *pizzicato* and *staccato* notations; numerous *sforzandi* accents; the minor mode; and a *Presto* tempo that reinforces the overall fervent character.[22]

Schumann's reference to the *verbunkos* idiom in conjunction with various formal irregularities suggests that he saw the style as connoting freedom from established norms. The surprising confirmation of the secondary key within the primary theme, for example, prevents the tonal contrast so typical of Classical sonata forms. It also forces us to rethink the formal functions served by subsequent transitional and closing materials. In addition, by not anchoring the movement definitively in the home key, the finale evokes the un-rootedness that many Europeans associated with so-called Gypsy life. Given the above, Schumann's use of the *verbunkos* idiom within this movement seems not merely incidental but rather supportive of the finale's recasting of sonata-form procedure. Ultimately, his atypical exposition provides the springboard for rethinking the recapitulatory process. As we shall see, this process resolves the question of tonic identity not only in the finale itself, but within the work as a whole.

To anchor the movement in the home key, Schumann does not merely recapitulate A minor, he reverses the tonal and thematic events of the exposition. After the development section, he restates transitional and closing materials first, transposing them a fifth below their original pitch level (mm. 152–205). Returning thus in F major—the key that has challenged A minor from the outset of the quartet—these materials now serve as a large-scale harmonic upbeat to the tonic return of the primary theme, which enters in measure 214. Thus what once dominated the theme now capitulates to it, and where A minor was once subsumed into C major, a diatonically symmetrical resolution uses F major to prepare A minor:

$$a - C$$
$$F - a$$

Schumann undercuts the prominence of returning transitional and closing materials in other ways as well. First, where the exposition punctuated the onset of transitional materials via an emphatic C-major cadence (m. 23), Schumann now merges the transition seamlessly with developmental materials, preceding the transition with a chordal passage that prevents any cadential motion (mm. 148–51). As a result, the recapitulatory process becomes evident to the listener only gradually. Second, to make clear the preparatory role that F now plays in relation to A minor, Schumann changes the conclusion of the closing materials. Where a full cadence concluded these materials in the first ending of the exposition, here Schumann substitutes a variation of the closing idea that clearly functions retransitionally (mm. 206–13). Instead of its original stable tonic drone, this version emphasizes V of A minor via Phyrgian motion from F; specifically, F underpins a surface-level predominant, serving as the bass of an augmented-sixth chord resolving to V of A minor (cf. mm. 204–13 with mm. 75–80 of the first ending). In this way, the closing idea becomes destabilized, forced to prepare the tonic return of the primary theme that immediately follows. Although the elision with developmental materials blurs a sense of thematic recapitulation, the tonal return is clear-cut (m. 214), reserved for the very theme whose tonic identity was compromised from the outset.[23]

Several events consolidate the A-minor return of the theme. Schumann now concludes the theme forcefully in the tonic, though only after evoking, then subduing, its original impulse toward the relative major (mm.

214–42). That is, the theme again suggests a cadence in C major, but an extension (mm. 236–41) thwarts closure to prepare a more emphatic cadence in A minor (m. 242). In this way, Schumann ensures that the home key now contains the relative key as an embedded tonicization. The following passage—an imitative version of the closing theme (mm. 242–53, derived from mm. 84–103 of the development)—confirms the role reversal: rather than solidifying C major (as it did in the exposition), this variant of the closing theme now secures the tonal control of the home key. As if to confirm such control, and the role that the *verbunkos* idiom had in challenging such control, Schumann now propels us into an otherworldly realm beginning in measure 254. For the first time in the entire quartet, the tonic major is emphasized, a significant mode change that protectively moves A farther from both F major and C major. Increasing our sense of distance from what has come before, a dramatic change in character occurs: instead of the passionate *verbunkos* idiom that has permeated the finale, we hear an abrupt drop in volume and sudden slowing of tempo and surface rhythm that brings, first, a lyrical musette (mm. 254–63), then a solemn hymn-like passage whose white notes produce a distant, archaic-like effect (mm. 264–85). Although both passages transform motives from the main body of the movement, they still make clear a break from the preceding sound world. Only then does Schumann resume the *style hongrois* character of the overall finale, although not the minor mode: maintaining distance from both F major and C major, the concluding materials sustain, and eventually close within, A major (mm. 286–320).

What makes Schumann's recapitulation even more interesting is that its response to the exposition, and to the a/F dichotomy overall, is itself foreshadowed in the "Introduzione" that opens the string quartet. As noted earlier, Schumann added this Andante after the quartet's composition. In so doing, he imbued the passage with elements that foreshadow not just the interplay between A minor and F major but even its eventual resolution. Using the head motive of the opening fugal subject as a point of departure (E–F–E, highlighting $\hat{5}$ and $\hat{6}$), Schumann develops a bass-line interaction between these same two pitches to show how F can thwart, but also facilitate, cadential definition of A minor (see Example 2.2). Two deceptive cadences occur that prevent closure in A minor, with bass E moving to F (mm. 16 and 20); these maneuvers intimate the role that F will subsequently play in questioning the tonal sovereignty of A minor. On the other hand, the bass note F also prepares V of A minor two times as a predominant, with F resolving to E. Schumann even foreshadows the Phrygian motion of the finale's retransitional passage by having an augmented-sixth chord built on F prepare first the dominant arrival that ends the opening section (mm. 11–12), and then the final full closure in A minor (mm. 22–25). The latter's $\hat{6}$–$\hat{5}$ movement even serves as the goal of the Andante's climax, culminating a rise in register and volume and highlighted via *sforzandi* accents and a subsequent drop in volume. In this way the Andante portends the finale's large-scale resolution of F as a harmonic anacrusis to V of A minor.

Schumann's string quartet gains additional significance by referencing the music of Beethoven. Writers have perceived several Beethovenian echoes in this quartet. The Adagio's main theme, for example, strongly evokes the main theme of the corresponding movement in Beethoven's Symphony No. 9 in D Minor, Op. 125.[24] Especially singled out for comparison is Beethoven's own late String Quartet in A minor, Op. 132, a work that—as Marie Sumner Lott has argued—became the touchstone for a number of nineteenth-century quartets in A minor, a key with virtually no presence in the eighteenth-century quartet repertory.[25] Like Schumann's quartet, Beethoven's Op. 132 highlights F-centered music: F major is the secondary key in the first movement sonata form, and F Lydian underpins the famous "Heiliger Dankgesang" slow movement. John Daverio also suggests that the texture of Schumann's slow introduction "conflates the detached character (and A minor tonality) of the opening Assai sostenuto of Beethoven's Opus 132 with the fugal texture of the first movement of Opus 131." Finally, Lott compares the brief A-major musette appearing near the end of Schumann's quartet with the A-major musette-based trio in Beethoven's second movement.[26]

These Op. 132 echoes notwithstanding, what interests me is the way in which Schumann sets his a/F interaction into play. Where Op. 132 introduces these keys within the context of a first-movement sonata form, Schumann juxtaposes them much more unexpectedly, between the A-minor "Introduzione" and the following F-major sonata form, thereby assigning F a more independent status. Through this surprising maneuver, Schumann conjures another Beethovenian reference unnoticed by scholars, namely the Cello Sonata, Op. 102, No. 1. Like Schumann's quartet, the sonata opens with a slow Andante in the tonic key of the work (here C major), followed by a fast sonata form in the submediant key (A minor). Like Schumann's, Beethoven's Andante also subverts its seeming function as a slow introduction by ending with full closure in C major: the dominant arrival in measure 24 (accompanied by a fermata) unexpectedly resolves to tonic harmony, sustained for several measures until another fermata highlights 1̂ in the top voice (mm. 25–27). Thus, although the formal plan of Schumann's quartet movement is highly atypical, it is not, as John Gardner has suggested, unprecedented.[27] As in Schumann's first movement, Beethoven takes care to highlight the unusual C/a dichotomy in other ways. First, the exposition of the A-minor sonata form modulates not to III but to minor V (E minor); in this way, Beethoven avoids treating C (the true tonic) as an internal area of departure, preserving it instead as an outside contrasting key. Second, the thematic character of Beethoven's Allegro remains mostly uniform, with forceful rhythms and explosive dynamic accents pervading the whole; Beethoven's use of a continuous exposition also means that a contrasting second theme never appears, although E minor—the secondary key area—is solidly established.[28] Therefore, thematic contrast occurs more outside than within the sonata form, a contrast of character that reinforces the larger interaction between C major and A minor.

As with Schumann's quartet, Beethoven's unusual movement requires that subsequent materials resolve the question of tonal identity, an issue I will briefly address since it also throws into relief Schumann's own unique response. In Beethoven's sonata, tonal clarification occurs in the interior of the work, with a section that evokes a slow movement but that ultimately serves as an introduction to the finale. (See Figure 2.2 for an overview of the work.) After a fantasia-like Adagio—the materials of which are both tonally and thematically vague (mm. 1–9)—a varied cyclic return of Andante materials re-establishes the key of C major (Tempo d'Andante, mm. 10–16), a tonal focus confirmed by the sonata-form finale. As if to redress the odd

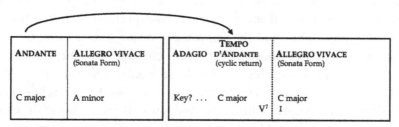

Figure 2.2 Formal overview of Beethoven's Cello Sonata in C Major, Op. 102, No. 1.

format of the first movement, Andante materials now remain open, ending with a dominant arrival (m. 16, accompanied by a fermata) that leads smoothly into the finale. That is, the Andante now seems to self-consciously fulfill its traditional function as a slow introduction to a C-major sonata form, the very thing we expected at the outset. The result, however, further confuses the question of movements in this work: although we hear the opening Andante as introductory, it ends with tonal closure, thereby suggesting its status as a separate movement; the Adagio and Tempo d'Andante, on the other hand, evoke the character of a slow movement, yet ultimately introduce the concluding C-major sonata form. We are left to ask, then, whether Beethoven has presented us with a two-, three-, or four-movement sonata.[29]

While Schumann's string quartet strongly recalls the opening tonal maneuver of Beethoven's cello sonata, it nevertheless remains strikingly different. Although his quartet also explores a submediant relationship, its paired keys are more distantly related: a/F versus the relative keys C/a (and I have shown that the proximity of the latter pair serves to undermine A minor in the finale, thereby reformulating the larger question of tonic identity in the quartet). The arrangement of movements within Schumann's quartet is also more regular than in Beethoven's sonata, with the first movement followed by a scherzo, slow movement, and fast finale. Rather than movement confusion, Schumann emphasizes tonal ambiguity, sustaining his split focus far longer than found in Beethoven's cello sonata. Indeed, by compromising A minor at the finale's outset, Schumann forces postponement of tonal resolution until near the work's end. This sustained tonal ambiguity begets a sense of absence, a longing for what tradition has normalized—the definitive control of a home key—but what cannot here be perceived. In this regard, the reference to the *verbunkos* idiom within the finale gains added significance. As discussed earlier, Schumann saw within that idiom the possibility of inexpressible longing produced by intimations of the unknown, a sort of musical poetry that embodied romantic yearning and distance. Schumann's finale captures something of these qualities by renewing at its outset the tonal ambiguity of the whole, with longing for resolution forcibly extended toward a more distant, unknowable horizon. And through this rebirth of ambiguity, the finale again highlights its creative distance from Beethoven's cello sonata while paving the way for Schumann to reimagine sonata form.[30]

Competing Tonics on an Intra-movement Level: The Finale of the Op. 44 Piano Quintet

Despite many irregularities in the Op. 44 piano quintet finale (or perhaps because of them), commentators have tried squaring its structure with classical norms. Almost invariably they label the movement a "sonata-rondo" with extensive coda, a reading prompted largely by the recurring refrain (A in Figure 2.3) and the thematic "recapitulation" that begins at measure 137.[31] At that precise moment, however, the music reveals tremendous distance from the opening G-minor tonic, for it begins in G-sharp minor, then quickly switches to D-sharp minor, a tonal remoteness that problematizes the notion of a recapitulation. Also odd is the key of this so-called sonata-rondo, for in beginning and ending in G minor it usurps the primacy of E-flat major, the key of Schumann's piano quintet. Although E-flat appears in the short first episode (B, mm. 21–29), it sounds like VI of G minor, the key underpinning the substantial opening refrain (mm. 1–21), which presents a rounded-binary form without repeats: aa,baa. (Example 2.4 reproduces the opening measures). The key of G minor will return not only at the end of the so-called sonata-rondo but also in a subsequent fugato within the lengthy

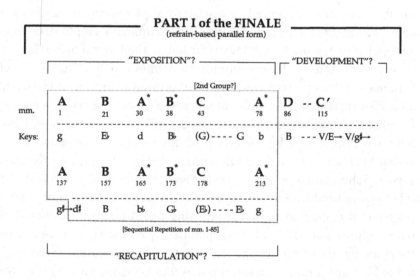

* truncated returns

Figure 2.3 Schumann, Piano Quintet in E-flat Major, Op. 44: formal overview of the finale, part I (mm. 1–220).

COMPETING TONICS 51

Example 2.4 Schumann, Piano Quintet in E-flat Major, Op. 44, finale: beginning of the opening theme (mm. 1–12).

coda. Given the above, G minor assumes a strong tonic status, yet it must ultimately capitulate to E-flat major, the key in which the finale ends. While writers have commented on the directional tonality of the finale, my analysis will offer a new understanding of the movement's unusual form, specifically its strategies for bringing about the gradual subversion of G minor, the roots of these strategies in earlier works by Schumann—even in earlier movements of the quintet, and the expressive role of the *verbunkos* idiom within these processes.

The tonal weakening of G minor begins through an unusual reimagining of rondo procedure. Instead of the refrain functioning as a tonal landmark, it adopts ever-changing harmonic guises. While the opening refrain strongly establishes G minor, we subsequently hear either full or truncated returns in D minor (mm. 30–37), B minor (mm. 78–85), G-sharp and D-sharp minor (mm. 137–56), and B-flat minor (mm. 165–72), before returning once again to G minor (mm. 213–20). In other words, Schumann loosens the grip of G minor from the refrain principle, allowing the theme to roam into diverse harmonic landscapes, both near and far.

I would argue that this surprising take on rondo procedure receives additional meaning through its evocation of the *style hongrois*, aspects of which saturate the refrain in its multiple appearances. The refrain is heavily textured, featuring double stops in the violins and a propulsive tremolo accompaniment that evokes the cimbalom, a dulcimer-like instrument used in Hungarian-Roma bands. The theme adopts a minor mode, and Schumann accents each note in a forceful *sempre marcato* style. The Hungarian anapest (short-short-long) reinforces this heavy peasant character, beginning and ending each of the five phrases and often appearing with a *sforzando* accent. The theme's four-square phrasing and exact repetition of ideas also suggest a folk-like character.[32] By imbuing the refrain with the *style hongrois* and facilitating its "travel" through multiple keys within an unusual refrain-based form, Schumann evokes cultural stereotypes attached to the Gypsy figure, one who (despite large numbers of settled Roma in the nineteenth century) was seen as rejecting the conventions of stable bourgeois life in favor of a wandering lifestyle. As in the finale of the first string quartet, the style also suggests that Schumann saw it as connoting freedom from established norms.

Further evidence that the alliance between the *verbunkos* idiom and formal experimentation is more than coincidental appears when we consider the roots of the finale's design. About two months before composing the quintet, Schumann wrote the third of his Op. 41 string quartets, a work in A major.

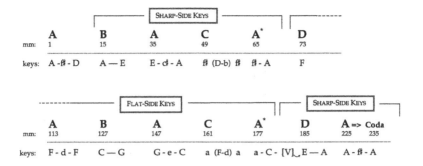

Figure 2.4 Schumann, String Quartet in A Major, Op. 41, No. 3: formal overview of the finale.

As I have discussed elsewhere, the finale of this quartet, and the early piano work from which it took its cue—the finale of the Op. 11 piano sonata—also combine references to the *style hongrois* within unusual, extended rondo-like forms: specifically, refrain-based "parallel" structures that feature sustained tonal ambiguity and multiplicity, with true tonic definition treated only as an end-oriented goal. For instance, in the quartet finale (see Figure 2.4), Schumann presents a sectional rondo form not once but twice. Moreover, instead of a refrain with periodic phrasing in a stable key, Schumann writes one that is sequential in nature, with the aphoristic main idea—a brief cadential gesture (mm. 1–2)—appearing six times in three different keys. Schumann also reverses the functions of refrain and episode. Because subsequent refrains preserve the modulatory nature of the opening theme, they appear more unstable and transitional in nature; the episodes, however, feature symmetrical periodic phrasing, rounded-binary forms, and (in the case of episodes C and D) begin and end in the same key. Also unusual is the multiplicity of keys, among which A major (the key of the overall quartet) surfaces in unexpected ways: sometimes initiating refrains, other times terminating them, perhaps disappearing altogether, and even appearing within episodes. Thus the so-called tonic—if one can yet call it that—behaves in a "migratory" manner, appearing in unexpected ways. Furthering our sense of harmonic confusion is the lengthy tonal journey that juxtaposes sharp-side keys with flat-side ones. Given the almost dizzying array of keys, and given the lack of a stable tonal home until near the movement's end (not until the coda does A major become definitively established), the music projects a palpable sense of longing, a state characteristic of the wanderer trope. In this regard, Schumann's use of the *verbunkos* idiom is surely significant. The idiom permeates the refrain in its seven appearances, adopting pronounced syncopations, abrupt tonal shifts, a *molto vivace* tempo, and pervasive dotted rhythms that evoke a Hungarian military recruiting dance (the more specific meaning of *verbunkos*). The C episodes continue the reference, stressing syncopation by continuously pelting the fourth beat with *fp* accents, and emphasizing tremolo affects common to the cimbalom. In other words, Schumann's evocation of the *style hongrois* seems not happenstance, but relevant for his recasting of rondo procedure.[33]

The finale of the Op. 44 piano quintet seems more indebted to this quartet finale (and to the earlier Op. 11 finale on which it was based) than to the sonata-rondo model proposed by others. Once again, Schumann adopts a refrain-based form that falls largely into a parallel design. Indeed, as Figure 2.3 shows, the shift to D-sharp minor in measure 149 makes the parallel restatement almost wholly sequential. (Compare mm. 149–220 with 1–85; the intervening passage, sometimes called the "development," lies outside this parallelism, however.) And like the earlier finales, Schumann again stresses non-tonic returns of the refrain amid a lengthy sojourn through numerous keys. If indebted to the earlier finales, the quintet nevertheless used them as a point of departure, for Schumann adopts a more ambitious design for this movement. First, because he establishes G minor as a competing tonic key, Schumann blurs our sense of the quintet's home key, E-flat major, even more. Second, the quintet's refrain-based structure travels more extensively around the circle-of-fifths; indeed, to generate greater tonal distance, Schumann now frames his parallel form with a symmetrical chromatic pitch structure (Figure 2.5). In the first half, long-range motion from G minor to B

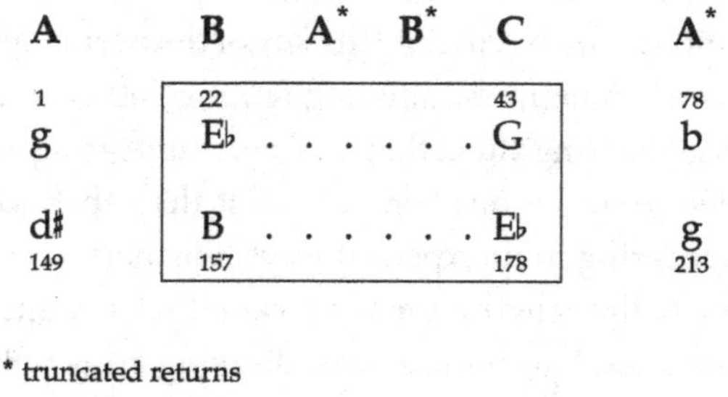

A	B	A*	B*	C	A*
1	22			43	78
g	E♭	.	. . . .	G	b
d♯	B	.	. . . .	E♭	g
149	157			178	213

* truncated returns

Figure 2.5 Schumann, Piano Quintet in E-flat Major, Op. 44, finale: symmetrical pitch structures around G minor and E-flat major.

minor (mm. 1–85) becomes balanced in the second half by similar motion from D-sharp minor to G minor (mm. 149–220), creating transpositional symmetry that divides the octave by major third (one that must assume enharmonic equivalence): g–b–d♯–g. Nested symmetrical motion occurs around E-flat as well, emphasizing the same tonics but in their parallel mode versions: E♭–G–B–E♭. Such chromatic symmetry, while having precedents in Schumann's earlier music, was quite uncommon in large-scale instrumental works of the time.[34] It presented him, however, with another strategy for subverting the tonal control of G minor.

By pairing G minor with E-flat major at both ends of his refrain-based parallel form, Schumann created the opportunity for recasting their hierarchical relationship, thereby weakening the control of G minor even further. As described earlier, the opening refrain strongly establishes G minor through a rounded-binary form minus repeats (aa,baa). This formal stability clearly projects any E-flat flavorings as VI, both in the theme's contrasting middle section (b, mm. 10–11) and in the brief pedal idea that follows (B in Figure 2.3). By the end of the parallel form, however, the tables have turned. E-flat major now returns with idea C (mm. 178–212), a lengthy episode that modulates from its initial tonicized key, only to return and make it the goal of a climactic push toward cadential closure. Thus E-flat receives much dramatic emphasis here. G minor returns with the final refrain (mm. 213–20), but its presence is now quite diminished. The theme returns in truncated form (aa), and a *descrescendo* undermines the impact of its return, creating a G-minor fade-out effect. Thus, although the parallel symmetry completes itself, the shift in tonal emphasis leaves the music open to further exploration.

Departing from earlier examples, Schumann now treats the parallel structure as part of a broader formal plan. Subsequent materials shift the focus entirely (see Figure 2.6). A series of E-flat-centered closing passages (mm. 221–48, 287–318, and 372–427) surround two fugatos: the first based on the finale's *verbunkos*-inflected theme (A, mm. 249–74), the second based famously on the first movement's main theme (mm. 319–71). Because of this cyclic return, Hans Kohlhase aptly describes part II of the movement as doubly oriented: measures 221–318 provide a coda to the finale, measures 319–427 a coda to the entire quintet.[35]

Although this second part seems to occupy a different world, I would argue that it continues a pattern introduced in the earlier parallel form and evocative of the Gypsy wanderer trope: namely, a pattern of continuously shifting perspectives. In part I, the parallel form ends by returning us once again to

	CLOSING IDEA #1	FIRST FUGATO	C′	CLOSING IDEA #2	SECOND FUGATO	CLOSING IDEA #1 + EXTENSION
	(1st appearance)	(based on main theme of Finale, A)	(cf. 115)		(based on main theme of first movement)	(2d Appearance)
mm:	221	249	275	287	319	372 402
keys:	E♭	g → V/c	E♭	E♭	E♭	E♭ E♭

PART II (doubly-oriented coda)

CODA TO FINALE ──────────────── CODA TO QUINTET ────────

Figure 2.6 Schumann, Piano Quintet in E-flat Major, Op. 44: formal overview of the finale, part II (doubly oriented coda).

G minor, yet the hierarchy of tonal relations has changed dramatically. The effect is spiral-like, imbuing the tonal return with new meaning. The parallel form also brings a series of thematic returns, yet refrains surface in different keys, propelling us further around the circle-of-fifths and ultimately down the path of changing key relations. Thematic sameness thus brings harmonic difference. By disavowing the hegemony of the "double return," Schumann's treatment of key bears closer resemblance to Baroque practice—like that of ritornello form and fugal procedure—than to Classical rondo practice. In this regard, the fugatos of part II provide an appropriate complementary response, for each requires us to hear familiar themes from new textural and harmonic perspectives. Indeed, as we shall see, the fugatos generate these new perspectives partly by responding to subdominant shadings established in previous movements. In the case of the first fugato, subdominant shading—a facet also connected with the *verbunkos* idiom—provides a final strategy for definitively conquering the tonal control of G minor.

In the first fugato (mm. 249–74), a fugal transformation of the *verbunkos*-styled main theme restores the key of G minor. By the end, however, the passage undercuts its tonal control via a plagal move: the final harmony—an emphatic G chord (m. 274)—now functions not as tonic, but as V of C minor, the subdominant of G minor and the relative key of E-flat major. This transformation arises from the fugato's unusual harmonic structure, which balances the opening tonic-dominant statements (mm. 249–56) with subdominant-tonic presentations (given in stretto, mm. 257–62). This harmonic symmetry paves the way for C minor to assume control, for a second subdominant statement now appears (mm. 263–66), the final entry of the fugato and its culminating moment: the subject occurs *forte*, the goal of the crescendo begun with the first subdominant statement; the entry is doubled, appearing in both the piano and violin; and all parts are active, making these bars the most expanded in register and texturally thickest yet. The following episode confirms the transformation in tonal perspective by treating as its goal a G chord that functions not as tonic, but as V of C minor (m. 274), a tonal capitulation that facilitates the subsequent primacy of E-flat major. In all, the fugato provides a new slant on the earlier parallel form, using nontonic returns to undermine the control of G minor.

The fugato's plagal orientation also magnifies an aspect of the original *verbunkos*-inspired theme, which opened with an emphatic full measure of C-minor harmony (Example 2.4). Thus the initial phrase and its subsequent repetitions (mm. 6, 14, and 18) consistently began with a subdominant upbeat, a flavoring enhanced by an internal tonicization of C minor (mm. 12–13). The first fugato reconfigures this plagal element by now collapsing G into C minor as V.

Shay Loya has identified within Liszt's *verbunkos*-related works the importance of various plagal elements: for instance, passages that generate ambivalence between I/V and IV/I functions, and the related phenomenon of resolving a perceived tonic into a subdominant coloring ("subdominant directionality").[36] Schumann also linked subdominant elements with the *style hongrois*. In the finale of the A-major string quartet, the opening refrain concludes in the subdominant key, anticipating subsequent flat-side keys (Figure 2.4).[37] In the piano quintet, Schumann expands this practice, and not just within the finale but throughout the entire work. As we shall see, each movement begins with a theme that highlights IV at its outset. Moreover, in the second and third movements, episodes in the subdominant minor also bring passages influenced by the *style hongrois*: measures 92–109 in the slow movement, and measures 123–96 in the scherzo. Because the slow movement also foreshadows the "subdominant directionality" of the finale's first fugato, I will focus attention there.[38]

Cast as a sectional rondo form (ABACABA), the slow movement evokes the analogous movement in Schubert's *Divertissement à l'hongroise* by presenting a funeral march in C minor, the very key that in Schumann's finale definitively subverts G minor. Unlike Schubert's theme, however, Schumann's march stresses the subdominant: outlining the chord in its melody, the theme opens with a full measure of F-minor harmony over a C pedal (see Example 2.5a), a coloring reinforced in the theme's middle section by a tonicization of F minor (mm. 15–18). The following episode in C major

Example 2.5 Schumann, Piano Quintet in E-flat Major, Op. 44: comparison of themes in the slow movement.

(a) Opening of the funeral march theme (mm. 1–2).

(b) Opening of the *Agitato* theme (mm. 92–93).

(B, mm. 29–61) recalls these plagal shadings, presenting a lyrical theme over a C pedal with $\hat{1}$–$\hat{4}$ lower-voice motion.

All of these "flat" elements receive full expression in the central F-minor episode (C, mm. 92–109), a turbulent *Agitato* inflected with traits of the *style hongrois*: numerous syncopated *sforzandi* accents, pervasive triplets, *staccato* articulation, and (beginning in the second half) numerous string "licks" in the form of rapid anapest rhythms. Especially striking is how this subdominant episode reflects on the movement's initial subdominant emphasis (see Example 2.5b). The *Agitato* theme traces the march's opening gesture, punning its pitches by transforming their harmonic function from iv–i in C minor to i–V^6 in F minor. This metamorphosis will have telling consequences.

Illustrating the powerful effect of this *Agitato* episode, subsequent materials return in ways that bear its influence. The funeral-march tune recurs considerably altered (mm. 110–32), for it is no longer solemn, but restless and impassioned. Adopting frenzied tremolos, the march continues the triplet eighths of the *Agitato* while also interjecting fragments of the *Agitato* theme into the second bar of each phrase (mm. 111, 115, 119, etc.). The triplet eighths continue into the reprise of B, also straining its original sense of repose (mm. 132–64); moreover, this episode returns transposed down a fifth, a tonal shift from C major into the major subdominant, F major. Lastly, the final reprise of the march theme (mm. 165–93) begins not in C minor, but in the subdominant key of F minor; and while a shift to C minor prevents closure in F (mm. 171–73), the subsequent tonicization of, and cadence within, F minor now sounds like a tonal return (mm. 177–80). Most strikingly, F-minor coloring thwarts tonal closure at the movement's end. The theme's final phrase is unable to cadence, stuck momentarily on a first-inversion C tonic chord (mm. 185–86). Suddenly, a dynamic surge brings an emphatic dissonance foreign to C minor, but diatonic to F minor: over a G pedal, the notes D♭–F slide into C-major harmony (mm. 187–88). The effect is remarkable: a Phrygian inflection of C minor, combined with resolution into major tonic harmony, suggests a possible function of C as V of F minor, a "subdominant directionality" presaged by the *Agitato*'s pun on the march tune. And while the following bars stabilize the C-major triad, this Phrygian approach prevents full closure in the tonic key. As a result, the last cadence of the movement is the earlier one tonicizing F minor (m. 180).

In all, the growing presence of the subdominant drastically alters conventional procedures in this movement. Given the *Agitato*'s influence in this regard, the slow movement links traits of the *verbunkos* idiom once again with experimental harmonic practice. By preventing full closure, the subdominant colorings also leave boundaries open, suggesting the possibility of further exploration. Ultimately, the movement's transformation of tonic function becomes spun once again by the finale's first fugato: reorienting the plagal directionality now toward C minor (the relative key of E-flat major), the fugato cinches the tonal capitulation of G minor and hence facilitates the subsequent tonal autonomy of E-flat major.

In the finale, the second fugato continues the pattern of evolving perspectives, most famously by transforming the first movement's main theme into a fugal subject, while also subduing the finale's main theme into an accompanying countersubject (mm. 319–71). Critics have pointed out various motivic elements that prepare this cyclic return.[39] Equally striking, however, is how this second fugato builds upon, while also surpassing, a web of plagal associations built across the entire quintet. Like the main themes of the second and last movements, this cyclic theme—in its original appearance at the outset of the quintet—also highlights the subdominant (see Example 2.6a): its opening leap to D♭ turns the initial tonic into V^7 of IV. Yet instead of destabilizing E-flat major, here the subdominant inflection prolongs it, with motion from I to IV balanced by motion from vii^{o7} to I, the whole underpinned by an E-flat pedal. Significantly, this opening progression and tonic pedal characterize *all* of the E-flat themes in the piano quintet (see Example 2.6b–c, though V^7 replaces vii^{o7}).

Example 2.6 Schumann, Piano Quintet in E-flat Major, Op. 44: comparison of harmonic structure in E-flat major themes.

(a) First movement, opening theme (mm. 1–3; reduction).

(b) Third movement, opening scherzo theme (mm. 1–8; reduction).

(c) Last movement, idea "B" (mm. 22–25; piano part).

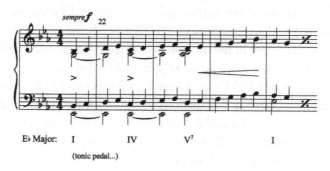

Nevertheless, given the tonal procedures of the slow movement and finale's first fugato, it is surely significant that the cyclic return of the theme ultimately expunges this subdominant inflection by transposing it down a fourth (Example 2.7a). That is, in a symbolic protection of the tonal sovereignty of E-flat major, the theme rids itself of the subdominant inflection that ultimately compromised the tonal control of its third-related keys: C minor in the slow movement, and G minor in the finale's first fugato. In so doing, the theme's opening gesture now becomes a dominant-prolonging idea. This functional transformation first occurs in the opening movement when the main theme returns eight bars later in varied form (mm. 17–25; see Example 2.7b). The real tour de force occurs much later, however, with the theme's contrapuntal transformation in the finale's second fugato, a passage that, unlike the first fugato, stresses only tonic-dominant entries of the subject. In the fugato's climactic conclusion (mm. 355–71), a sixteen-bar dominant pedal underpins eight statements of the subject's head motive in augmentation (see Example 2.7c). Each occurs two bars later and a fourth higher than the last—thereby emphasizing each scale degree of E-flat major—with the entire series framed by statements beginning on B♭ (mm. 355 and 369). Indeed, as evidence of its capacity to define (versus destabilize) the key of E-flat, the final gesture delivers the authentic cadence ending the fugato. In this way, the second fugato does not merely cinch E-flat major by reviving the theme that originally established this key, it responds to previous moments by definitively conquering the plagal tendency—and its association with the *style hongrois*—that brought about the downfall of its third-related keys, C minor and G minor. Thus the second fugato brings us to a new summit, affording a fresh vantage point on earlier harmonic processes.

In his 1858 biography of Schumann, Wilhelm Joseph von Wasielewski held out generous praise for the quintet, extolling its "rich power and originality of invention." Though supplying no particulars, nor commenting on the *style hongrois* aspects of the work, he nevertheless captured its continuously shifting perspectives with a metaphor by now familiar to us: "In a sense this work offers an image of a wanderer, who—drawn by the rich, blooming scenery extending across the mountain slope—climbs higher and higher to enjoy from the summit a final sweeping view while contemplating the path left behind."[40]

The marriage diary of Robert and Clara Schumann provides a striking parallel experience, one that Wasielewski would not have known. Just weeks before Robert composed the piano quintet, the couple vacationed in the

62 ROBERT SCHUMANN'S LEIPZIG CHAMBER WORKS

Example 2.7 Schumann, Piano Quintet in E-flat Major, Op. 44: reincarnations of the first movement's main theme, with the subdominant inflection expunged.

(a) Abstracted transformation.

(b) First movement, varied return of the main theme (mm. 17–21; reduction).

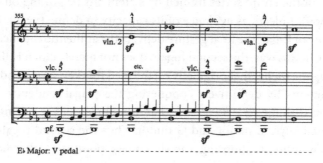

(c) Finale—climactic conclusion of the second fugato (mm. 355–71; reduction).

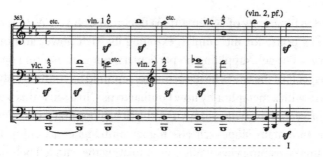

Erzgebirge region of Bohemia. Prior to their departure, Clara wrote that "I feel driven to go out into the mountains," and this desire was partly fulfilled through different hikes.[41] An entry by Robert for August 11, 1842, indicates that "we climbed the Schlossberg. It was very straining for Clara, also myself. The reward at the top is great, however." On the following day, they climbed the Milischauer, a "beautiful giant mountain" whose ascent made for a day that, as Robert writes, "will remain unforgettable for me." He continues:

> The ascent took place in already great heat and caused me much trouble.... Finally it was climbed. At the top one is addressed by lovely commemorative sayings [*Gedenksprüche*], and the comfortable facilities offer protection from storms and heat. And then the marvelous panorama! One should even see beyond Prague. But on mountains I don't like to slurp over particulars but prefer to let the whole thing wash over me. Then one feels God's beautiful world. I would have liked to remain up there easily for a week.

As for the Schlossberg, climbed the previous day, Robert notes that it "lies at one's feet like a mole-hill."

The higher perspective afforded by the Milischauer then becomes a metaphor for artistic progress, for Robert continues: "So it is also in life and in art. Only when one is on greater mountains does one perceive the smallness of those previously conquered, and if only yesterday one imagined themselves to stand high, then on the following day one feels how with effort and exertion they can reach even higher." Taking his leave late in the day, Robert returns these accomplishments (both figurative and literal) to a distant realm, one that initiates through its departure a state of infinite romantic yearning: "Towards 5 o'clock we left the beautiful giant mountain, which bid us farewell for a long time and finally shrouded itself (again) in total darkness."[42]

The piano quintet seems to enact this idea of artistic journeying. Composed just weeks after their Bohemian trip, the quintet manipulates tonal and thematic returns so that they continually yield new perspectives, ones that in the finale help to resolve the intra-movement dichotomy between G minor and E-flat major. But perhaps the climbing metaphor could be extended further, such that Schumann himself becomes an idealized Gypsy wanderer, building upon past accomplishments by continually seeking out new possibilities from the *verbunkos* idiom. Indeed, at the outset of their Bohemian trip, a chance encounter with an acquaintance from Zwickau reminded Schumann of his youth: "Lovely hopes were placed on me [then], as I again noticed from the conversation with him; they have only just been partly fulfilled. It again occurred to me how much there remains for me to do."[43] With the composition that followed, Schumann reached a new artistic summit, creating what Wasielewski called "undoubtedly the most significant chamber artwork" since those of Beethoven, an opinion echoed by many others.[44] But if the Op. 44 piano quintet is the "beautiful giant" Milischauer, then the A-major string quartet is surely the Schlossberg (and the Op. 11 piano sonata a smaller mountain yet). For it seems clear that the quintet took as its point of departure the finales of these earlier works. And suffusing each of these pieces—and the finale of the A-minor string quartet (with its reinvented sonata form that responds to the larger a/F dichotomy of the work)—is the *style hongrois*, which seems to have opened for Schumann new avenues of formal experimentation. Thus Schumann must also be counted as one who uncovered new expressive effects from this popular musical idiom.

Notes

1. *GS*, vol. 1, 228.
2. For a discussion of related pieces from (adjusted) Schenkerian perspectives, see for example Peter Kaminsky, "Aspects of Harmony, Rhythm, and Form in Schumann's 'Papillons,' 'Carnaval,' and 'Davidsbündlertänze'" (PhD diss., University of Rochester, Eastman School of Music, 1990), especially 79–121; and Benjamin Wadsworth, "Directional Tonality in Schumann's Early Works," *Music Theory Online* 18 (December 2012), article 7. For a discussion of such works against the backdrop of Jean Paulian *Humor*, or the "contrast of incommensurable entities," see Daverio, *Nineteenth-Century Music*, 64–71. See also Erika Reiman's discussion of the fifth number from the *Intermezzi*, with its "war between the keys of F major and D minor"; Reiman, *Schumann's Piano Cycles and the Novels of Jean Paul* (Rochester, NY: University of Rochester, 2004), 67–71. For commentary on the dual-tonic focus of *Kreisleriana*, see for instance Charles Rosen, *The Romantic Generation* (Cambridge, MA: Harvard University Press, 1995), 672–77.
3. See for example Kaminsky, "Aspects of Harmony, Rhythm, and Form," 80–81; and Wadsworth, "Directional Tonality in Schumann's Early Works," paragraph 2.
4. My analyses present revised and updated segments from essays first published in 2011 and 2013: pp. 407–22 from Julie Hedges Brown, "Study, Copy, and Conquer: Schumann's 1842 Chamber Music and the Recasting of Classical Sonata Form," *Journal of Musicology* 30 (2013); used with permission of the University of California Press, with permission conveyed through Copyright Clearance Center, Inc.; and pp. 265–68 and 280–91, with re-use of figures 13.1, 13.3, and 13.5, from Julie Hedges Brown, "Schumann and the *style hongrois*," in *Rethinking Schumann*, eds. Roe-Min Kok and Laura Tunbridge (Oxford: Oxford University Press, 2011); reproduced by permission of Oxford University Press (https://academic.oup.com/book/11444).
5. Jonathan Bellman, *The style hongrois in the Music of Western Europe* (Boston: Northeastern University Press, 1993). Shay Loya, *Liszt's Transcultural Modernism and the Hungarian-Gypsy Tradition* (Rochester, NY: University of Rochester Press, 2011). I will use the terms *style hongrois* and *verbunkos* idiom interchangeably. While I substitute "Hungarian-Roma" for "Hungarian-Gypsy," elsewhere I follow Loya's example (xv) by using the term "Roma" for the actual people, and "Gypsy" when referring to representations of them within popular

imagination and in visual, literary, and musical works, ones often weighted with problematic cultural stereotypes. The term *verbunkos* also requires clarification. In a more specific sense, the Magyar word *verbunk*—derived from the German word *Werbung* ("recruiting")—referred to a military recruiting dance. According to Loya, the term eventually assumed a more "collective generic" meaning in the hands of twentieth-century Hungarian musicologists. For more on this terminological flexibility, including Loya's definition of the *verbunkos* idiom, see Loya, *Liszt's Transcultural Modernism*, 60–61, and 253, note 1. For an overview of defining traits of the *style hongrois*, see Bellman, *The* style hongrois, 93–130. Loya has expanded Bellman's "lexicon," considering additional structural and harmonic features, especially in relation to Liszt's works; Loya, "The *Verbunkos* Idiom in Liszt's Music of the Future: Historical Issues of Reception and New Cultural and Analytical Perspectives" (PhD diss., King's College, 2006), 141–52.
6. Bellman, *The* style hongrois, 65.
7. Quoted in Litzmann, *CS*, vol. 2, 402.
8. Bellman, *The* style hongrois, 144–46. For an overview of Gypsy stereotypes propagated in literature and culture of the time, see ibid., 69–92. See also Jonathan Bellman, "The Hungarian Gypsies and the Poetics of Exclusion," in *The Exotic in Western Music*, ed. Jonathan Bellman (Boston: Northeastern University Press, 1998), 74–103.
9. Bellman, *The* style hongrois, 161. For a chronological list of Schubert's music using the *style hongrois*, see ibid., 225–26.
10. For a list of these works, see my essay, "Schumann and the *style hongrois*," 266. The first person to discuss the *style hongrois* in relation to Schumann was John Daverio, who in 2002 briefly mentioned Schumann's 1840 choral piece "Zigeunerleben" and the late Op. 131 *Phantasie* for Violin as examples (his essay emphasizes Brahms); Daverio, *Crossing Paths: Schubert, Schumann, and Brahms* (Oxford and New York: Oxford University Press, 2002), 213–14, and 239. Daverio opened the portal for my 2011 essay, which was the first substantial study of how the *style hongrois* influenced Schumann in both amateur and more ambitious large-scale works. Since then, Alexander Stefaniak has offered a more in-depth discussion of the Op. 131 *Phantasie*; Stefaniak, *Schumann's Virtuosity*, 228–35.
11. Schumann reviewed a number of Schubert works inflected with the *verbunkos* idiom: the Grand Duo Sonata, Op. 140; the F-minor *Moment Musical* from Op. 94; the Sonata in D Major, Op. 53; the F-minor Impromptu from Op. 142; and the Symphony in C Major, D. 944—a work in which Schumann heard a "wild, gypsy-like bustling of folk;" *GS*, vol. 2, 132. Schumann also recognized the *style hongrois* in the music of other composers. For example, in an October 1842 review of Loewe's oratorio, *Johann Huß*, Schumann expressed disappointment in the Gypsy chorus opening part 2, arguing, "Euphony and charm should never be lacking, even when Gypsies are the singers. Weber knew how to do this better in *Preciosa*." *GS*, vol. 2, 103. For a discussion of *style hongrois* elements in Weber's opera, see Bellman, *The* style hongrois, 138–44 and 163.
12. Entry of August 20, 1831; *Tb*, vol. 1, 363–64. Tambourines are more associated with Turkish style in Western music, a style that shared ties with the *verbunkos* idiom but that nevertheless remained distinct from it; see Bellman, *The* style hongrois, 11–16 and 47–68; and Catherine Mayes, "Turkish and Hungarian-Gypsy Styles," in *The Oxford Handbook of Topic Theory*, ed. Danuta Mirka (New York: Oxford University Press, 2014), 214–37. Nevertheless, composers frequently mixed the two in a kind of pan-exotic referencing. For example, in Schumann's 1840 choral piece "Zigeunerleben" (Gypsy Life), the score indicates an *ad libitum* role for the triangle and tambourine.
13. Robert Schumann, "Aufzeichnungen über Mendelssohn," in *Felix Mendelssohn Bartholdy*, ed. Heinz-Klaus Metzger and Rainer Riehn, Musik-Konzepte series, vol. 14/15 (Munich: Dieter Vollendorf, 1980), 101; date of reminiscence marked October 9, 1836.
14. On the literary and sociological aspects of the wanderer trope within the nineteenth century, including the ability to intuit meaning incapable of being expressed in words, see David Gramit, "Schubert's Wanderers and the Autonomous Lied," *Journal of Musicological Research* 14 (1995): 147–68. On Schumann's responsiveness to the notion of romantic distance in Schubert and in general, see Berthold Hoeckner, "Schumann and Romantic Distance," *Journal of the American Musicological Society* 50 (Spring 1997): 55–132; reprinted as chapter 2 of his book, *Programming the Absolute: Nineteenth-Century German Music and the Hermeneutics of the Moment* (Princeton, NJ: Princeton University Press, 2002).
15. *Österreichische National-Encyklopädie*, vol. 6 (Vienna, 1837), 247; cited in Bellman, *The* style hongrois, 78–79.

16. See Bellman, *The style hongrois*, 90–92. As George Sand stated in the concluding pages of her 1837–1838 novel, *La Dernière Aldini*, "Gaily let us dispense with wealth, when we have it, let us accept poverty without worry, if it comes; let us keep above all our liberty, enjoy life all the same, and long live the Gypsy!" Cited in Bellman, *The style hongrois*, 69. For a more panoramic view of how perceptions of Roma culture and music—including that linked with Russian and Spanish Roma—influenced European culture even beyond the nineteenth century, see Anna G. Piotrowska, *Gypsy Music in European Culture from the Late Eighteenth to the Early Twentieth Centuries*, trans. Guy R. Torr (Boston: Northeastern University Press, 2013).

17. Shay Loya has made a similar argument for Liszt, suggesting that the *verbunkos* idiom influenced Liszt's modernist treatment of tonality and form in works composed particularly in the later 1840s and beyond, including late works that may not even carry outward signs of the style. For an overview of his approach, see *Liszt's Transcultural Modernism*, 1–16.

18. C. Böhmer, review of June 12, 1850, *Neue Berliner Musikzeitung*, 185; original and translation found in Kohlhase, "Kritischer Bericht/Critical Report," 170.

19. On the notion of the continuous exposition and how it differs from expositions using a medial caesura, see James Hepokoski and Warren Darcy, *Elements of Sonata Theory: Norms, Types, and Deformations in the Late-Eighteenth-Century Sonata* (Oxford and New York: Oxford University Press, 2006), 51–64 and 23–50. For a more in-depth discussion of this facet of Schumann's sonata form, see Smith, "Schumann's Continuous Expositions and the Classical Tradition," 27–31.

20. As his *Haushaltbuch* entries show, the sketch of the quartet was begun on June 4, 1842 ("Quartett in A Moll angefangen") and was completed on June 10. The fair copy was made from June 20–24, with the slow introduction added a day later ("Nachmittag Introduction z. 1sten Quartett auch fertig gemacht"); *Tb*, vol. 3, 216–18. Linda Correll Roesner has shown that physical evidence also supports this chronology. Roesner, "Studies in Schumann Manuscripts: With Particular Reference to Sources Transmitting Instrumental Works in the Large Forms" (PhD diss., New York University, 1973), vol. 1, 83–88; the entire sketch is helpfully transcribed in vol. 2, 38–50.

21. F. C. Kist, review of March 26, 1849, performance in Utrecht, published in *Caecilia* 6 (1849), 78; original and translation in Kohlhase, "Kritischer Bericht/Critical Report," 168. The 1850 reviewer cited in note 18 also seemed to see the passage as separate but asserted that "it would surely have been better not to isolate the Introduction by bringing it completely to an end, but to link it directly to the following movement [the sonata form]." This assertion stems from his view of the Introduction as almost extraneous: "Since we cannot find any reference to [it] in the entire quartet, we naturally wonder why it is there at all. The only reason we can see is that the main key of the quartet is meant to be in A minor." As we shall see, the manner through which Schumann ultimately resolves his a/F dualism is in fact foreshadowed in the slow introduction.

22. Peter Gülke has also noted in passing this character of the finale ("All'ongharese"), though without describing its traits or significance. Gülke, "Mutmaßungen über waghalsiges Komponieren: Robert Schumanns Streichquartette op. 41," in *Ereignis und Exegese: Musikalische Interpretation—Interpretation der Musik*, ed. Camilla Bork (Schliengen: Edition Argus, 2012), 415.

23. I first described this recapitulatory process in 2000; Brown, "'A Higher Echo of the Past': Schumann's 1842 Chamber Music and the Rethinking of Classical Form" (PhD diss., Yale University, 2000), 234–37. Peter Smith has subsequently squared it with the type 2 sonata described by Hepokoski and Darcy in their *Elements of Sonata Theory*; Smith, "Schumann's Continuous Expositions and the Classical Tradition," 32–36. For an analysis that views the return of secondary materials in F major as only furthering—versus resolving—the a/F dichotomy, see Roesner, "The Chamber Music," in *The Cambridge Companion to Schumann*, ed. Beate Perrey (Cambridge: Cambridge University Press, 2007), 127; see also Taylor, *Music, Subjectivity, and Schumann*, 108–9. As I subsequently show, however, the process through which Schumann resolves F major into A minor in the finale (what Smith also sees as an unequivocal resolution of the quartet's a/F "vacillations," 35) inspired him to foreshadow it in the slow introduction that he subsequently added. Recall, too, that Schumann described the work as a "Quartett in A moll."

24. See for example Kohlhase, *Die Kammermusik Robert Schumanns*, vol. 2, 37; Daverio, *Robert Schumann*, 252; A. E. F. Dickinson, "The Chamber Music," in *Schumann: A Symposium*, ed. Gerald Abraham (London: Oxford University Press, 1952), 144; and Nicholas Marston, "Schumann's Heroes: Schubert, Beethoven, Bach," in *The Cambridge Companion to Schumann*, ed. Beate Perrey (Cambridge: Cambridge University Press, 2007), 54.

25. Lott, *The Social Worlds of Nineteenth-Century Chamber Music*, 111–15.

26. Daverio, *Robert Schumann*, 252; Lott, *The Social Worlds of Nineteenth-Century Chamber Music*, 131–32. I would argue that another similarity occurs through the shared E/F half-step emphasis within A-minor material. As Joseph Kerman describes it within Op. 132: "it is the step F-E which the Finale salvages from the *cantus-firmus* motif of the opening"; Kerman, *The Beethoven Quartets* (New York and London: Norton, 1979), 263.
27. John Gardner, "The Chamber Music," in *Robert Schumann: The Man and His Music*, ed. Alan Walker (London: Barrie and Jenkins, 1972), 203. Although Schumann never mentioned the C-major sonata in his criticism or diaries, the *Neue Zeitschrift für Musik* published several concert reviews that cite performances of Beethoven cello sonatas, including three in the years 1841–1842. *NZfM* 15 (July 27, 1841): 31; 16 (March 25, 1842): 100; and 16 (June 28, 1842): 208. (The last-named review mistakenly labels the F-major Cello Sonata "Op. 8" instead of Op. 5.) Bodo Bischoff has noted a November 1834 entry in Clara's diary that indicates a likely performance of a Beethoven cello sonata; Bischoff, *Monument für Beethoven: Die Entwicklung der Beethoven-Rezeption Robert Schumanns* (Cologne: Dohr, 1994), 425. The C-major sonata had also been well disseminated. Within several years of its composition in 1815, the piece had been published by Simrock and Artaria; arrangements for violin and piano followed, as did several reprintings. See Kurt Dorfmüller, Norbert Gertsch, and Julia Ronge, *Ludwig van Beethoven: Thematisch-bibliographisches Werkverzeichnis* (Munich: G. Henle Verlag, 2014), vol. 1, 643–49. All of the above indicates that Schumann likely knew the composition.
28. Arrival on V of E minor occurs early on (m. 46), with subsequent materials prolonging E minor, but a medial caesura never occurs. Instead, transitional materials eventually drive to full closure in m. 66, with subsequent closing materials recalling the dotted rhythms and $\hat{1}$–$\hat{3}$–$\hat{5}$ emphasis of the main theme (mm. 66–75).
29. On movement ambiguity in this sonata, see Lewis Lockwood, "Beethoven's Emergence from Crisis: The Cello Sonatas of Op. 102 (1815)," *Journal of Musicology* 16 (1998): 306 and 312–13. On the nostalgic character of the cyclic return (Tempo d'Andante), see Kristina Muxfeldt, *Vanishing Sensibilities: Schubert, Beethoven, Schumann* (Oxford and New York: Oxford University Press, 2012), 140–47. For a discussion of middle movements in Beethoven that problematize closure, and their psychological effect within the work as a whole, see Lewis Lockwood, *Beethoven: Studies in the Creative Process* (Cambridge, MA: Harvard University Press, 1992), 181–97.
30. As I have discussed elsewhere, other movements from the 1842 repertory rethink the tonal argument of sonata form while also referencing—and departing from—specific Beethovenian precedents: the first movements of the piano quartet and third string quartet; see Brown, "Study, Copy, Conquer," 369–407. Curiously, Schumann's second string quartet reverses the tonal focus of the first one by treating F major as its home key, although without engaging in the dualistic play of the first quartet. Indeed, as Kohlhase and Roesner have discussed, Schumann briefly considered a thematic link between the two works: the four-bar transitional idea that connects the "Introduzione" of the first quartet to the following F-major sonata form (mm. 30–33; see Example 2.2) reappeared in the manuscript of the second quartet as the opening gesture, a link that failed to appear in the published version, however. Kohlhase, *Die Kammermusik Robert Schumanns*, 47; and Roesner, "The Chamber Music," 128, who argues for other links between the three quartets. Schumann's interest in coloring A minor with F major also occurred in later works: for instance, the Op. 73 *Fantasiestücke* for piano and clarinet, especially the first of the set; the Op. 54 Piano Concerto; and the late Op. 105 Violin Sonata. For compelling discussions of the latter work, see Peter Smith, "Tonal Pairing and Monotonality in Instrumental Forms of Beethoven, Schubert, Schumann, and Brahms," *Music Theory Spectrum* 35 (2013): 89–91; and Smith, "Harmonies Heard from Afar," 47–86.
31. For instance, see Joan Chissell, *Schumann*, 162–63; Dickinson, "The Chamber Music," 153–54; Gardner, "The Chamber Music," 233–38; Kohlhase, *Die Kammermusik Robert Schumanns*, 1: 162–66; Frieder Reininghaus, "Zwischen Historismus und Poesie: Über die Notwendigkeit umfassender Musikanalyse und ihre Erprobung an Klavierkammermusik von Felix Mendelssohn Bartholdy und Robert Schumann," *Zeitschrift für Musiktheorie* 5, no. 1 (1974): 43; and Michael Talbot, *The Finale in Western Instrumental Music* (Oxford and New York: Oxford University Press, 2001), 96–98. Commentators have also asserted other so-called sonata-form elements: mm. 43–77 (C) as the secondary theme group, and mm. 86–136 as a "development" section. However, writers too often fail to qualify their reading by detailing the surprising departures from sonata-rondo practice; Talbot and especially Kohlhase are notable exceptions in this regard.

32. Jonathan Bellman has graciously drawn my attention to a "cognate" of this theme found in another piano quintet: the finale of Brahms's Piano Quintet in F Minor, Op. 34. There, the main theme also begins on the half bar, suffuses itself with anapest rhythms, and features a detached articulation (here *staccato*), simple rhythms (though Brahms incorporates ornamental figures as well), and much repetition of ideas. With its many repeated notes in sixteenth-note rhythms, the accompaniment also evokes cimbalom playing. Bellman, personal communication.
33. For a more detailed analysis of the A-major quartet finale, see Brown, "Schumann and the *style hongrois*," 269–73; for a discussion of the earlier Op. 41 finale and the ways in which it simultaneously references and departs from Schubert's *Grand Duo* Sonata, Op. 140, see 273–79. The concept of parallel structures has been associated with Schumann's early piano sonatas and *Fantasie*, as shown by Roesner ("Schumann's 'Parallel' Forms," 265–78), and Charles Rosen, *Sonata Forms*, rev. ed. (New York: Norton, 1988), 369 and 380–83. Yet Schumann resumed their use in 1842, and not only in the finales discussed above, but also in the finale of the Op. 47 piano quartet, as I have discussed elsewhere ("Higher Echoes of the Past in the Finale of Schumann's 1842 Piano Quartet," 511–64); however, the latter work extends sonata form instead of refrain-based form and does not reference the *verbunkos* idiom.
34. The opening number of Schumann's *Novelletten*, Op. 21, for instance, progresses through the keys F–D♭–A–F, a scheme foreshadowed in the opening theme. Even as early as 1831, Schumann showed interest in symmetrical key relationships. An early sketchbook begun in May of that year contains (among other items) ideas for such key schemes; arranging the circle-of-fifths horizontally, Schumann connects the keys with different arcs showing various possibilities, for instance: C–E–G♯–C and C–A–F♯–D♯–C. For a facsimile of these pages, see Bischoff (*Monument für Beethoven*, 485–87), who links this interest with Schumann's concurrent study of harmonic processes in Beethoven's "Hammerklavier" Sonata (121–31 and 163).
35. Kohlhase, *Die Kammermusik Robert Schumanns*, vol. 2, 94.
36. See Loya, *Liszt's Transcultural Modernism and the Hungarian-Gypsy Tradition*, 41–46. As Loya shows, Liszt principally engaged with the *verbunkos* idiom in the later 1840s onward. Thus it is difficult to assert Liszt's influence on Schumann's plagal practices in the 1842 quintet. Liszt's well-known remark in 1848 that the quintet was too "Leipzigerish" itself suggests a lack of identification on his part. On this episode, see the conclusion of Chapter 1.
37. The coda of the string quartet also features significant "subdominant directionality": while grounding the music in A major, the coda prevents final closure by turning an expected tonic resolution into V^7 of IV (mm. 278–79). Although a stable, root-position A-major chord occurs three bars later (m. 282), Schumann syncopates it as a *sforzando* accent on beat four and provides it with no cadential preparation. Thus, in a striking act of irony, the movement technically ends without full closure, a fitting conclusion given that the refrain's cadential gestures have previously served to confuse tonal focus by tonicizing other keys.
38. The slow movement also provides the basis for much of the finale's motivic materials, as Hans Kohlhase has shown: *Die Kammermusik Robert Schumanns*, 1: 71; and "Robert Schumanns Klavierquintett op. 44: Eine semantische Studie," in *Musik-Konzepte Sonderband: Robert Schumann, I, November 1981*, ed. Heinz-Klaus Metzger and Rainer Riehn (Munich: Johannesdruck Hans Pribil, 1981), 167.
39. See for example Daverio, *Robert Schumann*, 257–58; Kohlhase, *Die Kammermusik Robert Schumanns*, vol. 2, 96; and Tovey, *Essays in Musical Analysis*, vol. 7, *Chamber Music*, 154.
40. Josef W[ilhelm] von Wasielewski, *Robert Schumann: Eine Biographie* (Dresden: Verlagsbuchhandlung von Rudolf Kunze, 1858), 214–15.
41. Clara Schumann, *Tb*, vol. 2, 234.
42. Robert Schumann, *Tb*, vol. 2, 238. Schumann used mountain imagery as a metaphor for artistic progress in his criticism as well. For example, an 1836 review of W. Schüler's piano concerto criticizes the composer's desire to return to "older simplicity" in the rondo movement. Schumann comments: "We are not friends of backward steps.... Thus let us go forward, friends! We want to look back from the summit, not before." GS, vol. 2, 312.
43. Robert Schumann, *Tb*, vol. 2, 235.
44. Wasielewski, *Robert Schumann*, 214.

3
Nested Forms

"We must now find new middle movements of a different character." So proclaimed Schumann in 1836 while reviewing chamber music by a variety of composers. For him, slow movements could serve as portals through which true artists "uncover[ed] the reserves and richness of inner life," and scherzos were vessels for "immense imagination and wit." It was not enough to merely include inner movements "because it is the custom," nor to duplicate styles of earlier times. As Schumann admonished one composer, "write no more adagios, or write them better than Mozart's. If you put on a wig, does it make you wiser?" The work under review was also wanting in its scherzo movement, where Schumann had "dearly hoped to find something livelier and more original."[1]

This chapter provides new perspectives on Schumann's creative approaches to two inner-movement forms, one a scherzo-trio drawn from the A-minor String Quartet, Op. 41, No. 1, the other a variation-based slow movement from the F-major String Quartet, Op. 41, No. 2. For a listener, these two forms are the most predictable classical models, involving exact or varied levels of repetition. In the movements covered here, however, Schumann imbues these forms with new expressive effects by reimagining the repetition concept, and in ways that yield novel nested forms that create surprise at various turns. The chapter also explores diverse influences that illuminate these striking movements, including ones from Schumann's own musical past. Both movements, for instance, allude to earlier works (among other intertextual references) while also adopting devices more typically associated with his youthful output. The literary writings of Johann Wolfgang von Goethe and Jean Paul—two of Schumann's most admired authors—also help to illuminate Schumann's unusual approach to form in these movements, if not the character of the music. Finally, both movements betray the influence of past and contemporary composers, with Mendelssohn and Beethoven assuming particular significance.

Robert Schumann's Leipzig Chamber Works. Julie Hedges Brown, Oxford University Press. © Oxford University Press 2024. DOI: 10.1093/9780197749494.003.0003

Fantasy with "a More Profound Thought": The Scherzo of the A-Minor String Quartet, Op. 41, No. 1

The A-minor string quartet was especially admired among Schumann's three quartets, and its scherzo movement was singled out for pointed praise. After hearing a January 1843 performance given before invited guests, Robert Friese—publisher of the *Neue Zeitschrift für Musik*—wrote to Schumann that the scherzo "left me almost delirious; it is enchantingly beautiful." Upon the quartet's publication in score format, an 1850 reviewer identified the scherzo as having "just claim to preeminence" among the four movements, and he remarked upon its "vitality and élan." Schumann himself identified scherzos as a release valve for a composer's "champagne-like effervescence," and as we shall see, the "enchanting" and "effervescent" qualities of the quartet's scherzo movement arise by engaging with elements of the fantastic, ones indebted to specific works with otherworldly associations.[2] My analysis explores these influences and their stylistic markers within the scherzo-trio portions, all of which become challenged by an unexpected "Intermezzo" that I argue provides a counterpole with quasi-religious associations. The discussion investigates various sources that may have inspired this juxtaposition of sacred and fanciful elements, from the writings of Goethe, to works by Mendelssohn, to medieval folklore and religious figures whose reputations yet resonated in Schumann's day. Ultimately, Schumann negotiates the alterity of the Intermezzo in a way that suggests a reconciliation of seemingly opposed parts, a resolution that also prompts a scherzo movement unique in Schumann's instrumental output.

Writers have briefly observed different influences for Schumann's scherzo, all of which deserve greater attention for understanding the movement's play with fantasy. Some, for instance, have identified the scherzo of Heinrich Marschner's 1841 Piano Trio in G minor, Op. 111, as a source of inspiration, the earliest being Philipp Spitta.[3] As he rightly notes, Robert became familiar with this work around the time he wrote his quartet (Clara even gave a private performance of it in early July 1842), and in early August he reviewed the trio in his journal. In addition to remarking on the "wild and passionate character" of the scherzo and outer movements, Robert highlighted an aspect well-known within Marschner's operas—like his 1828 *Der Vampyr* and his circa 1833 *Hans Heiling*—but which Robert also perceived in the trio, namely, supernatural evocations: Marschner enters into "that sphere where he often moves so happily, the realm of the spooky and fantastic, less so in the first movement, but in the scherzo and finale with outright pleasure in his creations."[4] Spitta suggests that Marschner's scherzo "reappears" in Schumann's analogous movement, "in a modified form certainly, but yet recognizable enough," although without providing details. While Schumann's scherzo theme adopts a different melody, the two movements do share similar traits (compare Example 3.1a and b). In particular, both cultivate Presto tempos, a lilting meter (3/8 in Marschner, 6/8 in Schumann), and perpetual eighth-note motion, although Marschner's theme lacks the gallop motive—two sixteenths followed by an eighth—so prominent in Schumann's theme. Together the shared traits seem to "fix" an otherwise "fleeting impression," an ephemeral effect that Spitta perceived within Schumann's theme but one also captured in Marschner's music. Other aspects bind the themes, especially in the middle sections of their rounded-binary forms (mm. 9–16 in Marschner, and mm. 11–18 in Schumann): both feature syncopated *sforzandi* accents and octave leaps over prolonged dominants.

Notwithstanding these similarities, I would argue that an intermediate work—also with fantastic associations—likely fostered the resulting connection between the two scherzos. Although we cannot pinpoint Schumann's first encounter with Marschner's trio, if he heard it before sketching his A-minor quartet in early June 1842, it may well have reminded him of a song he composed in 1840: "Es leuchtet meine Liebe." Originally planned as song 15 in *Dichterliebe*, Schumann subsequently removed it (along with three other songs) and released it much later as song 3 of *Lieder und Gesänge*, Op. 127, published in 1854 (see Example 3.1c).[5] Like Marschner's scherzo, the song shares the key of G minor, a lilting meter (though 12/8 instead of 3/8) and continuous eighth-note motion. In addition, the song evokes an otherworldly realm, signaled at the outset by Schumann's heading "Phantastisch, markirt." Like song 11 before it ("Ein Jüngling liebt in Mädchen," originally song 13), this song shifts attention from the poet's pained expressions in first person by evoking another tale of unfulfilled love; here, however, references to a "magic garden," a knight, and a destructive giant suggest a medieval temporal remove. If Schumann heard a "spooky and fantastic" character within Marschner's scherzo, his own song may well have contributed to that impression. Of course, even more unmistakable is the song's likeness to Schumann's scherzo theme. The song's opening phrases—both in terms of melodic contour and harmonic disposition—strongly resemble the scherzo's opening parallel period, albeit without the gallop motive so prominent in Schumann's scherzo. Such similarity may partly explain why Schumann removed the

Example 3.1 Comparison of themes by Marschner and Schumann.

(a) Heinrich Marschner, Piano Trio in G Minor, Op. 111: opening of the scherzo movement (piano part, mm. 1–24).

NESTED FORMS 73

Example 3.1 Continued

(b) Schumann, String Quartet in A Minor, Op. 41, No. 1: opening of the scherzo movement (mm. 1–13).

Example 3.1 Continued

(c) Schumann, *Fünf Lieder und Gesänge*, Op. 127, Song 3 (mm. 3–6); originally Song 15 of *Dichterliebe*, Op. 48.

song from *Dichterliebe* upon the latter's publication in August 1844, a mere year and a half after the Op. 41 quartets appeared in print. The song also provides another source for the scherzo's "phantastisch" nature, one that—as I will later show—resonates with other medieval associations.

Schumann's scherzo also evokes another piece unacknowledged in scholarship, one that he would have certainly known: the first of Clara Schumann's Op. 5 *Quatre pièces caractéristiques*, a collection published in 1836 and notable for the programmatic titles attached to its individual pieces (rare in Clara's output). The first one is an Impromptu subtitled "Le Sabbat" (see Example 3.2); according to Nancy Reich, it was Clara's most performed "girlhood work." So popular was this first number that two years later it was published individually, though now under the name "Hexen-Tanz" or Witches' Dance (Op. 5a).[6] In depicting a witches' sabbath, Clara engaged with a subject that was popular in the romantic imagination. As Janina Klassen has described, a number of works that dealt with the uncanny would have provided examples for Clara: for instance, Paganini's 1813 *Le Streghe* (Witches) variations; Berlioz's 1830 *Symphonie fantastique*, with Liszt's piano arrangement appearing three years later; Spohr's 1816 opera *Faust* (which Clara saw in Leipzig in 1828); and operas by Marschner. (While visiting Hanover in 1835, Clara and her father spent time with Marschner, with Friedrich Wieck reporting that "on the second day" Clara "reveled" with the composer "in nothing but devils, witches, and doppelgängers.")[7] In Germanic lands, a particularly influential literary source for such imagery would have come from Part I of Goethe's *Faust*, published in 1808. In the famous "Walpurgisnacht"

Example 3.2 Clara Schumann, *Quatre pièces caractéristiques*, Op. 5: the opening of No. 1, "Impromptu. Le Sabbat" (mm. 1–14); also published independently as "Hexentanz," Op. 5a.

or Walpurgis Night scene, Mephistopheles brings Faust to the top of the Brocken—the tallest mountain in the rugged Harz region of northern Germany—to participate in an annual witches' sabbath that, according to medieval folklore, begins on the night of April 30 and continues through May 1. Clara and especially Robert became familiar with the writings of Goethe in the 1830s and beyond; he was a man who, in Robert's words, deserved "boundless reverence," and Robert regularly quoted the poet in his letters, diaries, criticism, and other writings.[8] Of course, two years after writing the A-minor string quartet, Robert began work on his own musical response to *Faust*, a decade-long project that eventually culminated in the *Szenen aus Goethes Faust*, WoO 3, for soloists, chorus, and orchestra. Although this ambitious work does not depict the scenes related to "Walpurgisnacht," Robert knew them from his multiple readings of *Faust*. Furthermore, in September 1844, Robert and Clara visited the Harz area, traveling through the same regions featured in Goethe's "Walpurgisnacht"—Schierke and Elend—and subsequently climbing the Brocken. In a diary entry, Robert noted the ever "rougher and more barren" landscape, and then referenced lines from the "Walpurgisnacht" scene that captured the soundscape: "the noses of the rock, 'how they snore as they blow' (Goethe's *Faust*)."[9] As a critic, Robert also encountered other musical evocations of Walpurgisnacht. In an 1835 review, he remarked that "the new age has produced so many ghost effects of the kind that it seems we have heard them all before." One work under review, a set of impromptus by Wilhelm Taubert, contained a piece called "Walpurgisnacht" that sketched the scene especially "clearly... for we can see witches riding through clouds on brooms and hot pokers." Robert wrapped up his review by humorously recommending the work "to those who seek compensation in the illusions of art for the many deceptions of reality."[10]

In her own musical "illusion," Clara, as Reich observes, generates various "demonic" effects through "wide leaps, reiterated chromatic appoggiaturas that provide sharp dissonances, accents on weak beats," and various chromatic lines (especially in the middle section), with the whole encased in an "Allegro furioso" tempo.[11] In the scherzo of his first string quartet, Robert echoes aspects of Clara's programmatic piece: the A-minor key, recurring octave leaps, and (especially notable) the pervasive rhythmic motive of two sixteenths followed by an eighth. Robert's music, though, strikes a lighter tone. Where Clara consistently presents this rhythmic motive on the downbeat, Robert treats it as an anacrusis gesture. Moreover, instead of abrupt dynamic contrasts at the outset (*piano* followed by *sforzandi* accents in Clara's piece), Robert's scherzo favors gradual crescendos; and while *sfp* designations do occur in the trio section of his movement (mm. 27–47), continuous light staccato articulations temper their effect. Additionally, while Robert's scherzo adopts a "Presto" tempo, it avoids the "furioso" character of Clara's piece. Although Robert's movement references Clara's "Le sabbat," its airier tone conjures a final intertextual reference also tied to the otherworldly: the elfin style developed by Felix Mendelssohn.

Some writers have briefly referred to Schumann's scherzo as evoking a "Mendelssohnian fairyland,"[12] an aural effect famously depicted in the Overture to *A Midsummer Night's Dream*—composed in 1826 when Felix was just seventeen—but first fully developed in the scherzo movement of his Op. 20 Octet, written nine months earlier. According to his sister Fanny Mendelssohn (later Hensel), the "new and strange" sound of the Octet's scherzo was inspired by Goethe's *Faust* but by a different side of fantasy: the "Walpurgisnachtstraum" or Walpurgis Night's Dream, which follows on the heels of the witches' sabbath.[13] Here Faust watches an amateur play featuring mythical creatures who come to celebrate the reconciliation of the king and queen of elves. (The scene is subtitled the "Golden Wedding of Oberon and Titania.") A vehicle for Goethe to satirize "dilettantes and snobs," among other things, the scene implies what R. Larry Todd has called a "backdrop of phantasmagoric music" played by an amateur "orchestra of flies, mosquitos, frogs and crickets, and a bagpipe that blows bubbles," the whole directed by a "miniscule Kapellmeister."[14] According to Fanny, Felix's delicate scherzo sound was inspired by the final verse of this dream scene, in which the magical tableau vanishes among clouds, mist, and breezes in the leaves and reeds. Todd, however, has convincingly shown how various gestures in the music also evoke the diminutive members of the orchestra.[15]

Fanny claimed that "to me alone" Felix described the inspiration behind his new scherzo sound. Yet Felix referenced this literary influence in at least two other ways. An 1832 Paris performance of the Octet during a Mass service commemorating the fifth anniversary of Beethoven's death prompted Felix to remark: "it is difficult to imagine something more absurd than a priest at the altar accompanied by my Scherzo," but it was "impossible to discourage them." Subsequently he compared the experience to the amateur musical performance in the "Walpurgisnachtstraum," even quoting lines from it: "To see the priest busy at the altar during the Scherzo was exactly like watching 'nose of fly and snout of midge, wretched dilettantes.'"[16] An event that occurred three years earlier provides another clue about the programmatic source of the Octet's scherzo. During the 1829 London premiere of his Symphony No. 1 in C Minor, Op. 11, Felix substituted the Octet scherzo for the original minuet, arranging it for reduced orchestra. According to Todd, the movement was titled "Intermezzo" for this performance.[17] This term is the very subtitle that Goethe assigned to his dream sequence in *Faust*, which functions as a digression from the main narrative portraying the "Walpurgisnacht" pagan revelries. The digression occurs after Faust—while engaging in an erotic dance with a witch—becomes startled by a mouse that escapes from her mouth; the shock prompts him to remember Gretchen, the young woman he has forsaken. To distract him from his guilt, Mephistopheles leads Faust to a theater on the mountain where the amateur "Intermezzo" play unfolds. It seems likely that this association explains the alternative title of the scherzo when it replaced the minuet of the C-minor Symphony.[18]

Schumann would have had many opportunities to hear firsthand accounts about the Octet from Mendelssohn, especially after the latter arrived in Leipzig in 1835 to assume directorship of the Gewandhaus orchestra. The Octet also drew admiration from Schumann, as made clear in reminiscences he sketched in 1847 after Mendelssohn's untimely death. On the first page he indicated that Mendelssohn saw the work as "probably the dearest thing from his youth . . . ; he spoke with joy of the beautiful time when it came into being." On a later page, Schumann indicated that the Octet was written in Mendelssohn's "15th year," prompting the comment that "No master of older or more recent times can boast of greater perfection at such a young age." Although we do not know for certain if Mendelssohn ever told Schumann about the literary basis of his scherzo movement, it is curious indeed that on the same page as the latter comment, just two lines earlier, Schumann reminded himself of a conversation he had with Mendelssohn: "His travels (Harz—as a boy)."[19] This comment suggests that Schumann knew the programmatic inspiration behind Mendelssohn's famous scherzo. Schumann also admired Mendelssohn's Overture to *A Midsummer Night's Dream*. As a youth, Mendelssohn "reached his highest flight" in this work, one that brought "fame enough for one man." It is a piece of "delicate intellectual construction," one in which the composer captured, "in fantastic outlines, the whole wild din of a 'Summer Night's Dream.'" Overall, Mendelssohn moves "poetically" within "adventurous and fairy-like spaces."[20] Given that Schumann recognized Mendelssohn's elfin style, and given that Schumann knew Goethe's Walpurgisnacht scenes and musical settings related to them—including plausibly the scherzo of Mendelssohn's Octet—to what extent might we perceive these additional influences in the scherzo movement of Schumann's A-minor quartet?

To begin, we can pinpoint traits of the "Mendelssohnian fairyland" style that writers have more generally perceived. From the outset, the scherzo features continuous rapid rhythms in a fast tempo (Presto) that are played in a light, detached manner within a minor key. (Mendelssohn used E minor in the Overture and G minor in the scherzo of his Octet, a key that perhaps reminded Schumann of his earlier song and Marschner's trio.) Although Mendelssohn's Overture favors high strings, Schumann's scherzo music, like that of the Octet, uses a fuller string range. It also unfolds in regular four-bar units, a periodicity in the Octet that Todd likens not only to the "rhythming quatrains of Goethe's burlesque-like review" but also one present in the Overture.[21] Rhythmically, Schumann's scherzo presents continuous eighth-note motion that more nearly resembles that of the Overture, though in $\frac{6}{8}$ instead of duple meter. Significantly, Schumann's recurring motive of two sixteenths followed by an eighth also pervades the Octet's scherzo movement, with both composers treating the motive as an anacrusis gesture (unlike its version in Clara's "Le sabbat"). In the Octet, this pervasive motive evokes yet another insect-like gesture played by the miniature orchestra in the "Walpurgisnachtstraum." First appearing as an inner gesture within the main theme (mm. 9–11), the motive then surfaces prominently within the transition (starting in m. 16, where it travels between all parts) and in the secondary theme (starting in m. 25; Mendelssohn used sonata form for his movement rather than scherzo-trio form). In the transition, the motive appears as an ascending scalar gesture; however, in the main theme and particularly the second theme, accompanimental parts emphasize a repeated-note version of the motive not unlike that found in Schumann's scherzo (mm. 9–11, 25–29 and 37–41; for the second theme, see Example 3.3). Schumann, however, highlights this gallop version much more: a two-bar introduction presents it in all four parts (mm. 1–2); it initiates every melodic phrase within the scherzo's rounded-binary form (mm. 3–26); and it appears in almost every measure as an accompanimental drone gesture, usually as an open fifth. (Mendelssohn's Octet movement also features prominent drone fifths at the end of the exposition, though cast as long-held notes—an effect likened by Todd to the bagpipe that plays in the miniature orchestra.)[22] Also relating the two scherzos is a momentary timbral effect in the high strings. In both movements, melodic playing at the octave directly precedes thematic

Example 3.3 Felix Mendelssohn, Octet in E-flat Major, Op. 20, Scherzo: gallop motive in the secondary theme (mm. 25–29).

returns, first heard in measures 33–36 of the Octet (which leads to a restatement of the secondary theme in m. 37), and first occurring in measures 17–18 of Schumann's quartet (which prepares the thematic return in the second half of the theme's rounded-binary form).

If Schumann's scherzo music reflects a variety of influences centered around fanciful topoi, a separate section offers a completely different sound world (mm. 79–110; see Example 3.4). Especially curious is the heading Schumann assigned to it: "Intermezzo." Of course, this term has a rich history in Schumann's earlier piano music, used variously as the name of independent character pieces (the Op. 4 *Intermezzi*); character pieces within piano cycles (the subtitle of "Paganini" from *Carnaval*, and the fourth piece of *Faschingsschwank aus Wien*); and interior episodes within individual refrain-based character pieces (the *Humoreske*, no. 2 of *Kreisleriana*, and nos. 2–3 of the *Novelletten*).[23] In the A-minor scherzo, however, I would argue that this term plays with different associations, especially those stemming from Goethe's "Walpurgisnachtstraum" (subtitled "Intermezzo") and the scherzo movement of Mendelssohn's Octet (which carried this term for the 1829 London performance). If Goethe's scene digressed from the main

Example 3.4 Schumann, String Quartet in A Minor, Op. 41, No. 1, Scherzo: opening of the Intermezzo (mm. 79–88).

narrative, Mendelssohn's movement inverted that relationship, treating the dream scene as inspiration for an entire scherzo movement. If Schumann knew about the literary source of Mendelssohn's Octet movement, he surely appreciated the play between subsidiary and principal materials, with Mendelssohn turning what was initially *Beiwerk* into *Hauptwerk*. As Erika Reiman and John Daverio have shown, such play was a common feature in Jean Paul's novels, with main narrative threads interrupted by other literary "works" ranging from philosophical essays to secondary works of fiction inserted by Jean Paul or "written" by characters. Sometimes these digressions are substantial enough to stand on their own, further confusing the line between subsidiary and principal content. In *Hesperus*, for instance, we read (among other parenthetical items) an essay describing "the relation of the self to bodily organs." In *Flegeljahre*, the identical twins whose adolescence forms the book's subject themselves write a separate novel (*Hoppelpoppel*) that periodically interrupts the main plot.[24] Of course, Schumann's early piano music provides many examples of confusion between *Beiwerk* and

Hauptwerk. John Daverio has likened the famous "Im Legendenton" of the Op. 17 *Fantasie*, first movement, to digressions within Jean Paul's novels, and Reiman has devoted an entire book comparing Jean Paul's novelizing techniques, including digressive effects, to Schumann's piano cycles of the 1830s.[25] While *Beiwerk*—or what Jean Paul called "Extrablätter"—are generally embedded within main narratives, they could also appear as appendices to seemingly completed works, thereby compromising our sense of conclusion. *Die unsichtbare Loge*, for example, "ends" with a new tale about a simple village schoolmaster that differs from the main story and its higher-class characters. Schumann did something similar in the seventh number of *Kreisleriana*, "ending" with a passage ("Etwas langsamer") that not only presents a new lyrical theme but also compromises closure in the C-minor tonic key by first emphasizing B-flat major, then closing in E-flat major.[26]

Although ambiguity between principal and subsidiary materials is generally associated with Schumann's earlier piano music, we experience a similar effect in the scherzo of the A-minor quartet, one comparable to the last examples cited above. The Intermezzo comes as a surprise partly because Schumann adds it to a form that has completed itself. Indeed, up to this point, the scherzo has behaved quite regularly from a structural point of view. After a short introduction, the opening section (A) presents a rounded-binary form in A minor—albeit without repeats—that unfolds in regular four-square phrasing, from the parallel period of the opening statement (mm. 3–10) and its return (mm. 19–26) to the contrasting middle passage (mm. 11–18). The following section (B, mm. 27–51) "is of such a kind that it could ... easily be taken for the Trio," as an 1850 reviewer remarked.[27] Like traditional trios, it presents another rounded-binary form in the same meter and tempo while also providing a degree of contrast: switching to C major, the trio presents a new melody within a thinner texture, all while forefronting light staccato articulations. Thereafter the opening scherzo music returns in full, written out by Schumann instead of using a *da capo* designation (mm. 53–78). The ABA form has thus fully materialized. Nevertheless, an unexpected *attacca* leads us directly into the Intermezzo. It seems that Schumann now presents us with a new sort of digression, a further play with *Beiwerk* that beckons us into a realm wholly different from the scherzo-trio music and its intertextual links with the fantastic.[28]

The Intermezzo presents a striking change in character. While it echoes the earlier trio by providing a complete rounded-binary form in C major, the Intermezzo presents calmer music that contains hymn-like traits. Legato articulation replaces detached playing; a slower tempo (initially titled "Moderato" in the sketch) removes us from the whirlwind of earlier Presto sections; and cut-time meter now replaces the compound $\frac{6}{8}$ meter. While the first violin presents a lyrical melody that moves mainly in quarter notes, the other parts move largely homorhythmically in half notes. (The cello, while emphasizing longer durations at the outset and in the contrasting middle, joins in the chordal motion elsewhere.) Curiously, the Intermezzo is dusted with markers of the fantastic, even the demonic: repeated diminished sonorities (two in the opening measures alone—the main source material of the Intermezzo) and descending chromatic lines that appear at different times in all four parts. Especially interesting, however, is how the Intermezzo contains these markers. For one, the cello's tonic pedal anchors the diminished sonorities within a clear-cut C-major environment. (The contrasting middle, mm. 95–102, tonicizes the dominant, with the cello grounding the diminished sonorities over a G pedal tone.) For another, the chromatic head motive of the Intermezzo is repeatedly balanced by a version of itself in retrograde-inversion: the notes E–G–F♯–F♯ are simultaneously mirrored by C–C♯–D–B (twice in the viola, mm. 79–82, and twice in the cello, mm. 87–90). In these ways, the Intermezzo seems to harness facets of the demonic within a quasi-hymnic environment.

Non-musical aspects of this passage also indicate a sort of religiosity. At the end of his sketch for the scherzo movement, in close proximity to the Intermezzo's conclusion, Schumann not only marked the date on which he completed it—a fairly regular practice of his—he also added a comment virtually absent in all of his other musical manuscripts: "Mit Gott" (with God).[29] Sources indicate that Schumann composed the scherzo quickly, beginning on Saturday, June 4, 1842, and completing it a day later on Sunday, "5 Juni," as the sketch indicates.[30] This latter date also seems significant, for it represents the Feast Day of St. Boniface (ca. 675–754), a figure commemorated in both Catholic and Lutheran traditions. A medieval English missionary who gained the confidence of Frankish and Roman church authorities, Boniface led a decades-long effort of Christianizing pagan Germanic tribes, including Saxon tribes referenced in various fictional accounts of Walpurgisnacht-related activities. Boniface died at the hands of pagans while preaching on June 5, 754; his remains—along with the Bible he was holding while killed—are said to be preserved in Fulda, Germany, in the present-day cathedral there.[31] While veneration of Boniface became especially important in the Catholic tradition, Siegfried

Weichlein has shown how the eighteenth century produced a more ecumenical image of this "Apostle of the Germans," one taken further during the first half of the nineteenth century. Boniface was portrayed more as a "virtuous teacher and monotheistic preacher" and less as the "Roman ambassador and church reformer." In numerous biographies published "at the beginning of the nineteenth century, Boniface came out against paganism. He converted the unbelievers. This view of Boniface facilitated a nondenominational veneration of him." Weichlein suggests that this image "found its most striking expression in the Fulda Boniface Monument," established in 1842 to celebrate the 1,100th anniversary of Boniface's elevation to archbishop. As Weichlein emphasizes, the statue depicts him "in the preacher's cloak, not in the bishop's robe," thereby presenting him "as a Christian preacher, not as a Catholic bishop." In addition, the plinth contains a biblical quotation significant for Lutherans: "Verbum domini manet in aeternum [The word of God shall stand forever]."[32] The year 1842 produced another event with which Schumann may have been familiar: the completion of Karl Grosse's two-volume history of Leipzig "from the oldest to newest time," the first volume of which had appeared several years earlier. In discussing the medieval period, Grosse acknowledged the importance of Boniface's missionary work in Saxon lands, although he cast doubt on legends asserting that Boniface introduced Christianity to Leipzig and established the first church there.[33]

Given contemporary notice of Boniface and related events, Schumann likely recognized the religious significance of June 5th, the date he completed the scherzo. This date, in conjunction with his "Mit Gott" comment, and certain hymn-like qualities of the Intermezzo, together suggest that Schumann envisioned a kind of sacred counterpole to the fanciful, supernatural qualities of his scherzo proper. In this regard, Schumann's movement reflects the dualistic nature of Walpurgisnacht celebrations. As Michael Cooper has discussed, surviving evidence indicates that the name "Walpurgis" had both heathen and Christian associations. In terms of the former, the name could derive from "a prehistoric Germanic cult of a goddess" (or goddesses), but it also references German and Norse mythology, specifically the place in Walhalla where Wuotan/Wotan chooses new virgins for his consort, though only after they have morphed from their previous vile nature as "shrieking accursed hags." Both mythologies were associated with the arrival of spring and celebrations of fertility, and both underpin demonic associations attached to the Walpurgisnacht legend, like those found in *Faust*. On the other hand, Walpurgis also refers to Boniface's niece, a Benedictine nun who responded to her uncle's call for aid by joining his mission in Saxon lands in 748. A person with whom certain miracles are associated, Walpurgis became widely known for her benevolence toward German pagans and Christians alike. After her death in 779, a Christian cult rapidly developed in her name, with her canonization following almost a century later on May 1, 870, the subsequent Feast Day for St. Walpurgis.[34]

Other sources known to Schumann would have provided further examples of the sacred and secular being juxtaposed in Walpurgisnacht-related works. As mentioned earlier, Mendelssohn saw his Octet scherzo as incompatible with religious observance, and its famous cyclic return in the development of the finale has prompted Todd to read a struggle between the diabolical and the divine, a central theme of *Faust*. Here a new fugal passage alludes to a melody from Handel's famous Hallelujah chorus, specifically that accompanying the words "And He shall reign for ever and ever." When scherzo material subsequently returns, it preserves its initial fairy-like character through *pianissimo* statements in F major and E-flat major, but then it recurs, as Todd notes, "in a sinister *fortissimo* G minor, the key of the scherzo," and (one might add) is quickly sequenced into A minor, the tritone-related key to the E-flat major tonic (evoking the *diabolus in musica*). This sequential motion and subsequent liquidation of material, along with the ever loud dynamic, impart a frenzied effect to the scherzo music; suddenly, however, this music "disappears, as if banished by the return to E-flat," which then brings a triumphant statement of the Handel theme "over a resounding dominant pedal." This aural sense of struggle between sacred and profane forces has also led Todd to "test" a Faustian reading for the finale, comparing it with the Dungeon Scene that concludes Part I of Goethe's play. Here Gretchen—wracked by guilt—refuses help from Faust to free her, prays for divine mercy after seeing Mephistopheles, and ultimately receives spiritual redemption.[35]

A separate Goethean source, also set to music by Mendelssohn and familiar to Schumann, provides a different and especially compelling example of pagan and Christian elements interacting: the 1799 ballad "Die erste Walpurgisnacht," written while Goethe also worked on the Walpurgisnacht scenes for *Faust*. As Cooper remarks, this ballad is "unique among [Goethe's] treatments of the Walpurgis Night topos in that it addresses its subject not by investing in the supernatural lore of the Brocken, but by recounting *a rational and natural hypothetical explanation* for that lore."[36] The poem depicts Saxon pagans ("druids") coming together to celebrate the "Allvater" (Wuotan/Wotan) but under duress, for practicing their rites can bring death by the Christian sentinels who guard them. (The poem harks back to the post-Boniface time of Charlemagne and his bloody imposition of Christianity on Saxon tribes.) The pagans decide to scare off the "foolish cleric-Christians" by disguising themselves as the Christians' own "fabled devil," which procures at least a temporary victory.[37] Cooper notes the ironies within Goethe's poetic staging of the scene: first, the Christians "flee in fear of a ruse, not a reality," and second, they fail to recognize "the truth that their adversaries celebrate values they themselves share." Cooper describes how Goethe "downplays the differences between Christianity and paganism" by portraying the pagans "as monotheistic or quasi-monotheistic." In addition, Goethe gives the two groups a comparable number of lines in a similar call-and-response structure, while also using "imagery and action" that evoke both pagan and Christian customs cultivated during Walpurgisnacht celebrations in Goethe's own day. For instance, the pagans' fire atop the Brocken evokes the Christian practice of lighting "enormous bonfires to defend against witches," and the tremendous noise made by the pagans parallels Christian customs of "cracking whips" or "rattling tin cans... in order to chase away the witches and demons." As Cooper describes, "these protagonists are not pagan Others to the poem's intended readers; they are reflections of the readers themselves."[38] Seeming alterity is thus a matter of perception.

Goethe saw his ballad as appropriate for musical treatment, and in 1799 he sent it to the Berlin composer Karl Friedrich Zelter, the year initiating their famous thirty-three-year-long correspondence. The project never materialized, and it was only much later that Zelter's student, Felix Mendelssohn, undertook the task. Composed primarily during his 1831 Italian sojourn, Felix's *Die erste Walpurgisnacht*, written for soloists, chorus, and orchestra, received its first private performance in one of Fanny's October 1832 Sunday Musicales, and its public premiere in Berlin in January 1833. Felix, however, remained hesitant about the work, never publishing this version, nor performing it during his Düsseldorf years. When he arrived in Leipzig in 1835, Felix brought the score with him, and evidence from the late 1830s and the year 1840 indicate his desire to revise the work, especially the first part. It is unclear exactly when such revision began in earnest, but 1842 proved to be a critical year: evidence shows that the revised score was completed sometime in December 1842, with the premiere occurring in Leipzig in early February 1843.[39]

Schumann would have known about Goethe's ballad if not by reading the poem itself, then by reading the Goethe-Zelter correspondence (published in 1833–1834 shortly after the poet's death, and which Schumann had in hand at least by 1838),[40] and by conversing with Mendelssohn about his setting of the text. Indeed, on sheets that survive containing "Conversations with Mendelssohn in the years 1835, 1836, 1837," Schumann indicates that "I asked him about his setting of Göthe's 'Walpurgisnacht,' which he had composed much earlier. 'The first part he now would find dislikable; the second part, on the other hand, pleased him a great deal.' 'He wanted to wait for the time at which he could write a new first part for it.'" It is unclear if Mendelssohn showed Schumann a score version at this point, or even prior to Schumann sketching the A-minor quartet in early June 1842.[41] At the very least, Schumann gleaned further insight on Goethe's poem as his conversation with Mendelssohn in the later 1830s makes clear: "softly...he told me of a letter he had received from Goethe concerning the poem."[42] This letter was written on September 9, 1831, after Goethe learned that Mendelssohn had finished his musical setting, at least in its first version. In the letter, Goethe described his ballad as "elevated symbolism" that explores the tension between old and new forces: "For in the history of the world it must eternally be repeated that something old, established, proven, [and] reassuring will be compacted, pushed aside, dislocated, and if not abolished, then corralled into the tightest space by emergent new forces."[43] Goethe's ballad, however, suggests that such conflict need not be inevitable. By highlighting pagan "imagery and action" that resonated with Christian customs of his own day, Goethe's poem, as Cooper puts it, portrays "the past as something indestructible and still very much a part of the present." Thus, Goethe "enfranchises the reader in his own skepticism" regarding "usual portrayals of alterity in a predominantly Christian society." In other words, the poem—and, Cooper argues, Mendelssohn's composition—invite the reader on a process of discovery that leads to a reassessment of perceived dichotomies (Christian/non-Christian, old/new, real/imaginary), viewing them not as "mutually exclusive subclasses, but dualities, individual parts of a coherent whole."[44]

Given Schumann's predilection toward viewing the past as inspiration for the future, such a perspective would surely have been appealing. And indeed, Schumann's scherzo presents a similar illusory tension between old and new. On the one hand, the Intermezzo is appended to a completed traditional form, and it suggests further alterity by presenting a quasi-religious counterpole to the supernatural character of the scherzo-trio portions. On the other hand, I would argue that this very passage ultimately provides the impetus for renewing the expressive power of an older form. If Schumann sided "with God," this orientation did not prevent him from finding a reconciliation of seeming opposites. Following the Intermezzo, Schumann restates not just the scherzo music (A) but the entire large-scale ternary complex (ABA, mm. 111–91), as Figure 3.1 shows.[45] Thus, what was initially heard as outside the form now becomes the nexus of a larger nested design. Indeed, this design allows Schumann to magnify what was already an inherent part of traditional scherzo (and minuet) movements, namely, their quasi-fractal nature. In traditional examples, the statement-departure-return principle occurs on two levels: in the rounded-binary forms that constitute the scherzo and trio sections proper, but also in the large-scale ABA form. Schumann echoes this principle on yet a higher level, creating a third tier of analogous activity. In an 1840 review of "Impromptus in the form of scherzos" by Hermann von Löwenskiold, Schumann praised the sense of "foreground, perspective, [and] background" levels coming together to create a "pleasing whole." Schumann's scherzo, with its various nested forms, presents a new take on this kind of multidimensionality.[46]

The 1850 reviewer who so admired the scherzo also remarked on its "unusual form," describing its sequence of formal parts.[47] To better appreciate its novelty, however, we may contrast the scherzo with others found in Schumann's multi-movement instrumental works. About half of his scherzos evoke a traditional ABA format, with a few examples repeating the trio in an ABAB-type format.[48] Schumann also frequently employed double trios, a concept we might be tempted to associate with the C-major sections in the A-minor scherzo movement. In the 1842 piano quartet and piano quintet, for instance, double trios occur in their respective scherzo movements, with both labeled as such ("Trio I" and "Trio II"). In these cases, however, the second trio is followed by a single repetition of the opening scherzo

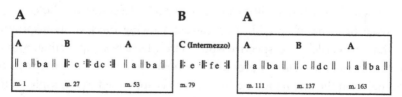

Figure 3.1 Schumann, String Quartet in A Minor, Op. 41, No. 1: formal overview of the scherzo movement.

theme, creating an overall ABACA form. The same characterizes other scherzo movements with double trios: those in the B-flat major Symphony, Op. 38; the C-major Symphony, Op. 61; the G-minor Piano Trio, Op. 110; the D-minor Violin Sonata, Op. 121; and one early example, the F-sharp minor Piano Sonata, Op. 11.[49] Thus, the scherzo movement of Schumann's A-minor quartet, with its mid-level ABACABA form, is unique in how it amplifies the fractal quality of traditional scherzo (and minuet) form. Through this idiosyncratic approach, Schumann imbues an old form with new expressive power. An initially disruptive entity—the Intermezzo—ultimately becomes the means for reimagining the most predictable of classical forms. Not unlike Goethe's 1799 ballad, the scherzo invites the listener on a process of discovery that allows seemingly conflicting elements to emerge as dualities of a larger design, a process that reconciles not just disparate formal parts, but also the different sound worlds of the fanciful and quasi-religious. Schumann appreciated how scherzos might engage such different aural effects. As he remarked in an 1842 review of an independent scherzo by Stephen Heller, only a "lively, amiable mind" may "jest and amuse" while also allowing "a more profound thought" to emerge.[50]

If Schumann's scherzo illustrates how such dualism could aid his reinvention of a traditional form, it also illustrates another reconciliation of sorts: between his seemingly more traditional music of the early 1840s and the more overtly experimental works of earlier years. The scherzo appears as a movement within a classical genre, the string quartet, yet by introducing the Intermezzo it also engages with aspects more commonly associated with Schumann's youthful piano music: musical digressions, and a confusion between *Hauptwerk* and *Beiwerk*, aspects stemming from Schumann's love of Jean Paul. As we have seen, however, these very elements facilitate Schumann's reinvention of traditional scherzo-trio form. As I have discussed elsewhere, a similar process occurs in the sonata-form finale of the Op. 47 piano quartet, written several months after the A-minor quartet. There, a lengthy lyrical digression—also in rounded-binary form—appears four bars into the recapitulation, undermining a crucial moment of formal articulation. In so doing, the finale evokes a description offered by John Daverio for the first movement of Schumann's Op. 17 *Fantasie*, composed in the later 1830s. But where Daverio argues that the digression "preserv[es] the past by writing its demise into the very fabric of the music," I show how the analogous moment in the 1842 piano quartet provides the rationale for re-enacting another tonal-thematic return, yielding a successful reinterpretation of sonata form.[51] In using digressive passages as ironic agents of renewal, the finale of the piano quartet and the scherzo of the A-minor string quartet thus illuminate Schumann's stylistic development in telling ways: the works of the early 1840s could affirm tradition not by rejecting his earlier experimental tendencies, but by reorienting them toward new compositional ends.

The Variation Concept "Bathed in Fresh Imagination": The Slow Movement of the F-Major String Quartet, Op. 41, No. 2

In the F-major string quartet, Schumann again explores nested forms within an interior movement. Such nesting—with confusion once again arising between principal and subsidiary materials—also serves to reinvent an older form, here theme and variations, the reference point of the quartet's slow movement. Writers typically describe the Andante in straightforward ways, referring to sections after the opening theme as its numbered variations. Superficially the movement may evoke a typical theme-and-variation model: a lyrical opening theme unfolds in rounded-binary form (mm. 1–16), followed by a series of clearly defined sections, each delineated by a double bar, each presenting a rounded form in the tonic key of A-flat major, and (with the exception of two sections) each preserving the sixteen-measure length of the opening theme, the whole capped by a coda. As we will see, however, the Andante is anything but straightforward, with Schumann mapping a different structure onto his chain of passages. In this regard, he was perhaps inspired by the slow movement from Beethoven's String Quartet in E-flat Major, Op. 127, a work Schumann once described as having "grandeur for which we cannot find words."[52]

Daverio has noted in passing that Schumann's Andante "adopts the tone, if not the thematic substance" of Beethoven's slow movement, and Schumann's opening theme—while different in contour—does evoke the gentle, lilting character of Beethoven's main theme (compare Example 3.5a and b). Daverio also notes that Schumann's Andante shares "the same form (variations), tonality (A♭), and meter $\frac{12}{8}$."[53] To these we might add other similarities: a freer treatment of variation form (Joseph Kerman notes Beethoven's "organic" approach to the "classic model"), the weightiness of the movement (even doubling or more the length of other movements), and a larger formal concept imposed on the sequence of passages. Kerman suggests that Beethoven's

Example 3.5 Comparison of themes by Schumann and Beethoven.

(a) Schumann, String Quartet in F-Major, Op. 1, No. 2: opening of the slow movement (Theme 1, mm. 1–4).

Example 3.5 Continued

(b) Beethoven, String Quartet in E-flat Major, Op. 127: opening of the slow movement (mm. 1–4).

variations constitute not just a chain but "a symmetrical ABA design," the result of a central variation breaking from A-flat to E major "with a spasm," and the last three variations returning to the original tempo and tonic key of the movement.[54] Schumann's Andante—tellingly subtitled "quasi Variazioni"— also reveals a formal concept larger than a mere variation chain, but it takes a breathtakingly different tack, one that, as we shall see, conjures the novelizing techniques of Jean Paul. For one thing, the Andante adopts a bait-and-switch approach, for the opening theme turns out *not* to be the source of internal variations. An 1850 reviewer discerned this departure from custom, noting generally that the "variations are not related to the subject in as specific a manner as is customary, but rather coexist with it in a generally parallel way."[55] Hans Kohlhase comes closer to pinpointing Schumann's unusual approach, observing that the internal variations "orient themselves, more or less strongly on the first variation" (by which he means section two, mm. 16–32), which thus makes this passage "the actual theme of variations 2–5" (in other words, sections three through six, mm. 32–89).[56] For the sake of clarity, and because of its striking difference, this "actual theme" will be labeled Theme 2. Yet Schumann does not stop there, for after two variations on Theme 2, he introduces yet another theme—henceforth called Theme 3 (mm. 65–76)—that then spawns its own variation (mm. 77–89).[57] In other words, Schumann embeds not one but two sets of theme-and-variations within the Andante. And when the opening theme reappears once more prior to the coda, its "bookend" function becomes clear, framing as it does these nested variations. (See Figure 3.2 for an overview of the movement.) In all, Schumann accomplishes here a goal similar to that found in the scherzo of the A-minor quartet: a traditional form known for its predictability instead thwarts expectations at various turns, thereby renewing its rhetorical force.

The second section (mm. 16–32) immediately makes clear Schumann's break from tradition, for it presents not a variation on the opening theme but a new theme (Theme 2, see Example 3.6). Instead of a lilting melody aligned with the notated $\frac{12}{8}$ meter, we hear a spare, descending-scalar idea in the cello that, heard in isolation without a score, seems to unfold as dotted-quarter notes; in fact, the theme as a whole is metrically displaced, with almost every gesture in every part blurring the true beat by consistently beginning on the same offbeat, including the imitative entries at the outset. As noted by Harald Krebs, who provides a lengthy metrical analysis of the Andante: "This takeover of the entire texture by the displaced layer" creates "a total suppression" of the notated meter.[58] Theme 2 also generates a harmonic structure different from Theme 1. Its first half ends not with a full but half cadence (m. 24) and tonicizes different keys prior to that. The contrasting middle section especially provides

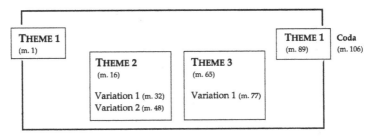

Figure 3.2 Schumann, String Quartet in F Major, Op. 41, No. 2: formal overview of the slow movement.

Example 3.6 Schumann, String Quartet in F Major, Op. 41, No. 2, slow movement: opening of Theme 2 (mm. 17–19).

contrast (mm. 24–28): instead of tonicizing F minor as Theme 1 does (mm. 8–12), an enharmonic shift reinterprets E♭ from the preceding half cadence as D♯ of a prolonged B-major sonority, stressed via *forte* and *sforzandi* accents (mm. 24–26), with sequential chromatic motion eventually leading back to A-flat major.

The next two sections clearly vary not the opening theme, but Theme 2. Both adopt essentially the same harmonic structure, ending their first halves on the dominant, followed by the striking enharmonic shift to B major, loud dynamics, and subsequent chromatic approach to A-flat major. In addition, both sections adopt the same descending-scalar idea. The first variation (mm. 32–48) presents it in the first violin, though metrically adapted so that each pitch now occurs on a main beat, and with the idea now accompanied by a new counterpoint in imitation. The second variation (mm. 48–64) embeds the scalar descent in a swirling arabesque line of sixteenth notes, initially passed between the violins in the first half, then kept within the first violin for the tonal-thematic return in the second half.

Instead of another clear-cut variation on Theme 2, the following section emphasizes contrast, presenting a new theme (Theme 3, mm. 65–76) that differentiates itself from prior sections in multiple ways (see Example 3.7). First, the theme brings the first change in tempo, shifting from Andante to "Molto più lento." Second, it presents a new melody that highlights a recurring descending-second "sigh" gesture over a tonic pedal and its fifth. Third, while still notated in 12/8, the grouping of sigh gestures strongly implies a shift toward simple meter, though different triple and duple groupings suggest hemiola.[59] Finally, where earlier sections all comprise sixteen-measure

Example 3.7 Schumann, String Quartet in F Major, Op. 41, No. 2, slow movement: opening of Theme 3, showing hemiola in an implied simple meter (mm. 65–68).

lengths, Theme 3 compresses its rounded-binary form into twelve measures. At the same time, it expands the form by repeating each of its halves, something that no earlier sections have done; thus, the opening idea (a) becomes repeated in measures 67–68 with slight adjustment at its end, and the contrasting middle (b) and thematic return (a) in measures 69–72 become repeated in measures 73–76. Overall, this section emphasizes dissimilarity from preceding sections, offering not a straightforward variation of Theme 2 (or Theme 1) but yet another new theme. The following section (mm. 77–89) clearly varies Theme 3: it preserves the theme's repetitions in compressed form, adopts the same harmonic structure except for alterations at the ends of its thematic (a) returns (one of which expands the section from twelve to thirteen measures), incorporates the "sigh" gesture in its variation, albeit in a slightly livelier tempo ("Un poco più vivace"), and actualizes the implied simple meter within Theme 3 by switching to common time.

Given all of the above, we must grapple with a most unusual question: what is the main theme of the Andante? Theme 1 is prominent because of its opening position, but it does not comprise the basis of variations to come, but rather the first half of a frame that contains within it two other themes that separately deliver on the promise of "quasi Variazioni." This design undermines a hierarchy of themes, a leveling process not unlike that found in Schumann's earlier piano cycles, with their sequence of individual character pieces. Indeed, we could hear the themes within the Andante as three such pieces, each with their own thematic and formal identity. The Andante recalls Schumann's earlier repertory in other ways as well. As various writers have noted, Theme 1 evokes an actual character piece by Schumann, a short "Larghetto" composed in the early 1830s but only published much later as No. 13 of the *Albumblätter*, Op. 124 (compare Example 3.8 with Example 3.5a).[60] Both themes share the same meter, key (though the Larghetto ends in F minor), mood, and texture, with the melody doubled in octaves and accompanied by the bass a tenth below. Of course, the Andante theme veers from the original melodic contour after just five notes, defamiliarizing its older precedent. In so doing, Theme 1 anticipates

Example 3.8 Schumann, *Albumblätter*, Op. 124: opening of No. 13, Larghetto (mm. 1–4).

the very process of the movement, which also begins in a familiar way (with a theme in rounded-binary form that we assume will underpin the variations to follow) only to continue in a wholly new fashion.

Other traits of the Andante resonate with Schumann's earlier piano music. In conflating character pieces with variation principles, the Andante evokes a similar concept in Schumann's earlier piano works, identified by Daverio in early compositions like the 1833 Variations on Schubert's *Sehnsuchtswalzer* and the Op. 5 *Impromptus* and other works.[61] Such conflation may be subtle (e.g., the transformations of ASCH-related ciphers in different pieces of *Carnaval*) or more obvious (e.g., the combination of the D-major waltz that opens *Papillons* with the "Großvatertanz" that ends it, or the variations embedded within the central "Intermezzo" of piece 3 from the *Novelletten*). Schumann's early piano music also provides examples of bait-and-switch techniques. In *Papillons*, for instance, pieces 7, 8, and 9 each begin with a substantial thematic idea that we assume represents the main melody (or at least its beginning); in retrospect, however, these thematic ideas serve only an introductory function, for each one ends on an unstable harmony that is followed not by the expected continuation but by wholly new material in a different key. While initially digressive sounding, these new materials ultimately comprise the principal substance of each piece because each gives rise to a complete musical form (a sixteen-measure period in no. 7, and rounded-binary forms in nos. 8 and 9). A longer-range questioning of principal thematic material occurs in the fifth *Novellette*, which—despite its rondo-like construction—shows what Anthony Newcomb has described as "an almost riddling play with the functions of the various sections." As the piece unfolds, the refrain gradually loses its thematic dominance; on the flip side, two different lyrical episodes gradually take over, eventually "supplant[ing] the A material . . . to achieve formal closure and end the piece."[62] By drawing on diverse influences like these from the 1830s, the Andante of the F-major quartet illustrates a point also raised in the scherzo of the A-minor quartet: that Schumann's earlier piano music proved foundational for, rather than antithetical to, his instrumental works of the early 1840s.

Not surprisingly, such stylistic threads imply the continued influence of Jean Paul's writings, especially the play between principal and subsidiary content. In the Andante, the second section neglects to offer a variation on Theme 1 and thus sounds digressive; yet Theme 2 ultimately provides the basis for two subsequent variations. Thus, seeming *Beiwerk* assumes its own status as interiorized *Hauptwerk*. This process evokes parenthetical elements in Jean Paul's novels that go beyond fragments to attain their own formal coherence, either individually or through an incremental process. As mentioned earlier, in *Flegeljahre* a series of interruptions constitutes a complete novel (*Hoppelpoppel*) written by the adolescent twins. Schumann's Andante also provides not one but two sets of themes that receive variation treatment, which in turn evokes Jean Paulian novels where multiple, self-contained digressions appear. In *Hesperus*, for example, we read not only the protagonist's essay on "the relation of the self to bodily organs" (referenced earlier), but also a eulogy written for himself, letters to his teacher, and (among other items) what Reiman has described as "a wildly fantastic, pseudoscientific dissertation" on the promised land of humankind.[63] Reiman notes that Jean Paul's narrative style is "essentially digressive," and that the "levels and types of digressions" can be so "numerous and overlap to such an extent" that it becomes difficult to discern the central plot line, a situation not unlike that found in Schumann's Andante. Here the most substantial content occurs in its interior, with variation sets that realize the promise of "quasi Variazioni" announced at the outset. Do these then comprise the true *Hauptwerk*? The coda (mm. 106–112) strengthens this perspective by adopting the arabesque figurations found in the second variation on Theme 2. On the other hand, Schumann heightens the opening theme's significance by having it return to frame the interior variation sets, much like Jean Paulian digressions that, as Reiman notes, "almost always lead back to the [main] story."[64]

Whether Theme 1 comprises *Hauptwerk*, or mere *Beiwerk*, to the variation sets, the movement illustrates another influence of Jean Paul: namely, "witty" links between markedly different sections. As Reiman describes: "In its widest sense, 'Witz' for Jean Paul is the art of comparison." In a narrower sense, it unveils what Jean Paul called "partial sameness masked by a greater difference." Thus, although the writings by the protagonist in *Hesperus* digress from the main storyline, they nonetheless provide insight into his own character development. In *Siebenkäs*, a "supplement" to the second chapter—which "details the governance and social structure" of a small village with a "ridiculous amount of bureaucracy"—itself reflects the "narrow social world" in which the protagonist of the main plot struggles.[65] In *Flegeljahre*, the embedded novel becomes a portal of discovery for the main characters; for instance, as Daverio notes, one twin discovers his brother's love for a young woman by reading their coauthored story. We also learn that *Hoppelpoppel* was almost called "Flegeljahre," and it reflects its own status within the larger novel by itself incorporating digressive turns.[66]

The Andante of the F-major quartet displays similar "witty" links between its disparate parts. Theme 2 and hence also its variations magnify details hidden within the opening theme. Its head motive—a scalar descent through a third (mm. 16–17)—derives from similar but inconspicuous gestures in the cello line of the opening theme: the ascent to the final cadence that occurs moments earlier (mm. 15–16), and the descent/ascent near the end of the contrasting middle section (mm. 10–11). These instances within Theme 1 also relate to Theme 2 in their metrically displaced nature, for all begin on similar off-beats. Ultimately, their syncopated nature derives from the opening viola line (m. 1), whose offbeat E-flat pedal tone is veiled by the lilting melodic qualities of the other three parts. Krebs describes how the viola line ultimately prompts an "intensification of [metrical] dissonance" within the opening theme, but its expression through scalar movement of a third only rises to prominence with Theme 2; thus, once-obscure details now become forefronted, a micro-level play with subsidiary and principal content.

Theme 3 links subtly not just to Theme 1, but also to Theme 2. Just as Theme 2 forefronts details once obscure in Theme 1, Theme 3 does the same. Its ever-prominent "sigh" motive derives from the first-violin line in the middle section of Theme 2 (mm. 25–26). As if to make this relationship clearer, Theme 3 subsequently preserves within its own middle section the surprising turn toward a *forte* B-major sonority, with a subsequent chromatic descent, albeit in compressed form (compare mm. 69–70 with 24–28). Theme 3 also picks up on threads from the opening theme: it not only provides a new take on metric disruption by exploring hemiola within an implied simple meter, it also foregrounds the pedal tone first introduced in m. 1 of the viola part, though E-flat now becomes coupled with A-flat as a pervasive cello drone.

A final element links the three themes together: all of them blur formal boundaries. In particular, they all compromise definitive closure at the ends of their rounded-binary forms, a blurring that arises either through metrically weakened cadences or through incomplete thematic returns. Theme 1 illustrates the former: while the melody provides a strong melodic approach to $\hat{1}$ on the downbeat of measure 16, the other parts are tied over the barline, with the cello providing a delayed $\hat{5}$–$\hat{1}$ resolution; the same holds true for the "bookend" return of Theme 1. Theme 3 behaves similarly, though it now metrically undermines IAC-type cadences. As noted earlier, only with Theme 3 do repetitions of each formal half finally occur; however, in both statements of the second half, the returning 'a' idea (mm. 71–72 and 75–76) each time ends on the offbeat of a weak beat, and not just in the notated $^{12}_{8}$ meter but also in the duple meter implied at its cadence. (Compare these returns with Example 3.7.) In the variation on Theme 3, the return of 'a' materials suggests compensation by rewriting the harmonic approach to the cadence, the second even more emphatic than the first (mm. 83–84 and 87–89). Yet once again, both yield off-beat resolutions to tonic harmony. Schumann compromises endings not only through metrically weakened cadences, but also by featuring incomplete returns. The first half of Theme 2 presents a sentence that leads to a half cadence (mm. 16–24); in the second half, however, only the basic idea (with its beginning adjusted) and its varied repetition reappear (mm. 28–32), thereby neglecting any sort of cadential articulation. The same holds true for the first variation on Theme 2. The second variation suggests rectification by rewriting the 'a' material in the second half of the form: a strong PAC in B-flat minor (m. 62) raises hope for a similar cadence in A-flat major; and while the subsequent continuation (mm. 63–64) "ends" with tonic harmony, it appears without cadential preparation and brings a *ritardando*, creating a "fizzling-out" effect. All in all, these shared compromised endings—while achieved in different ways—create linkages between the heterogeneous sections while also downplaying the structural seams between them.

The first compromised ending—that of Theme 1—ultimately has its raison d'être in the opening viola line, with its disruption of the $^{12}_{8}$ meter. As described earlier, the viola part also provides the embryonic source for pronounced syncopations in both Themes 2 and 3 (and their variations), along with the pedal that permeates Theme 3. As if to acknowledge this fundamental source, Schumann isolates the viola part before the return of Theme 1, thereby raising its once low-profile gesture (mm. 89–90; see Example 3.9). In this regard, the Andante provides another nod to Beethoven's Op. 127 quartet, for its slow movement begins with an isolated E-flat syncopated pedal tone on which subsequent pitches are layered (see Example 3.5b). Through this intertextual link, we see yet another micro-level play with principal and subsidiary content: the conspicuous opening pitch of Beethoven's slow movement becomes submerged in the opening of Schumann's Andante, with its motivic significance slowly revealed as the movement unfolds, and the pitch only laid bare near the movement's end.

As a music critic, Schumann had many opportunities to review variation-based works, particularly because of their prominence among virtuoso

Example 3.9 Schumann, String Quartet in F Major, Op. 41, No. 2: return of Theme 1 near end (mm. 89–91).

pianist-composers, for whom variations served as vehicles for demonstrating technique. While appreciative of the form's historical legacy, Schumann dismissed its use for shallow display, with variations used in this way provoking his ire. In a series of 1836 reviews, categorized into different "courses," Schumann began thus:

> The man who invented the first variations was certainly not bad (after all it was Bach again). One cannot write and listen to symphonies every day, and so the imagination came up with such graceful games from which Beethoven's genius even evoked ideal artistic forms. But the true glorious period of the variation is approaching its end and giving way to the caprice. May it rest in peace! For in no other genre has such botched, amateurish work been unearthed, and still will be. One has little idea how much poverty and shameless vulgarity flourishes in these depths.[67]

If variation form were to survive, it had to move beyond superficial content toward a poetic reimagining. As Schumann remarked in the "second course" of reviews, "Gone are the days when one was amazed by a sugary figure, a languishing suspension, a rapid E-flat-major run on the keyboard; now we want ideas, inner connection, poetic unity, with everything bathed in fresh imagination."[68] The Andante of the F-major quartet realizes this poetic vision while simultaneously positioning itself within the historical legacy that Schumann admired. The Andante clearly shows its debt to Beethoven's analogous movement in the Op. 127 quartet, yet also treats it as a point of departure for a wholly new formal structure. Equally important in "bathing" the Andante with "fresh imagination" is Jean Paul's influence, whose works provided models not only for nested structures, but also for discerning poetic links between seemingly disparate parts.

Notes

1. *GS*, vol. 1, 168, 346, and 172.
2. Robert Friese, letter of January 9, 1843. C. Böhmer, review of June 12, 1850, *Neue Berliner Musikzeitung*, 185; original and translation in Kohlhase, "Kritischer Bericht/Critical Report," 155 and 171. Schumann, *GS*, vol. 1, 171.
3. Spitta—who mistakenly identifies Marschner's trio as Op. 112 instead of Op. 111—compares the two scherzos in his "Robert Schumann" entry for *A Dictionary of Music and Musicians*, ed. George Grove (London: Macmillan, 1879–1890), vol. 3, 414. His comparison has since been echoed by Chissell, *Schumann*, 159; and Davies, "Schumann, Robert Alexander," 372.
4. *GS*, vol. 2, 90–91. Despite finding faults with the trio, Robert appreciated Marschner's "ever curious freshness." Clara, however, found the trio "very flat." *Tb*, vol. 2, 232. Nevertheless, the work proved to be a best-seller for the Leipzig publisher Hofmeister, with sixteen printings from 1841 to 1896; on this point, see Lott, *The Social Worlds of Nineteenth-Century Chamber Music*, 31, table 1.3.
5. For an edition that contains all twenty songs of the original cycle, see Arthur Komar, ed., *Dichterliebe: An Authoritative Score, Historical Background, Essays in Analysis, Views and Comments*, Norton Critical Scores (New York: W. W. Norton, 1971); Komar labels "Es leuchtet meine Liebe" as Song 12a. For a survey of *Dichterliebe*'s compositional history, see Beate Julia Perrey, *Schumann's* Dichterliebe *and Early Romantic Poetics: Fragmentation of Desire* (Cambridge: Cambridge University Press, 2002), 116–21. Joan Chissell, J. A. Fuller-Maitland, and Basil Smallman have also noted the similarity between the song and the scherzo, but they mistake the chronology by asserting that the latter inspired the former. Chissell, *Schumann*, 159; J. A. Fuller-Maitland, *Schumann's Concerted Chamber Music* (London: Oxford University Press, Humphrey Milford, 1929), 7–28; and Basil Smallman, *The Piano Quartet and Quintet: Style, Structure, and Scoring* (Oxford: Clarendon Press, 1994), 48.
6. Nancy Reich, *Clara Schumann: The Artist and the Woman*, rev. ed. (Ithaca, NY: Cornell University Press, 2001), 224 and 293–95. The final piece in the Op. 5 collection—"Le ballet des revenants" or Ballet of the ghosts—also engages with the uncanny.
7. Janina Klassen, *Clara Schumann: Musik und Öffentlichkeit* (Cologne: Böhlau Verlag, 2009), 86–87; Wieck's comment is quoted on 86.
8. Quotation from a letter to Clara of February 11, 1838; *Briefedition* I/4, 225; cf. *CC*, vol. 1, 99. On Robert and Clara's personal reactions to Goethe's *Egmont* in the late 1830s and early 1840s, see Brown, "Higher Echoes of the Past in the Finale of Schumann's 1842 Piano Quartet," 550–58.
9. Diary entry of September 13, 1844; *Tb*, vol. 2, 389. The passage in *Faust* occurs near the beginning of the Walpurgisnacht scene and is sung in alternation by Faust, Mephistopheles, and a Will-o'-the-wisp.
10. *GS*, vol. 1, 191.
11. Reich, *Clara Schumann: The Artist and the Woman*, 224.
12. Chissell, *Schumann*, 159; and Melvin Berger, *Guide to Chamber Music* (New York: Dodd, Mead, 1985), 400.
13. Fanny's comment is quoted in R. Larry Todd, "The Chamber Music of Mendelssohn," in *Nineteenth-Century Chamber Music*, ed. Stephen Hefling (New York: Schirmer; London: Prentice Hall, 1998), 182–83.
14. R. Larry Todd, "Familiar and Unfamiliar Aspects of Mendelssohn's Octet," in *Mendelssohn Essays* (New York: Routledge, 2008), 176–77.

15. For Fanny's quotation of this verse, see Todd, "The Chamber Music of Mendelssohn," 182–83. For Todd's programmatic interpretation of individual scherzo gestures, see *Mendelssohn: A Life in Music* (New York and Oxford: Oxford University Press, 2003), 150–51.
16. Letters of March 15–17 and March 31, 1832; quoted in Todd, "Familiar and Unfamiliar Aspects," 172–73.
17. Ibid., 172, and Todd, *Mendelssohn: A Life in Music*, 207. A review of this concert described the scherzo as "unusually delicious, playful, and original" and indicated that it "was unanimously encored." *Athenaeum*, June 10, 1829, 364.
18. Todd does not relate the Goethean "Intermezzo" to the London anecdote, but elsewhere he reads the movement as a "musical digression or interlude that momentarily distracts us" from the "heavier, more fully wrought and formally complex second and fourth movements," and thus provides an analogy to Goethe's dream scene "that interrupts the principal dramatic action." Todd, "Familiar and Unfamiliar Aspects," 176.
19. Schumann, "Aufzeichnungen über Mendelssohn," 99 and 107. Schumann's recollections of Mendelssohn "from the year 1835 through his death" likely represent work for an intended publication, which never appeared, however.
20. *GS*, vol. 2, 156, and vol. 1, 24, 143, 246, and 46.
21. Todd, "Familiar and Unfamiliar Aspects," 177.
22. Ibid., 177.
23. Most usages of the term "intermezzo" stem from the piano works of the 1830s, though Schumann subsequently used it for certain slow movements in multi-movement works (the Piano Concerto in A Minor, Op. 54, and the Violin Sonata in A Minor, WoO 2) and occasionally within vocal works (no. 2 of *Liederkreis*, Op. 39, and nos. 2 and 6, respectively, of the *Spanisches Liederspiel*, Opp. 74 and 138).
24. For more, see Reiman, *Schumann's Piano Cycles and the Novels of Jean Paul*, 31; for an overview of Jean Paul's literary techniques, see ibid., 9–33. See also Daverio, *Nineteenth-Century Music*, 35.
25. Daverio, *Nineteenth-Century Music*, 19–47; Daverio also relates the passage in Op. 17 to Schlegel's notion of the romantic arabesque. Reiman, *Schumann's Piano Cycles and the Novels of Jean Paul*.
26. For Reiman's discussion of the *Kreisleriana* number, see ibid., 138–42.
27. Böhmer, review of June 12, 1850, *Neue Berliner Musikzeitung*, 185; original and translation in Kohlhase, "Kritischer Bericht/Critical Report," 171.
28. So set apart is the Intermezzo that an 1849 reviewer even listed it as a separate "movement" within the quartet: "Introduzione, Allegro, Scherzo, Intermezzo, Adagio, and Presto." F. C. Kist, review of March 26, 1849, performance in Utrecht, published in *Caecilia* 6 (1849): 78; original and translation in Kohlhase, "Kritischer Bericht/Critical Report," 168.
29. For a transcript of this sketch, which largely provided melodic lines with some harmonic indications, see Roesner, "Studies in Schumann Manuscripts, vol. 2, 43; for a discussion of this sketch manuscript, see vol. 1, 385–401. See also Kohlhase, "Kritischer Bericht/Critical Report," 185–88, which labels the source EW; and McCorkle, *Robert Schumann: Thematisch-Bibliographisches Werkverzeichnis*, 182. The latter source helpfully provides marginalia found in all of Schumann's musical manuscripts. The only other instance in which he wrote "Mit Gott" occurs in a manuscript from late 1831/early 1832, containing a set of four variations on a theme with a free interlude; see McCorkle, 670, catalog no. F7. In general, marginalia of a religious nature are extremely rare in Schumann's musical manuscripts; I know of only one other (though less overt) instance, one that appears at the end of the sketches for *Das Paradise und die Peri*: "Leipzig mit Dank erfüllt beendigt/am 17ten Juni 1843" (Leipzig, finished with thanks/ June 17th 1843); see McCorkle, 221. As Daverio reminds us, in 1830 Schumann described himself as "religious, but without religion," a characterization that—according to Wasielewski— remained true into the 1850s; quoted in Daverio, *Robert Schumann*, 471. Daverio raises this aspect of Schumann's "religiosity without dogmatism" in relation to the composer's late Mass and Requiem, both of which straddle the sacred and the secular (471).
30. The *Haushaltbuch* also confirms this date; see *Tb*, vol. 3, 216.
31. Michael Cooper, *Mendelssohn, Goethe, and the Walpurgis Night: The Heathen Muse in European Culture, 1700–1850* (Rochester, NY: University of Rochester Press, 2007), 7; and Philip H. Pfatteicher, *New Book of Festivals and Commemorations: A Proposed Common Calendar of Saints* (Minneapolis: Fortress Press, 2008), 262–65.

32. Siegfried Weichlein, "Bonifatius als politischer Heiliger im 19. und 20. Jahrhundert," in *Bonifatius: Vom angelsächsischen Missionar zum Apostel der Deutschen*, ed. Michael Imhof and Gregor K. Stasch (Petersberg: Michael Imhof Verlag, 2004), 222–23. The biblical quotation comes from Isaiah, 40:8 (King James version).

33. Karl Grosse, *Geschichte der Stadt Leipzig, von der ältesten bis auf die neueste Zeit* (Leipzig: Verlag von C. B. Polet, 1839–1842), vol. 1, 34–36.

34. Cooper, *Mendelssohn, Goethe, and the Walpurgis Night*, 7 and 10–12.

35. Todd, "Familiar and Unfamiliar Aspects," 177–78. On a separate analogy he makes with Goethe's *Faust*, see note 18. For a different Goethean slant on the finale, see Benedict Taylor, *Mendelssohn, Time and Memory: The Romantic Conception of Cyclic Form* (Cambridge: Cambridge University Press, 2011), 52–102. Taylor argues that the cyclic return of the scherzo, with the larger course of thematic recall that it prompts, has analogies with both Goethean and Hegelian conceptions of time and self-consciousness.

36. Cooper, *Mendelssohn, Goethe, and the Walpurgis Night*, 63; my emphasis.

37. Quotations from lines 50 and 61. For Goethe's poem in both German and English translation, see ibid., 74–77.

38. Ibid., 64–67. On Goethe's pancultural and pan-religious viewpoints, see 43–49.

39. Ibid., 59–60 and 80–91.

40. Robert first described reading this correspondence in a letter to Clara of February 6, 1838 (*Briefedition* I/4, 215; cf. *CC*, vol. 1, 95), and in a diary entry of March 22, 1838 (*Tb*, vol. 1, 52).

41. Schumann's diary and household book indicate interactions with Mendelssohn in late April and early May 1842 before the latter's departure for Düsseldorf and beyond. No evidence exists that Mendelssohn's choral work was discussed, but these dates do coincide with Walpurgisnacht celebrations. *Tb*, vol. 1, 227, and vol. 3, 212–13.

42. These loose sheets from the late 1830s were added to the reminiscences Schumann wrote much later in 1847. Schumann, "Aufzeichnungen über Mendelssohn," 108. Translation of the earlier comment from Cooper, *Mendelssohn, Goethe, and the Walpurgis Night*, 88.

43. Quoted and translated in Cooper, *Mendelssohn, Goethe, and the Walpurgis Night*, 83. Mendelssohn subsequently included this comment on the title page of his piano-vocal edition of the work. Ibid., 92–93.

44. Ibid., 69 and 161. In her study of the nineteenth-century French *scherzo fantastique*, which was indebted to the elfin style created by Mendelssohn (and Weber, especially his opera *Oberon*), Francesca Brittan describes a similar blurring of seeming dichotomies. Depictions of fantastic miniature realms overlapped with advances in botany and entomology via improved microscopy, such that fairies became "materialized, recast as creatures secreted within rather than held outside the realm of the real." Similarly, in musical depictions of fairyscapes (like Berlioz's Queen Mab movement from *Roméo et Juliette*), the fantastic sounds were the products of contemporary advances in virtuosity and orchestration techniques; thus, "the experience of the supernatural was bound up with an awareness of the machinery producing it." Brittan, "Fairyology, Entomology, and the *Scherzo fantastique*," in her *Music and Fantasy in the Age of Berlioz* (Cambridge and New York: Cambridge University Press, 2017), 11 and 286.

45. The only change to the original ABA complex occurs at the very end of the movement, when a five-measure delay of the final cadence brings the whole to a more definitive conclusion.

46. *GS*, vol. 1, 478. In Schumann's *Szenen aus Goethes Faust*, WoO 3, John Daverio also perceives varying levels of structural symmetries, ones that counter the view of the work as a mere "sequence of isolated fragments." Daverio, *Robert Schumann*, 369–70.

47. Böhmer, review of June 12, 1850, *Neue Berliner Musikzeitung*, 185; original and translation found in Kohlhase, "Kritischer Bericht/Critical Report," 172.

48. For more traditional scherzo forms, see those from the F-major String Quartet (Op. 41, No. 2); the D-minor and F-major Piano Trios (Opp. 63 and 80); the A-minor Violin Sonata (Op. 105), and—in earlier works—the Piano Sonatas in F Minor and G Minor (Opp. 14 and 22). For examples of the ABAB type, see the scherzo movements from the D-minor Symphony (Op. 120) and the Overture, Scherzo, and Finale (Op. 52).

49. The Op. 11 scherzo provides the one other example where a trio—here also the second one—is called "intermezzo." Marked "alla burla, ma pomposo," the passage seems to parody a dance of Philistines. It dissolves into a recitative-like passage that neglects cadential preparation for the final return of the scherzo theme (ABACA).

50. *GS*, vol. 2, 114.

51. Brown, "Higher Echoes of the Past in the Finale of Schumann's 1842 Piano Quartet," 511-64. Daverio, *Nineteenth-Century Music*, 19-47; quotation from 42.
52. *GS*, vol. 1, 380. Schumann included Beethoven's Op. 131 quartet in this description.
53. Daverio, *Robert Schumann*, 252.
54. Kerman, *The Beethoven Quartets*, 212, 214, and 216-17.
55. Böhmer, review of June 12, 1850, *Neue Berliner Musikzeitung*, 185; original and translation found in Kohlhase, "Kritischer Bericht/Critical Report," 172.
56. Kohlhase, *Die Kammermusik Robert Schumann*, vol. 2, 46.
57. Kohlhase himself acknowledges that Theme 3, which he calls "variation 4" shows "very little reference" to the "actual theme," but without adapting his formal interpretation. Ibid., vol. 2, 48.
58. Krebs, *Fantasy Pieces: Metrical Dissonance in the Music of Robert Schumann*, 227.
59. For a detailed metrical analysis, see ibid., 229-30.
60. Kohlhase, *Die Kammermusik Robert Schumann*, vol. 1, 43-44; Tunbridge, *Schumann's Late Style*, 86-87; and McCorkle, *Robert Schumann: Thematisch-Bibliographisches Werkverzeichnis*, 526-29.
61. Daverio, *Robert Schumann*, 106-9.
62. Newcomb, "Schumann and the Marketplace," 297-98. Elsewhere I have discussed how this *Novellette* resonates with Schumann's personal reactions to Goethe's *Egmont* in early 1838, and how the finale of the Op. 47 piano quartet—which references this *Novellette*—provides an inverse response. Brown, "Higher Echoes of the Past in the Finale of Schumann's 1842 Piano Quartet," 545-60. As I also describe, this movement similarly challenges the concept of a "main theme."
63. Reiman, *Schumann's Piano Cycles and the Novels of Jean Paul*, 24 and 31.
64. Ibid., 27-28. The scherzo of the A-minor quartet does something similar: the Intermezzo initially sounds like a digressive appendix to the completed ABA scherzo-trio form; yet by restating the entire ABA complex after the Intermezzo, Schumann "returns to the main narrative," so to speak, though one that yields an unusual extension of traditional scherzo form.
65. Reiman, *Schumann's Piano Cycles and the Novels of Jean Paul*, 16 and 31.
66. Daverio, *Nineteenth-Century Music*, 35-36.
67. *GS*, vol. 1, 219.
68. Ibid., vol. 1, 224.

4
Dancing to Schumann

As scholars have long acknowledged, and as we've seen even in the Leipzig chamber repertory, extramusical influences—especially literary ones—affected Schumann's compositional output. Yet Schumann's influence has flowed outward as well, permeating many disciplines outside of music, especially in the twentieth century and beyond. His tantalizing life story—from the battle to marry Clara, to his long struggle with mental illness and demise in an asylum—has prompted a variety of biographies written by non-music specialists, including psychiatric readings by Peter Ostwald and more recently by Theo Payk, along with a collection of historical novels and theatrical pieces.[1] The experience of hearing Schumann's music has informed writings with a personal bent, from Roland Barthes's classic 1985 essay "Loving Schumann" to Jonathan Biss's 2012 Kindle Single, *A Pianist under the Influence*.[2] Robert and Clara have been the subject of various films—Clarence Brown's 1947 *Song of Love* starring Katherine Hepburn represents a notable early example—and quotations of Robert's music have figured in many more.[3] Schumann has also inspired visual art from different periods, from Henri Fantin-Latour's nineteenth-century work in different media to (it seems) more recent work by Leipzig-based artist Neo Rauch.[4]

Although Schumann never composed a ballet, his music has attracted a variety of prominent choreographers from across the twentieth century and beyond. Michel Fokine, for instance, choreographed *Papillons* (1912) and *Carnaval* (1910) for performance by the Ballet Russes, and the latter work was also set in 1922 by Heinrich Kröller for the ballet of the Vienna Staatsoper. In America, Martha Graham's 1926 *Novelette* set the ninth piece from Schumann's Op. 99 *Bunte Blätter*, and Bronislava Nijinska's 1951 *Schumann Concerto*—premiered by the American Ballet Theatre—choreographed the Op. 54 Piano Concerto in A Minor. The latter company also premiered Antony Tudor's 1980 *Little Improvisations*, set to Schumann's *Kinderszenen*, and the last major work by George Balanchine for the New York City Ballet was his 1980 *Robert Schumann's Davidsbündlertänze*, the music of which had also underpinned Jonathan Watts's earlier 1974 ballet, *Evening*

Dialogues, written for the Joffrey City Center Ballet. Schumann's music continues to be set in the twenty-first century as well, from Mark Morris's 2001 dance *V* (which uses the Op. 44 Piano Quintet), to Colleen Cavanaugh's 2004 *Schumann Songs* (set to music from *Frauenliebe und Leben*), to Uwe Scholz's 2006 *Schumann's 2nd Symphony* and Lauren Lovette's 2016 *For Clara*, choreographed to the Op. 134 Introduction and Concert Allegro.[5]

Modern-day scholars are in the early stages of exploring such Schumann-inspired repertory, including works in the realm of dance. In an illuminating 2011 essay, Wayne Heisler argues that a consistent tendency among choreographers is to "treat [Schumann's] biography as an essential ingredient in the experience of his scores," such that "the relationship between man, composer, and music seems to be indissoluble.... One might say that dancing to Schumann's music is to dance also with Schumann—that is, the biographical, imagined-to-be-real Schumann." To illustrate this identification of choreographer to composer, Heisler analyzes the ballets by Kröller and Balanchine cited earlier, contending that for both choreographers Schumann represented progressiveness and thus provided a kind of "spiritual authority for [their own] respective artistic visions." In the case of Kröller, Schumann's battle against the Philistines served as an "allegory to assert modern ballet in the ... conservative culture of theatrical dance in interwar Vienna"; as for Balanchine, Heisler suggests that the choreographer "explore[s] the legacy of dance modernism—including his own—and ultimately allies it with Schumann's legacy."[6]

Heisler suggests in passing that the figure of Schuman may have also informed a 1975 ballet by the Dutch choreographer Hans van Manen (b. 1932) entitled *Four Schumann Pieces*.[7] Commissioned by the London Royal Ballet, this work choreographed all four movements of Schumann's A-Major String Quartet, Op. 41, No. 3, which was played by a live ensemble during the premiere. The ballet attracted attention partly for how Van Manen forefronts a ballerino in place of a ballerina. (Anthony Dowell, a then-rising star for the Royal Ballet, performed the leading role.) As described by George Balanchine, *Four Schumann Pieces* is a "dramatic ballet without a story. It shows a man who stands alone but who is surrounded by persons he would wish to know"—the latter represented by five couples.[8] Heisler, after quoting Balanchine's description, suggests that perhaps "the subject of this ballet is 'pieces of *Schumann*'" himself, thereby summoning the presence of Schumann in his iconic representation as an outsider, the creative genius misunderstood by others.[9]

Heisler's conceptual framework has great appeal, but the attempt to uncover a "biographical, imagined-to-be-real Schumann" in Van Manen's ballet proves problematic. First, unlike the piano cycles set by Kröller and Balanchine, the A-major quartet is not programmatic and does not offer clear biographical meanings tied to Schumann. Second, none of my research on Van Manen revealed that such meanings shaped his choreographic process, nor that he even had any knowledge of Schumann's life and works at the time he wrote the ballet, and an interview with him corroborated just that. In addition, Van Manen indicated that the title was inspired by the four-movement structure of Schumann's quartet, thereby problematizing the notion that the ballet perhaps captured "pieces" of Schumann-the-figure.[10] If any one person inspired the work, it was Anthony Dowell, who went on to became one of England's greatest male dancers. Van Manen became acquainted with Dowell in 1972 while working with the Royal Ballet on his *Grosse Fuge*, and he later took the opportunity to showcase Dowell in his *Four Schumann Pieces*. (Figure 4.1 shows a rehearsal photograph of the two.) By his own admission, Dowell was an introvert (in 1975 he stated, "I'm sort of a hermit"), and Jochen Schmidt has proposed that the solo male dancer in *Four Schumann Pieces* perhaps evokes something of Dowell's personality.[11] Yet even this interpretation presents difficulties. Although Van Manen recognized an enigmatic quality about Dowell, he was ultimately attracted to the dancer's renowned classical technique and Dowell's willingness to foreground movement over individual personality. In this regard, Dowell differed from his famous colleague at the Royal Ballet, the extroverted Rudolf Nureyev, known for his flamboyant performances.[12] The focus on technique serving choreographic movement (rather than the person) thus makes the search for a "biographical Dowell" in *Four Schumann Pieces* problematic. This focus, however, helps explain why Van Manen chose chamber music for his ballet: its "delicate" texture suited the "simple steps" of the choreography, which in turn showcased Dowell's refined classical technique. As Van Manen noted in a 1976 *BBC* documentary about Dowell—one that forefronts *Four Schumann Pieces*—Dowell's "enormous technical abilities" are apparent even in "the most simple step, and I was interested to do it in the most simple steps I could find. So, I wanted to have a sort of chamber music, which is very delicate music. It had to be exactly for him."[13]

While not portraying the (real or imagined) figures of Schumann and Dowell, Van Manen's ballet offers other avenues of inquiry that resonate with

Figure 4.1 Hans van Manen rehearsing with Anthony Dowell in *Four Schumann Pieces*, 1975.

Photograph by Anthony Crickmay. Image supplied by the Hans van Manen Foundation at the Dutch National Opera and Ballet. © Victoria and Albert Museum, London. Used with permission.

his choreographic sensibilities while also illuminating Schumann's music. The ballet *Four Schumann Pieces* illustrates aesthetic principles in Van Manen's output as a whole, including ones inspired by his formalist-modernist role model, George Balanchine. Van Manen became familiar with Balanchine's work in the 1950s and was impressed by his functional, sculptural approach to classical ballet technique, with musical elements guiding movement instead of a storyline. (Balanchine, famous for his Stravinsky collaboration, among other things, was one of various choreographers to emerge from an early twentieth-century dance tradition that favored "music visualization." As he once remarked, "I must show them the music. Music must be seen!")[14] In 1980, while reflecting on his then already considerable output, Van Manen remarked that whenever he choreographs, Balanchine is always "looking over" his shoulder.[15] Not surprisingly, *Four Schumann Pieces*, like most of Van Manen's works, is plotless (or in Balanchine's words, a "dramatic ballet without a story"), with the choreography shaped by the artist's response to the music. In different program notes, Van Manen has indicated that the ballet is "music visualized," and that "for each of the four parts I have put the ballet in accordance with the different moods and rhythms of the music."[16] The stage backdrop used for the ballet's premiere, created by Van Manen's longtime designer Jean-Paul Vroom, also enhanced the visualization process: changing colors evoked temporal movement, while thin, black, horizontal lines conjured an abstract musical staff (see Figure 4.2). Thus, the dancers, as one blogger has suggested, appear like "representations of the notes themselves."[17]

While adopting a formalist approach to choreography, Van Manen has always wanted his ballets to reflect facets of human existence, albeit in abstract ways. The British dance critic Sanjoy Roy has perceptively noted that while Balanchine was an important influence, "Van Manen is less interested in 'pure movement' than Balanchine, and elements of drama and characterization are often quite explicit in his pieces."[18] Any glance at Van Manen–related literature will quickly reveal a recurring theme, namely, the importance of human relationships in all of his works. As Van Manen has stated, "The desire for abstraction is a determining factor in my ballets, but it shouldn't allow the human element to be submerged." For this reason, Van Manen has made stylized "looks" between dancers an important thumbprint of his style. He continues: "I've underlined that [importance of the human element] by always laying a great stress on the directional gaze of the dancers."[19] Although Van Manen has never described an explicit meaning for *Four Schumann Pieces*, the use of such looks and Balanchine's suggestion that the ballet "shows a man who stands alone but who is surrounded by persons he would wish to know" together give some sense of this "human element."[20]

I would argue that *Four Schumann Pieces*, in both its gestural and human dimensions, has much to tell us about the workings of Schumann's quartet.

DANCING TO SCHUMANN 111

Figure 4.2 Anthony Dowell in front of the original backdrop designed by Jean-Paul Vroom for *Four Schumann Pieces* (pose beginning Piece 1).

Photograph by Anthony Crickmay (cropped). Lillie F. Rosen, *Anthony Dowell*. Dance Horizons Spotlight Series. [Brooklyn]: Dance Horizons, 1976, 10–11. © Victoria and Albert Museum, London. Used with permission.

That is, the choreography does more than reveal Van Manen's sensitive response to the score; it also provides a new interpretive framework for rehearing the music. Even Stravinsky—who made no bones about which part of the music-dance relationship he saw as most important (and Balanchine tended to agree that it was the former)—remarked that the choreographer's 1963 setting of his *Movements for Piano and Orchestra* "has been a greater revelation to me, I think, than to anyone else. The choreography emphasizes relationships of which I had hardly been aware—in the same way—and the performance was like a tour of a building for which I had drawn the plans but never explored the result."[21] To show how *Four Schumann Pieces* might serve as a hermeneutic lens in this regard, the chapter focuses on Schumann's Adagio movement, the third "piece" of Van Manen's ballet and the most intimate of the four in that it features a series of *pas de deux*, including a duet for two male dancers. (For information on available performances and how to access them, see the Note on Performance Sources at the end of this chapter.) Van Manen's choreography explores identity as multivalent and relational, with the result that heteronormative boundary lines, hierarchies, and gestural protocols become reconfigured. This conceptual framework— buttressed by an investigation into Van Manen's own emancipatory attitudes about identity, especially gay identity—proves remarkably telling for Schumann's Adagio, a movement that has provoked a variety of contradictory formal interpretations. Indeed, the multivalent nature of Van Manen's choreography facilitates numerous insights into the music that have hitherto escaped notice: for instance, a "primary" theme that resists any fixed version of itself; a large-scale "form" that allows multiple structural principles to intersect; and a softening of boundaries that exposes ties between seemingly different materials. By bringing such aspects into view, *Four Schumann Pieces*—itself a classically based ballet—illuminates not only a continuing strain of experimentalism in Schumann's Leipzig chamber music, but also the ability of such experimentalism to renew the expressive power of older, inherited forms and genres.[22]

Van Manen and the Emancipation of Identity

The third piece in Van Manen's ballet has attracted attention because of a duet danced by the soloist with another male. Given the ballet's overall focus on a "man who stands alone," we might be tempted to assume that this pairing, and the homoerotic interest that it implies, accounts for the soloist's detached identity in earlier movements. After all, there he represents an asymmetrical element against which five male-female couples usually appear. Here, however, Van Manen presents us with a more interesting account of gender identity and sexual orientation, one that imbues the Adagio not with a sense of secretive isolation, but of inclusive, multifaceted intimacy. Only in this movement will the number of dancers be reduced—two men and two women, making a literal quartet of dancers—and only here will the soloist experience physical contact with others. Such intimacy illustrates the protagonist's evolving relationship with others, but it does so in ways that challenge balletic gender conventions, ones that Van Manen had already destabilized from the outset by spotlighting a ballerino in place of a ballerina. Although the quartet makeup might suggest a division into two male-female couples, Van Manen not only writes a male *pas de deux*, he also undermines the notion of heteronormative monogamy by joining the soloist with each female in separate duets. Indeed, the transition from the first female to the second briefly implies a threesome. Such flexible groupings are foreshadowed at the outset by Van Manen's positioning of bodies. Before a note sounds or any movement occurs, the soloist stands center stage with his arm extended to his left. But to whom does he beckon? One female stands downstage, the other male upstage. (The second female awaits him on stage right.) The soloist's gesture, directed toward a space "in between," seems to invite multiple possibilities. Thus, the Adagio as a whole appears to provide more than what Eva van Schaik has called an "emancipatory statement about homosexuality."[23] Indeed, as we shall see, its exploration of identity is multivalent: although the male duet receives particular emphasis, the Adagio ultimately poses different groupings as viable and interconnected, significant only when viewed collectively (a perspective reaffirmed in the coda). Reinforcing the fluid nature of identity, certain gendered movement protocols also become reconfigured. In his review of the ballet's 1975 premiere, Richard Glasstone pointed to the fluid nature of gender lines in the Adagio by asserting that the soloist "investigates the male and female sides of his personality."[24] An even more relational view of identity seems to emerge, however, because a woman dancer does so as well, suggesting that so-called masculine and feminine qualities may function pliably in relation to the male-female binary. Thus, the piece adopts different strategies for challenging conventional gender markers and boundary lines. To further understand the Adagio's choreography, let us turn once again toward Van Manen, for even though he objects to writers positing relationships between his biography and ballets, his views on gender identity and sexual orientation nevertheless will inform our understanding of the Adagio in both its gestural and musical dimensions.

Even as a boy in the 1930s and 1940s, Van Manen acknowledged his homosexual orientation and saw it as equally valid as heterosexuality. As Van Schaik has described, this stance likely resulted from several factors: (1) having an accepting mother, who saw that her son felt neither guilty nor unhappy about being gay; (2) coming of age during postwar years when many Dutch youth were redefining what older generations had seen as the social, religious, and moral "pillars" of society; and (3) befriending the older but influential Dutch designer Benno Premsela, a founding member and later director of the first (though initially anonymous) organization for gay men in the Netherlands, the *Cultureel Ontspannings Centrum* (COC), or the Center for Culture and Leisure, established in 1946. As a young man, Van Manen was attracted to Premsela's "emancipatory attitude" and involved himself in the club's cultural and recreational activities in the 1950s and beyond. Yet Van Schaik also notes that Van Manen approached the problem of homosexual anonymity differently than Premsela. On becoming director of the COC in 1962, Premsela made the organization's fight for recognition more public, evident not only in its well-publicized battles against sodomy laws, but also in the more explicit new name for the organization, the *Nederlandse Vereiniging voor Homofielen COC*, or the Dutch Association for Homophiles COC. For his part, Van Manen took a different approach: while publicly open about his sexual orientation, he has downplayed its significance for understanding his life and work and sought to pose it as merely one of various legitimate ways of being. This perspective clarifies his oft-repeated response to interviewers who have frequently raised the matter of his sexual orientation: it is a non-issue, he states, and raising it says more about the person asking than answering the question.[25]

Such democratic attitudes have influenced Van Manen's approach to dance, whether in terms of career outlooks, costuming, or choreography. When asked in 1980 to explain his contribution to the development of Dutch theatrical dance, he promptly replied: "That the job of choreographer is as respectable as any other profession."[26] Costumes for his ballets also reveal his leveling attitudes by perhaps featuring uniform outfits among men and women (his 1969 *Squares*, for instance, in which all dancers wore white t-shirts and tights), or by disrupting gendered dress associations. When asked why male dancers wore skirts in his *Grosse Fuge* (1971) and *Corps* (1985), Van Manen replied:

> A skirt is much more than just an indication of gender. It's a lovely feeling dancing in a long skirt, just like having a fan wrapped round you. In *Grosse Fuge* I wanted to convey aggression, and a skirt that keeps swirling open looks much more violent than moving legs. *Corps* was about uniformity: the women wore skirts and, therefore, so did the men as well.[27]

Van Manen's ballets also counter the traditional supremacy of the prima ballerina by acknowledging other possibilities: works that feature a male soloist alone or with others (occurring as early as his 1957 ballet, *Feestgericht*); works for groups (the 1969 *Squares*, for example) or for a small group of soloists (the trio of *Untitled*, from 1968, or the quartet in the 1978 *Dumbarton Oaks*, both mixed-gender ensembles); duets that treat each soloist equally in terms of technique and attention (rather than the traditional supporting role of a cavalier to a ballerina); and duets that may comprise either male-female pairings or male-male pairings. (Early examples of the latter that predate *Four Schumann Pieces* include the 1965 *Metaforen*, the 1970 *Situation*, and the 1974 *Le Sacre du Printemps*.) That roles may be unfixed and interchanged is represented in a work like *Tilt* (1972), which in its second half swaps individual-group patterns found in the first half, while doing the same with its male-female roles.

Van Manen's early willingness to explore non-heteronormative topics positions him as an innovator among choreographers, a status that deserves still more recognition. In a 1995 essay, the esteemed German dance critic Horst Koegler discussed the long unacknowledged presence of gay men in the ballet world while also giving a historical overview of works in which gay themes began to emerge.[28] Though citing a few examples from the late 1950s, Koegler asserts that "it was the sixties that witnessed the 'coming out' of ballet," and he draws immediate attention to an experimental Dutch dance group founded in 1959—the Netherlands Dance Theater (NDT)—and two people who at different times served as its directors: Van Manen and later Glen Tetley.[29] Koegler notes that, unlike older generations of choreographers (like Frederick Ashton, Antony Tudor, Serge Lifar, and many others, who "considered their sexual preferences their strictly private concern"), Van Manen and Tetley "did not hide their homosexuality;" yet neither did they "flaunt their private emotions," but rather "presented homosexuality as just a different variant of a 'normal' sexual relationship."[30] Koegler cites Van Manen's *Situation* and "breathtaking" *Metaforen*, along with Tetley's 1969 ballet *Arena*, and his insight receives additional support from Van Manen, who in reference to *Metaforen* has argued for a normative framing of its male *pas de deux*:

> Do you know what my sort of political statement is? It's the duet for two men in *Metaforen*. I had the devil's own fun making Han Ebbelaar and Gérard Lemaitre dance together without the excuse of an anecdote; simply to show that two men can partner each other at least as well and in just the same way as a man and a woman. The duet ends with a lift: a man lifted up to sit on the shoulder—a lift usually only done with women. That was my political stand. The ballet had no homosexual theme; the piece didn't need selling in the programme book by a reference to some deep underlying psychological background. It was just an emancipated male duet; the only problem being that there was no problem.[31]

Elsewhere Van Manen has remarked: "It never struck me that two men were dancing together; it seems quite normal to me. If it worries some people, that's not my problem." Pieter Kottman has pointed out the obvious, namely, that Van Manen understood the novelty of his male duet in *Metaforen*, yet notes that by positioning it as normative Van Manen attempts to repudiate the "irrational morality" of those who see homosexuality as deviant.[32]

In the comments above, both Koegler and Van Manen de-emphasize psychological probing into gay identities, something that distinguishes the latter's works from a number of other ballets with gay themes. Referencing examples from the 1960s, Koegler cites the well-known 1965 *Monument for a Dead Boy* by Van Manen's Dutch colleague Rudi van Dantzig (which shows the destruction of an adolescent tortured by his sexual orientation) and the 1962 *A Wedding Gift* by the British choreographer Peter Darrell (where a former "roommate" of the groom becomes "rejected when the bride discovers a compromising inscription in a book given as a wedding gift"). As Koegler notes, both works were of their time in that they "suggest that 'gay is sad.'"[33] For Van Manen the choreographer, gay has never been sad, nor a stigmatized identity. As one British critic remarked in 2010, unlike his contemporary Kenneth MacMillan, "another specialist in sexual relations" but who "is fascinatingly drenched in guilt, Van Manen takes a bold, guilt-free stand."[34] This stand occurs not only by making gay elements visible (rather than closeting them), but also by downplaying narrative and psychological explorations (which have the potential to particularize, versus universalize, such elements) and by adopting strategies that position gay identities alongside others. Even in the opening movement of *Four Schumann Pieces*, where the soloist remains unpaired, the choreography makes clear that he is not stigmatized, for the others eventually prove as curious about him as he is of them. The Adagio goes the furthest, giving the soloist free reign to join with multiple partners, be they female or male, and even to adopt gestures conventionally rendered as feminine. By allowing such different pairings and outlooks to coexist, the Adagio embodies Van Manen's emancipatory attitudes while simultaneously providing hermeneutic windows through which we might better understand Schumann's music.

The Adagio: Multivalent Identity in the Music and the Dance

In presenting identity as flexible and multidimensional, Van Manen visually enhances (and was surely responding to) a prominent aspect of Schumann's Adagio, namely, the continuous variation principle that plays out on both local and large-scale levels. The opening theme immediately sets such variation into play (mm. 1–19; see Example 4.1). Its first four-bar phrase (a) appears three times along with a contrasting middle part (b), generating a small rounded-binary form without repeats (aa,ba). Yet each statement of the 'a' idea differs in terms of its melodic trajectory, contrapuntal setting, dynamics, harmonization, and (in the case of its third appearance) phrase length. Even the opening phrase (mm. 1–4) projects a sense of instability and openness. This occurs partly by avoiding strong metric definition of the D-major tonic chord—the opening I^6 harmony serves as an upbeat to IV—but also by ending with a tonicization of that subdominant. The second phrase veers further from the home key (mm. 5–8): while the melody initially sounds consequent-like, the phrase thwarts any sense of "starting over" by inflecting toward the mediant key (F-sharp minor), then ending in A major. In its third appearance (mm. 12–19), the main idea diverges even more, expanding its upbeat gesture to two beats and beginning on $\hat{7}$ instead of $\hat{5}$ (m. 12), while also replacing its original 2 + 2 subphrasing with a *fortspinnung*-type extension that lengthens the phrase. Although this third statement provides yet another harmonization of the melody, it at least begins and ends

118   ROBERT SCHUMANN'S LEIPZIG CHAMBER WORKS

Example 4.1 Schumann, String Quartet in A Major, Op. 41, No. 3: the opening theme of the Adagio (mm. 1–19).

Example 4.1 Continued

in D major. Nevertheless, it also conjures earlier harmonic meanderings by tonicizing G major twice more (mm. 13–14 and again in mm. 15–16) along with E minor (mm. 16–17, a key emphasized earlier in part b). Collectively these statements suggest that the central 'a' idea resists fixed notions of itself. Of course, such thematic fluidity is in itself not exceptional; in eighteenth- and nineteenth-century examples, rounded-binary forms can accommodate variation of the 'a' phrase. In the Adagio, however, Schumann seems to take this capacity as a cue for engaging with it on a larger scale, for his subsequent treatment of the main theme only enriches its manifold nature and in ways that (as we shall see) challenge any single traditional formal reading.

Twice more the main theme will return, first transposed a fourth higher (mm. 45–58), then again at its original pitch level (mm. 78–94; for clarity, these three statements of the overall theme will be labeled A^1, A^2, and A^3). While the individual 'a' phrases largely retain the harmonizations found in A^1, they nevertheless undergo further variation. In A^2, new counterpoints appear that feature triplets and sextuplets against primarily duple divisions; in addition, the final appearance of 'a' (mm. 55–58) compresses its upbeat gesture from two beats to one while also expunging the original *fortspinnung* figuration. In A^3, duple and triple divisions return as accompaniment to the 'a' phrases, but in changed counterpoints and with a new *pizzicato* articulation; and while the *fortspinnung* figuration returns for the final 'a' phrase (mm. 88–94), its upbeat gesture remains compressed at one beat versus its original two beats. Given both small- and large-scale repetitions, we thus hear nine statements of the 'a' phrase in total, yet none are alike and no single version emerges as primary. Once again, even as the phrase maintains a recognizable identity, it continually leaves itself open to ongoing transformation.[35]

Resistance to a fixed identity also characterizes the overall form of the movement. Indeed, we may glean some sense of this resistance by noting the curiously varied interpretations offered by writers on its structure. John Daverio describes it in passing as a strophic variation form, while John Gardner calls it a rondo form. Hans Kohlhase echoes both interpretations: the movement adopts an A B A' B' A'' coda format, he asserts, but because "the accompaniments of section A are so greatly changed in the da capo sections," a "quasi-Variation form" also emerges. A. E. F. Dickinson offers a different perspective by calling the movement a "free sonata form."[36] Other writers who reference the Adagio skirt the matter entirely.[37]

Of all the movements in a traditional instrumental cycle, the slow movement tends to be the most malleable in terms of structure. As James Hepokoski and Warren Darcy note, its format is "nonobligatory. One cannot predict what the form will be in advance of hearing it."[38] Prompted partly by the ballet's cues, I would argue that Schumann plays with this tradition by allowing multiple structural principles to intersect. Thus, while each of the above formal interpretations touches on crucial aspects of the Adagio, each by itself is inadequate to account for the whole. A theme-and-variations perspective, for instance, explains the changing appearances of the main theme

(A), but it does not accommodate the contrasting episode (B, mm. 19–44), which emphasizes a new plaintive idea surrounded by dotted rhythms and minor-mode inflections, and which—aside from being truncated—is not thematically varied upon its return (B^2, mm. 58–77). Nor does a theme-and-variations reading explain the large-scale harmonic departure that occurs when both A^2 and B^2 recur a fourth higher (mm. 45–77); such a transposition counters the tonal constancy associated with theme-and-variation form. A rondo interpretation suits both the refrain principle and contrasting B episodes; however, a traditional rondo is not compatible with the continuous variation of A, nor with its transposed appearance in the middle of the movement (A^2). (In rondos the refrain traditionally serves as both a fixed tonal and thematic landmark.) A sonata-form perspective recognizes the recapitulation-like return of the main theme to its original harmonic framework (A^3, which follows the transposed statements of A^2 and B^2), but this interpretation does not explain the considerably changed character of A^3, nor does it accommodate section B, which functions more like a developmental episode than a stable secondary theme area. (Even Dickinson acknowledges that the tonality of B is "peculiar, ranging from E flat major to C sharp minor.") All of the above indicates that Schumann's treatment of form is multivalent: like the choreography, understanding its nature requires that we accept the coexistence of multiple identities.

Another choreographic element that illuminates the music has to do with Van Manen's treatment of sectional divisions, in particular, what seems to be a purposeful blurring of them. Such obfuscation stands in relief precisely because his choreography "visualizes" numerous other musical elements, whether they concern rhythmic accents, phrasing, formal parallelisms and the like, and whether they occur on small- or large-scale levels. In the opening theme, for instance, the movements of the soloist with his first female partner clearly reinforce the 2 + 2 subphrasing, with steps, lifts, rotations, and pauses marking beginning and end points. The dancers also echo the model-sequence pattern of part 'b' (mm. 8–12) by presenting their movements, then repeating them, facing first downstage, then upstage. At the same time, Van Manen reflects the ever-changing 'a' phrase within the theme by accompanying each statement with different gestural patterns: in the first, for instance, a female dancer approaches the soloist, after which they move in unison; in the second phrase, however, they take turns supporting each other in a new pattern of turns. On a larger level, the one example of extensive choreographic repetition occurs, not surprisingly, with B materials, the only section that—aside from being shortened and stated a fourth higher—recurs without variation; for this reason, Van Manen repeats the choreography of B^1 for B^2. To reflect Schumann's continual variation of the main theme, Van Manen changes the gestural movements for each of its appearances; on the other hand, he acknowledges the commonality of these three statements by marking the end of each A section similarly, with two dancers standing side by side and extending an arm either toward each other (the ends of A^1 and A^2) or toward the wings (end of A^3). In these various ways, Van Manen's choreography seems to reinforce sectional divisions in the music.

Or does it? Especially intriguing is how his choreography both acknowledges *and* questions conventional boundaries—what any act of resistance necessitates. Although Van Manen pairs the soloist with three different partners, he avoids aligning those pairings with the threefold appearance of section A. Instead, duets tend to overlap contrasting sections, with partner exchanges usually occurring "in the middle of things." While blurring borderlines that we expect to be straightforward, these off-center duets provide new frameworks for considering relationships between seemingly dissimilar things, be they contrasting musical sections or pairings that challenge the primacy of heteronormative monogamy. Figure 4.3 provides a formal overview of both the music and the soloist's pairings, and as it shows, the male-female duets especially contravene musical seam lines. Even the first duet begins *in medias res* (upbeat to m. 3), a delay prompted by Van Manen's prolonged "portraiture" of bodies on stage, with the soloist's hand beckoning to a space in between other dancers. We might expect the first partner swap to synchronize with A^2 but instead it occurs much earlier with section B, though not at its outset since the first duet perseveres for some

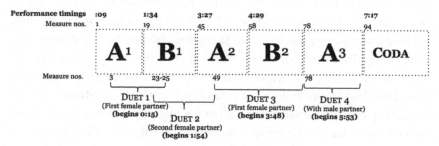

Figure 4.3 Schumann, String Quartet in A Major, Op. 41, No. 3: formal overview of the Adagio, showing placement of duets against main musical sections. Timings taken from the 1978 performance cited in the Note on Performance Sources at the end of the chapter.

six measures into the episode. Even when the handoff occurs, Van Manen imbues it with a hazy quality by having both women momentarily hold the soloist's hand (mm. 23–25), intimating the possible threesome mentioned earlier. The second pairing soon reveals a telling break when the soloist abruptly ceases to dance (upbeat to m. 35), an event that also brings a static C-sharp pedal and fragmented melodic gestures (mm. 34–37): here the soloist passionately grasps his partner's arms and looks into her eyes, only to slowly register a subtle look of disappointment (one made more pronounced in the 1978 performance by having both look down). Each walk away from the other, a moment that soon brings a cadence in the distant key of C-sharp minor (m. 38). The soloist will indeed return to his first female partner, but it does not happen here, nor is it correlated with the forthcoming varied return of the main theme (m. 45). Instead, he continues with his second partner, returning to his first only when A^2 is well underway (m. 49), another *in medias res* exchange. Because his first partner will dance up until A^3, she receives a disproportionate amount of stage time (another element of asymmetry), which nevertheless will end with the same expression of disappointment from the soloist, the result of repeating choreographic movements with the transposed return of B materials (mm. 58–77).

Even though male-female pairings dominate the Adagio, their misaligned, asymmetrical nature implies that the gender norms of classical ballet have been disturbed, something the all-male *pas de deux* will confirm. In challenging various borders, the choreography illuminates a similar facet of the music. Indeed, the Adagio shows a variety of strategies—ones more typically associated with Schumann's earlier output—for making musical borders porous; these strategies in turn prompt us to acknowledge a wider range of relationships that may transgress formal norms and hierarchies. One such strategy involves Schumann's intermixing of materials between sections that we assume will be separate. The B sections, for example, may sound like contrasting episodes, but each time they become infiltrated by A materials: the opening scalar ascent of phrase 'a' returns in varied form, leading toward a dominant arrival (mm. 27–28 in B^1, mm. 66–67 in B^2), after which the first half of phrase 'b' appears (mm. 28–30, with the whole sequentially restated a second higher, mm. 31–34; cf. mm. 67–69 and 70–73 in B^2). This chain of events generates a shift in hierarchical relations: in the opening theme, the 'a' phrase serves as an initiating, principal idea, with 'b' as secondary; in section B, both now appear as interior, subsidiary elements. The intrusion of 'a' material within section B also allows the former to undergo more variation; thus, the 'a' idea explores new representations of itself even outside of its "proper" thematic context.

Such intermixing of materials does not stop here, for B materials will also seep into subsequent A sections. In A² the contrasting middle part assumes a new identity: instead of part 'b', we hear a reference to section B, specifically a variant of the fragmented, sigh-like gesture that accompanied the brief but passionate embrace of the dancers (cf. mm. 53–54 with mm. 35–36). This same idea will also supplant part 'b' in A³ as well (mm. 86–87). As a result, the original setting in which part 'b' appeared—the opening theme—turns out to be an illusory "home" context: thereafter part 'b' surfaces only within B episodes, as if identifying more with something originally outside of itself.[39]

Schumann's movement uses other strategies to blur boundaries we typically assume to be clear-cut. As mentioned earlier, even at the outset we hear not a definitive tonic downbeat but a I^6 chord that serves as an upbeat to the subdominant, thereby undermining a strong harmonic beginning.[40] The subsequent weak treatment of cadences especially undercuts the articulation of formal junctures, both within and between major sections. Although the opening eight measures melodically imply an antecedent-consequent relationship, the cadences that traditionally define a period are missing here, not only because of the roaming modulations, but also because of contrapuntal writing in the bass: although G major and A major are tonicized at the end of the first and second phrases respectively, neither ends with the implied root-position IAC because the bass's upward linear movement avoids $\hat{5}$-$\hat{1}$ motion each time (mm. 3–4 and 7–8). Given the opening theme's harmonic wanderings, we might expect A¹ to at least conclude with the strong PAC that it briefly implies: I^6–IV–cad$^6_4$ (with the melody emphasizing $\hat{1}$–$\hat{4}$–$\hat{3}$ as harmonic tones, mm. 17–18). Yet once again the bass thwarts the implied root-position cadence through a linear ascent, with each bass note now receiving its own harmonization: vii^{o7}→vi–vii^{ø7}–I (mm. 18–19). The melody's ending on $\hat{5}$ further weakens the sense of conclusion. Subsequent appearances of the theme only confirm Schumann's unusual rethinking of cadential norms, for even though the main theme undergoes variation in subsequent occurrences, it preserves each of its original weakened cadences.[41]

As further evidence of blurred borderlines, the first root-position V-I cadence occurs not at the end of a section but within it, namely, with the IAC that occurs in B¹ after the soloist's look of disappointment with his partner (m. 38). Moreover, when this cadence arrives, it defines not the home key of D major but its leading-tone key, C-sharp minor. In other words, what normally functions as a decisive formal marker, a V–I cadence, is consigned to articulating a distantly related key within the interior of a section.[42] As if to confirm the diminished significance of this moment, the two dancers remain still, having walked—not danced—to their separate positions. In other words, by playing down this clear cadence, Van Manen implies that conventional musical markers have no ability to animate the dancers in this movement. (The choreography remains the same with the analogous cadence in B^2, one that now defines F-sharp minor, m. 77.) Indeed, the irrelevance of usual identifying markers becomes clear by the end, for nowhere in the Adagio will a PAC ever occur, not even within the coda.

Schumann also clouds structural seams by avoiding retransitional passages, thereby undercutting the force of thematic returns. In a sense, he thwarts the utility of such retransitions by composing a theme that at the outset avoids a strong tonic downbeat: a traditional "standing on the dominant" could not prepare the theme's downbeat on IV. Other factors also make thematic returns sound surprising rather than inevitable. The entry of A^2, for instance, sounds interruptive because it prevents an in-progress sequential pattern from completing itself (mm. 38–44; this pattern begins after the IAC in C-sharp minor, and recalls the eight-bar pattern found at the outset of B^1, mm. 19–26; the entry of A^2 usurps the pattern's concluding gesture). The move into A^3 sounds similarly unexpected. Because B^2 transposes its materials a fourth higher while also truncating them, it ends with the IAC in F-sharp minor (m. 77). Thus, this cadence provides no harmonic preparation for the return to D major in A^3 (m. 78). Moreover, because we assume that B^2 will continue as it did in B^1 (that is, with the sequential pattern that follows the IAC), the return of the main theme seems further surprising.

Against this backdrop of numerous blurred boundaries, both musical and choreographic, the male duet certainly stands in relief. Unlike the male-female pairings, Van Manen synchronizes this duet with the beginning of a section, specifically A^3, and as a result imbues it with more formal clarity (see Figure 4.3). Its unfolding within the theme's original key also does not seem accidental, as if the duet positions itself as an alternate normative pairing. Other aspects also throw the male *pas de deux* into relief. For one thing, it projects the greatest sense of intimacy thus far since they dance alone, the women having left the stage. For another, the dancers, at least initially, present new movements while also projecting a greater sense of equality than seen thus far: linked through extended straight arms (a challenging way to join two bodies, see Figure 4.4), the men take turns promenading each

Figure 4.4 Rudolf Nureyev (left) and Henny Jurriëns in a pose from the Adagio of *Four Schumann Pieces*. Performance by the Dutch National Ballet in 1976. Photograph by Jorge Fatauros and supplied by the Hans van Manen Foundation at the Dutch National Opera and Ballet. © Jorge Fatauros. Used with permission.

other and then perform a short but difficult series of parallel steps, skips, and back lunges (mm. 81–82). Finally, neither dancer seems disappointed with the other: indeed, at the end of their duet, both dancers turn to gaze at each other while standing center stage (m. 94).

Given the above, we might be tempted to read the choreography as privileging a homoerotic orientation. Especially telling, though, is how the male duet increasingly reveals the influence of what has preceded it. In other words, rather than disavowing his past, the soloist gradually seems to acknowledge it within his present male pairing, such that a more encompassing, multifaceted identity begins to emerge. First, as his duet progresses, he begins to assume a traditionally feminine role by receiving more support from his partner. Second, as if enacting memories of his past but through a new lens, he adopts gestures earlier associated with the women. In some cases, movements and poses that he previously enabled now become the means through which he must accept support. Especially striking is the floor work: two times the soloist's partner lies him on the ground (mm.

84–85 and 92), recalling earlier moments when the soloist himself had similarly directed his partners' bodies downward (mm. 12–14 and 51–52 with his first female partner, and mm. 44 and 46–48 with his second).[43] Each time the soloist is lifted from the floor, his male partner steers him into a deep backbend, evoking a similar backbend coaxed by the soloist from his first partner after her floor work (mm. 13–14). Stationary turn gestures also link all the duets. The soloist performs a rapid double turn in the air, steadied by his male partner (m. 83), and later they both perform parallel pirouettes (mm. 87). Together these movements recall a variety of pirouettes danced by the women with stationary support from the soloist (mm. 28 and its corresponding repetition in m. 67; m. 57 as well), but also danced by the soloist in parallel with them (mm. 32–34 and its corresponding repetition in mm. 71–73). By continuing such movements within the male duet, even by swapping out his earlier supporting roles, the soloist breaks down conventional gender lines, revealing cohesion between masculine and feminine identities, and between his all-male and male-female pairings. Thus, if the male duet receives particular emphasis, it does so partly by acknowledging other possible pairings and the roles that accompanied those pairings. Similarly, if the soloist seemed dissatisfied at certain moments in his earlier duets, I would argue that this feeling arose not necessarily because of an exclusive homosexual orientation, but because these pairings upheld a heteronormativity that was not (yet) inclusive enough for the soloist. As I will later show, this perspective becomes confirmed by the choreography in the coda.

By blending the past with the present, and the similar with the seemingly dissimilar, the male duet captures an overarching principle within the music, for each subsequent section shows the influence of what has come before. As earlier remarks illustrate, this concept manifests itself partly by intermixing materials between seemingly contrasting sections: both appearances of B incorporate gestures from the 'a' and 'b' phrases found in the opening theme, and, similarly, A^2 and A^3 incorporate an idea from B in place of the original contrasting middle section of A^1. The notion of cumulative coloring appears in other ways as well. Section A^2 generates striking rhythmic density by mixing various triplet-sextuplet divisions into the common-time metrical framework. In so doing, this section normalizes what were once isolated rhythmic irregularities in earlier sections: the one-time triplet in measure 5 of the opening theme, and the sextuplet figure that ornaments the C-sharp pedal in B^2 (mm. 35–37). In returning a fourth higher than their original appearance, both A^2 and B^2 reveal the influence of A^1 by magnifying its plagal tendencies, specifically its subdominant downbeat and multiple tonicizations of G major, the subdominant key. As for A^3, it seems to acknowledge A^2 by featuring mixed subdivisions for its first three phrases, though now primarily triplets against duple divisions (mm. 78–87). In addition, its prominent *pizzicato* accompaniment amplifies what was once a short-lived articulation within B^1 (mm. 39–41; these measures do not recur in B^2 because of its truncation). Section A^3 also references A^1 by returning both to the original rhythms that accompanied its last phrase (hence the triplets quickly disappear), and to the *fortspinnung* figuration that extended this very phrase (missing in A^2). All of these traits indicate a continuous referencing of the past, with the music—like the choreography—embracing elements from different contexts to yield ongoing, multifaceted identities.

The coda affirms the importance of this collective perspective, both choreographically and musically. Although A^3 ends with a telling gaze between the men, equally important is how both extend an arm toward the separate wings, inviting the women back on stage (an inside-out version of the gesture that ends A^1 and A^2, where the soloist and a female partner extend arms toward each other). For the first time in the movement, all four dancers join together, first by moving in a horizontal line holding raised hands (mm. 96–98), then by linking waists in a tight line that rotates in counterclockwise motion (mm. 98–100). The ordering of bodies (F–M–M–F) also encapsulates the pairing possibilities we have witnessed: an all-male partnering that simultaneously dovetails two male-female pairings. Eventually the center breaks so that, for the first and only time in the movement, we briefly witness two male-female couples, with each male playing a cavalier-like role as he carries his female partner in continuing rotations and supports her in various lifts (mm. 100–104). In other words, only after a range of possibilities has been explored does Van Manen briefly reference what audiences likely expected of his quartet of dancers in the first place, namely, a division into two heteronormative couples that behave according to the gendered norms of classical ballet.

Nonetheless, in conjuring these norms here, Van Manen reconfigures them in the final two measures of the coda, and in a manner that furthers the notion of multivalent identities. Although one couple remains on stage—the soloist and his first female partner—what we ultimately witness is an exchange of conventional masculine and feminine markers: she stands flat-footed, steadying him as he moves with raised arms into an arabesque on demi-pointe. This striking role reversal is foreshadowed near the outset of the movement when, in another flat-footed stance, she supports him on demi-pointe in a turn with an extended high leg (mm. 7–8). Indeed, this female dancer shows unusual initiative at several moments in this duet, not only by briefly supporting him here, but even by prompting this duet (she approaches him, taking his extended hand, mm. 1–2) and by later triggering the handoff to the second woman (to whom she scampers, with the soloist following; mm. 22–23). Nevertheless, these earlier moments appear isolated since she and the second woman mostly conform to classical balletic roles, relying on assistance from the soloist. By the end of the piece, however, the role reversal assumes particular significance: it now follows on the heels of the male duet, wherein the soloist received much support from his male partner by assuming gestures similar to those performed earlier by the women. Here at the coda's conclusion, where an exchange of traditional masculine and feminine qualities occurs between a male and female dancer, Van Manen suggests an identification of natures traditionally kept apart. The soloist's final pose also indicates how far he has come: in the last measure of the piece, he descends, one-legged, into a lunge, a tremendously difficult movement requiring great balance, and a final pose wholly different from the stiff, vertical posture he assumed at the outset. Although the soloist is left alone on stage, his final pose is not that of an outsider, but of an individual transformed by his interactions with others. Indeed, not only does his lunge—which he inflects backward—evoke a similar one performed with his male partner (m. 82), but by leaning forward he simultaneously recalls a give-and-take leaning gesture performed with his first female partner at the beginning of each B episode (mm. 19–20 and 58–59).[44]

Such interconnectedness draws attention to Schumann's music, especially to elements previously kept apart but which here become fused. As some have noted, the coda (mm. 94–105, Example 4.2a) recalls episode B: in particular, the coda's melodic gestures, combined with the accompanying dotted-pedal-note idea, derive from the opening phrase of B (see Example 4.2b, which reproduces the beginning of B^1). Equally important, though, is the new harmonic context provided for these materials. At the outset of each B episode, this phrase never achieves resolution for its V^7 chord; instead, the harmony switches to another V^7 chord with which it shares two tones (D–F in B^1, and G–B♭ in B^2), which in turn initiates a varied sequential restatement (mm. 23–26 in B^1 and mm. 62–65 in B^2). In the coda, however, this phrase assumes a new trajectory by finally attaining its implied resolution, albeit over a tonic pedal tone.

130 ROBERT SCHUMANN'S LEIPZIG CHAMBER WORKS

Example 4.2 Schumann, String Quartet in A Major, Op. 41, No. 3: thematic similarity between the Adagio's Coda and B materials.

(a) The coda (mm. 94–105).

Example 4.2 Continued

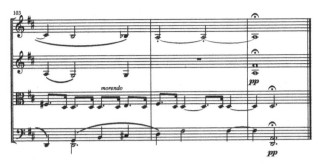

(b) The opening phrase of B¹ (mm. 19–24).

Significantly, the means through which it achieves this resolution clearly derive from A materials: by adding its seventh over what we hear as a D-major tonic chord (m. 95), the phrase creates an applied dominant that resolves toward the subdominant (m. 96)—the very maneuver that serves as a harmonic thumbprint of the main theme in each of its appearances.

The opening theme, for instance, inflects the tonic chord in just this way for its threefold tonicization of the subdominant key, G major (mm. 2–4, 13–14, and 15–16; see Example 4.1). As the coda unfolds, we will hear two more such inflections, thereby underscoring its importance (mm. 99–100 and 102–103; another turn to the subdominant—with a suspension—occurs in m. 101 but without the applied chord). Plagal inflections are common within codas, of course, and perhaps here they suggest that we have arrived home in some fashion. At the same time, they become another means for resisting V–I definition of the tonic; in other words, the subdominant inflections assume a new expressive force, occurring as they do in a movement that has assiduously avoided PACs in ways that further multidimensionality. Such avoidance only continues in the coda, for returns to the tonic occur not through the dominant, but rather—and without exception—through its leading chord. Moreover, this chord always appears as fully diminished, allowing it to bring something outside the realm of the home key, specifically the chromatic pitch B♭ (mm. 98, 100, 101, and 103).[45]

A Wrap

In staging different pairing possibilities, and by disentangling so-called masculine and feminine traits from the sexes, Van Manen's Adagio highlights the relational value of the male-female binary that had long dictated roles, movements, and qualities within classical ballet, a perspective that anticipates the work of later choreographers like Mark Morris, William Forsythe, Alonzo King, and others. I would argue, though, that Van Manen's reconfigured identities attain power not in spite of ballet's long-standing gender protocols but precisely because of them. That is, by using the vocabulary of classical ballet (rather than that of a modern dance idiom, for example), Van Manen allows such reconfigured identities to simultaneously conjure their absence within the historical repertory that such a vocabulary evokes. In populating the classical ballet idiom with these diversified identities, he also renews the idiom's expressive capacity for new generations of dancers and audiences. In the wording of Karmen Mackendrick, one might thus say that Van Manen's "transgressions" are not merely "*re*-active" but transformative, not "smash[ing] things to bits but ... push[ing] them into new and constantly mobile admixture with those forces that seem to oppose them."[46]

Schumann's innovations within the Adagio of this string quartet also stand in relief since (like Van Manen's reconfigured identities) they counter expectations established within the classical repertory. Schumann's reworking of older formal principles similarly imbues them with greater expressive force, for the music invites a more engaged manner of listening; no longer can we assume a sequence of familiar formal-rhetorical patterns. Recognizing such innovations in Schumann's Adagio—something that Van Manen's choreography helps to facilitate—once again prompts us to question the simplistic boundary line that writers have long posited between Schumann's so-called "objective" music of the early 1840s and the "subjective" works of the preceding decade. All the unusual traits found in the quartet's Adagio—avoidance of strong tonic downbeats, weakened and "misplaced" cadences, blurring of structural seams, infiltration of materials from outside sections—have precedents in Schumann's earlier music. Even the Adagio's conflation of multiple forms recalls earlier piano works like the opening movement of the Op. 17 *Fantasie* (where fantasia and sonata-form elements intersect) and the finale of the Op. 11 piano sonata (which evokes both rondo and sonata-form principles, though without resembling anything close to traditional sonata-rondo form).[47] In these ways, Schumann's Adagio illustrates his creativity working in harmony with, rather than struggling against, his own compositional past. Van Manen told me that when he first discovered Schumann's quartet, he heard it as very "intimate," more "inside than outside" in character. Thus, the ballet *Four Schumann Pieces*—created by someone working outside musicological realms and uninfluenced by the standard reception history of Schumann—provides an interpretive lens through which we may discover new subjectivities in Schumann's large-scale instrumental music.[48]

Note on Performance Sources

Establishing an authoritative identity of any dance "text" often poses difficulties, as Stephanie Jordan has described. Like operas, ballets often evolve as choreographers cater their works to new dancers and companies, or make improvements upon originals, or simply make changes because memory of past versions remains inexact. Choreographic notation is often lacking, and even when extant is usually produced by someone other than the choreographer, perhaps even in their absence, and ultimately reflects another interpretation of the work. Dancers themselves add another interpretive layer to the work.[49] For these and other reasons, it is important to clarify which performance(s) will inform a scholar's research.

Instead of choreographic notation, Van Manen has relied on video documentation since the early 1970s to record his ballets for posterity. Although slight changes may occur in revivals of his works, it seems clear—and certainly so in the case of *Four Schumann Pieces*—that he prefers faithful adherence to a ballet's original choreography as far as it is practical and achievable. Pieter Kottman has described the experience of watching a 1976 video of Rudolf Nureyev intently watching a 1975 video of Dowell dancing *Four Schumann Pieces*, all in an effort to learn the solo male role. (Nureyev subsequently played the part in Dutch, British, and North American revivals.) As Kottman remarks, "That video is vital in remounting the piece," and even Van Manen, who was present with Nureyev, "sometimes has to look three or four times at the same small section to jog his memory."[50] Because *Four Schumann Pieces* was written for the London Royal Ballet and for Dowell in particular, I have favored English video sources that feature him in the solo role. These, along with a more recent performance by the Dutch National Ballet, confirm a striking degree of continuity for performances spanning multiple years; any minor discrepancies had no effect on my analyses or arguments. The main sources consulted for this project are the following, all currently accessible to the public:

(1) A 1975 performance of the entire third movement, shown near the conclusion of the 1976 *BBC* documentary *Anthony Dowell: All the Superlatives*, directed by Colin Nears and produced by Barrie Gavin for the Omnibus series and first broadcast on October 21, 1976, on *BBC One London*. For the *BBC* catalog record, see: https://genome.ch.bbc.co.uk/search/0/20?q = Anthony+Dowell+All + the+Superlatives#top. The performance of the third movement is also available online as "Anthony Dowell: All the Superlatives," YouTube video, 9:37 [pt. 6 out of 6], posted by "quillerpen," July 11, 2010, https://www.youtube.com/watch?v = LWjOd_AIXfk (accessed July 22, 2023). *Four Schumann Pieces* played an active role in Dowell's repertory for 1975, with nine performances occurring from January through October of that year—hence the focus it receives in the *BBC* program. For performance documentation of the work by the Royal Ballet, see "Four Schumann Pieces," in "Performance Database," Royal Opera House: Collections Online, http://www.rohcollections.org.uk/production.aspx?production = 4476&row = 0 (accessed July 22, 2023). The database does not

indicate any 1976 performance, suggesting that the performance was filmed in 1975.

(2) A July 22, 1978, performance of the complete work by the Royal Ballet with Dowell in the solo role; the Adagio performance is the one from which I have squared timings with the formal overview found in Figure 4.3. The complete performance appeared as part of a larger program entitled *The Royal Ballet Salutes the U.S.A.*, hosted by Gene Kelley, and telecast live by satellite on *WNEW-TV/Channel 5*, New York, on July 22, 1978; videorecording, 3 cassettes, directed by Colin Nears, Bob Lockyer, and Brian Large, and produced by Brian Large; BBC Television production in association with Metromedia Television, New York, 1978. For the New York Public Library catalog record, see: https://digitalcollections.nypl.org/items/2ddbb4f0-ef9c-0133-7d58-60f81dd2b63c (accessed July 22, 2023). The Royal Ballet's complete performance of *Four Schumann Pieces* is also available online in four parts, "Four Schumann Pieces, pt. 1, 2, 3, and 4," YouTube videos posted by "quillerpen" (who conjectures the date as ca. 1980), January 20–23, 2010, https://www.youtube.com/results?search_query = Four+Schumann+Pieces + complete (accessed July 22, 2023). The Adagio movement is found here: https://www.youtube.com/watch?v = PNOMleHbc2U

(3) A more recent performance by the Dutch National Ballet, with the complete first piece, most of the second piece, and snippets of the third and fourth, available in the 2007 Dutch documentary and commemorative dance collection *Hans van Manen: Master of Movement*, DVD, disc 5 (out of 6), compiled and distributed by the Stichting Hans van Manen ([IJsselstein, Netherlands]: Cobra Records, 2007). Also available online as "Hans van Manen: Master of Movement (Disc 5 [incomplete])," YouTube video, 12:37, posted by Luis José, May 5, 2012, https://www.youtube.com/watch?v = WNQcocGc0S0 (accessed July 22, 2023).

Notes

1. Peter Ostwald, *Schumann: The Inner Voices of a Musical Genius* (Boston: Northeastern University Press, 1985); Theo R. Payk, *Robert Schumann: Lebenslust und Leidenszeit* (Bonn: Bouvier Verlag, 2006). For examples of recent historical fiction based on the lives of Robert and Clara, see Boman Desai, *Trio: A Novel Biography of the Schumanns and Brahms* (Bloomington, IN: AuthorHouse, 2015); Klaus Funke, *Am Ende war alles Musik* (Leipzig: Faber & Faber, 2005); Janice Galloway, *Clara* (London: Jonathan Cape, 2002); Peter Härtling,

Schumanns Schatten: Variation über mehrere Personen (Cologne: Kiepenheuer & Witsch, 1996); and J. D. Landis, *Longing* (New York: Harcourt, 2000). Examples of twenty-first-century theatrical works include Sven Holm's 2006 play *Schumanns Nacht*, and the 2009 dance theater piece by Yoshiko Waki and Rolf Baumgart, *Der Unvollendenich oder Warten auf den Tunnel am Ende des Lichts*. Robert also figures prominently in plays centered around Clara: for example, the 2007 play *Vater Wiecks Liebe* by Helfried Schöbel, and the 2008 play *Sein Bildnis wunderselig* by Nina Omilian. In a letter to Clara dated September 8, 1843, Robert himself acknowledged that the "exciting life we have led ... often sounds like a novel." *Briefedition* I/7, 572; cf. *CC*, vol. 3, 364. Laura Tunbridge has shown how fictionalizing tendencies occurred even in writings by Schumann's contemporaries, who in their reception of his *Manfred* (1849), for instance, often aligned Schumann with the protagonist of Byron's poem; Tunbridge, "Schumann as Manfred," *Musical Quarterly* 87 (Fall 2004): 546–69. For other essays that explore the fictionalizing of the Schumanns' lives, see David Ferris, "The Fictional Lives of the Schumanns," in *Rethinking Schumann*, ed. Roe-Min Kok and Laura Tunbridge (Oxford and New York: Oxford University Press, 2011), 357–94; Marik Froidefond, "'C'est encore du roman, ça': Fonctions des citations schumanniennes dans *Mademoiselle Else* d'Arthur Schnitzler," in *Musique et roman*, ed. Aude Locatelli and Yves Landerouin (Paris: Le Manuscrit, 2008), 153–69; Hans Martin-Plesske, "Robert und Clara im Roman und in der Novelle," *Sammelbände der Robert-Schumann-Gesellschaft* 2 (1967): 87–98; and Lars Oberhaus, "Spurensuche: Variationen zu Peter Härtlings Roman *Schumanns Schatten*," *Musik & Bildung: Praxis Musikunterricht* 36, no. 3 (2004): 10–19."

2. Roland Barthes, "Loving Schumann," in his *The Responsibility of Forms: Critical Essays on Music, Art, and Representation*, trans. Richard Howard (New York: Hill & Wange, 1985), 293–98. Jonathan Biss, *A Pianist under the Influence*, E-book, [2012]; reissued 2018; available at https://www.amazon.com/Pianist-Under-Influence-Jonathan-Biss-ebook/dp/B07BZRB 5RL/ref=sr_1_1?keywords=Jonathan+Biss+a+pianist+under+the+influence&qid=1639763 359&sr=8-1 (accessed July 22, 2023).

3. Other movies based on Robert and Clara's lives include Harald Braun's 1944 film *Träumerei*; Peter Schamoni's 1983 film *Frühlingssinfonie*; and Helma Sanders-Brahms's 2008 film *Geliebte Clara*. As for quotations of Robert's music, a search of the Internet Movie Database in September 2022 (before new restrictions appeared that only recognized film-score composers) indicated almost 400 soundtrack credits for Schumann; "Robert Schumann Soundtrack," Internet Movie Database (IMDb), https://www.imdb.com/filmosearch/?sort=year&expl ore=title_type&role=nm0006281&ref_=nmbio_ql_flmg_1 (accessed September 20, 2022). Writings that discuss the use of his music in film include Jeremy Barham, "Recurring Dreams and Moving Images: The Cinematic Appropriation of Schumann's Op. 15, No. 7," *19th-Century Music* 34 (Spring 2011): 271–301; Michelle Elizabeth Yael Braunschweig, "Biographical Listening: Intimacy, Madness, and the Music of Robert Schumann" (PhD diss., University of California, Berkeley, 2013), especially chapter 2; Berndt Heller, "Spiel beim Abschied leise Schumann: Zur Musik der Stummfilmzeit," in *Einblicke, Ausblicke: Gedanken, Erinnerungen, Deutungen zu musikalischen Phänomenen* (Berlin: Robert Lienau, 1985), 37–41; and Laura Tunbridge, "Deserted Chambers of the Mind (Schumann Memories)," in *Rethinking Schumann*, ed. Roe-Min Kok and Laura Tunbridge (Oxford and New York: Oxford University Press, 2011), 396–99. For other productions inspired by the Schumanns, see the "Film and Stage" link on the webpage "Publications/Releases," found on The Schumann Network, https://www.schumann-portal.de/veroeffentlichungen-en.html (accessed July 22, 2023).

4. In a discussion of Rauch's 2009 painting *Vater*, Laura Tunbridge discerns Schumannian resonances blended with images of the artist and his father; Tunbridge, "Deserted Chambers of the Mind (Schumann Memories)," 396 and 399–400. Some of Fantin-Latour's Schumann-inspired images can be found in Douglas Druick and Michael Hoog, eds., *Fantin-Latour: Exhibition* (Ottowa: National Gallery of Canada; National Museums of Canada, 1983); and Michelle Verrier, *Fantin-Latour* (New York: Harmony Books, 1978). Kathy Brown's monograph on Lotte Lehmann reproduces twelve paintings that the latter created in response to Schumann's *Dichterliebe*; Brown, *Lotte Lehmann in America: Her Legacy as Artist Teacher, with Commentaries from Her Master Classes* (Missoula, MT: College Music Society, 2012), 199–214.

5. The tradition of choreographing music never intended for dance began with the turn into the twentieth century, and is especially associated with Isadora Duncan, Michel Fokine, and others. For more on this formalist movement, see Stephanie Jordan, *Moving Music: Dialogues with Music in Twentieth-Century Ballet* (London: Dance Books, 2000), especially chapter 1.

6. Wayne Heisler, "Choreographing Schumann," in *Rethinking Schumann*, ed. Roe-Min Kok and Laura Tunbridge (Oxford and New York: Oxford University Press, 2011), 329–56; quotations from 330 and 332–33. For an alternative perspective on the meaning of Balanchine's ballet, one addressed to a dance-based readership, see Adam Pinsker, "*Davidsbündlertänze*," *Ballet Review* 30, no. 3 (Fall 2002): 79–93. Although noting parallels between the ballet and Schumann's biography, Pinsker sees death as the main subject of the ballet, specifically representing Balanchine's "farewell to his dancers and the company" (90); Balanchine was already sick with the illness that took his life three years later. Cécile Auzolle has discussed Fokine's setting of Schumann's piano cycle *Carnaval*: "Quand les Ballets Russes rêvent l'Allemagne romantique: *Carnaval* op. 9 de Schumann à Fokine," *Ostinato rigore: Revue international d'études musicales* 22 (2004): 203–18. In general, however, existing commentary on Schumann-based ballets occurs mainly in dance writings, whether performance reviews, biographies and articles on choreographers, or dictionaries like George Balanchine and Francis Mason's *Complete Stories of the Great Ballets*, rev. ed. (Garden City, NY: Doubleday, 1977) and Cyril Beaumont's *Complete Book of Ballets: A Guide to the Principal Ballets of the Nineteenth and Twentieth Centuries* (Garden City, NY: Garden City Publishing, 1941).
7. The most substantial book on Van Manen's life and output is Eva van Schaik's *Hans van Manen: Leven & Werk* (Amsterdam: Arena, 1997), although Jochen Schmidt provided an important precedent a decade earlier: *Der Zeitgenosse als Klassiker: Über den holländischen Choreographen Hans van Manen* (Cologne: Ballett-Bühnen-Verlag, 1987). For a summary of Van Manen's life and accomplishments, with numerous quotations by him, see Eddie Vetter, "Nooit te wijs om te leren. Een interview," in *Hans van Manen: Meer dan een halve eeuw dans*, edited by Bram van Baal (Amsterdam and Antwerp: Arbeiderspers, 2007), 7–30. A valuable source is the "Hans van Manen Foundation" website, which provides a survey of his career and an updated catalogue of his more than 150 ballets, among other items; the website is hosted by the Dutch National Opera and Ballet: https://www.operaballet.nl/en/ballet/hans-van-manen-foundation (accessed July 22, 2023). In general, substantive English literature on Van Manen is all but lacking, though a useful 1992 Dutch source—celebrating his 60th birthday—provides parallel English translations: Marc Jonkers, Pieter Kottman, Jhim Lamoree, and Divera Stavenuiter, eds., *Hans van Manen: Fotos-Feiten-Meningen/Hans van Manen: Photographs-Facts-Opinions* (Amsterdam: Nederlands Instituut voor de Dans, 1992). To gain a quick sense of the many ways in which Van Manen has emancipated theatrical dance, and ballet in particular, see Pieter Kottman's essay in this anthology, "Dat rokje, dat moest/That Skirt Was Essential," 31–41, especially 35–41. There are numerous videos of Van Manen's ballets. For ones celebrating his 75th birth year (2007) and featuring interviews with the choreographer, see *Hans van Manen Festival: Dutch National Ballet and Guests*, DVD containing dances by Van Manen and interviews with him and performers (portions in English and subtitles available), produced, directed, and edited by Altin Kaftira, Adrienne Liron, and Jeff Tudor (West Long Branch, NJ: Kultur, 2007, 2008); *Hans van Manen: Master of Movement*, DVD, 6 discs, containing dances by and interviews with Hans van Manen; compiled and distributed by the Stichting Hans van Manen ([IJsselstein, Netherlands]: Cobra Records, 2007); and *Hans van Manen*, DVD, 2 discs containing dances by and interviews with Van Manen (English subtitles available), performances by Het National Ballet and Nederlands Dans Theater ([Leipzig]: Arthaus Musik, 2007); the liner notes by Vetter—"Déja vu?," also translated into English—summarize Van Manen's life and accomplishments up to that point. For a video made to celebrate his 85th year (2017), see *Six Ballets: The Art of Hans Van Manen*, DVD, 2 discs, containing dances by and interviews with Van Manen (English subtitles available), directed by Wilbert Bank and Jellie Dekker, performed by the Nederlands Dans Theater and Het Nationale Ballet ([Halle]: Arthaus, 2016).
8. Balanchine and Mason, *Balanchine's Complete Stories of the Great Ballets*, 252. On the creation of this ballet and an overview of its four "pieces" from a choreographic perspective, see Van Schaik, *Hans van Manen*, 371–76. The latter acknowledges Van Manen's "tribute to the twentieth-century male ballet dancer," even asserting that "no classical ballet has done so much for the emancipation of the ballerino as *Four Schumann Pieces*, though it took many years before European critics realized this" (371). Important precedents for this emancipation occurred, however, in Diaghilev's Ballet Russes, as Lynn Garafola has discussed: "Reconfiguring the Sexes," in *The Ballet Russes and Its World*, ed. Lynn Garafola and Nancy Van Norman Baer (New Haven, CT: Yale University Press, 1999), 245–68.
9. Heisler, "Choreographing Schumann," 330; emphasis original. In her 1997 biography, Van Schaik offered a related interpretation: because the male soloist "was placed in the middle of,

but outside, a double quintet," thereby functioning as a kind of "hyphen," the ballet implied that "the leading dancer was the composer himself of this four-part string quartet." Van Schaik, *Hans van Manen*, 371.

10. Van Manen, phone interview of April 10, 2014. Van Manen explained, "Today I know more about him [Schumann], but [for the ballet] I started with the quartet." He also indicated that he discovered Schumann's quartet while listening to records in search of music for a Royal Ballet commission, which resulted in the 1975 ballet *Four Schumann Pieces*.

11. Dowell, quoted in John Gruen, "Antoinette Sibley and Anthony Dowell," in his *The Private World of Ballet* (New York: Viking Press, 1975), 120. Schmidt, *Der Zeitgenosse als Klassiker*, 76.

12. As Van Schaik notes, Van Manen disliked Nureyev's emphasis on "sex appeal" and his insistence on having special roles created for him. Dowell, however, did not obsess with stardom. Instead, he desired to "adhere to the dictates of choreographic issues" and hence "in Van Manen's eyes was much more an example of an emancipated ballet dancer." Van Schaik, *Hans van Manen*, 371–72. Eventually Van Manen and Nureyev become friends, and the latter took the solo role in Dutch performances of *Four Schumann Pieces* (see Van Schaik, 375–76). Nureyev also introduced the ballet to North American audiences, taking the lead role in performances by the National Ballet of Canada in 1976 (in New York) and in 1977 (in Toronto). On program notes made for these performances, see note 16.

13. Van Manen, quoted in *Anthony Dowell: All the Superlatives*, videorecording, 2 cassettes, directed by Colin Nears and produced by Barrie Gavin; BBC production made in association with RM Productions, Munich, and taped for the Omnibus series (March–April 1976). This documentary provides clips of Dowell rehearsing *Four Schumann Pieces*, and a complete performance of Piece 3 (the Adagio movement) near its conclusion.

14. Cited in Jordan, *Moving Music*, xiv. The term "music visualization" was coined by Ruth St. Denis and her husband Ted Shawn. On the history and practitioners of this concept, and the different theories that emerged to describe music-dance relationships, see ibid., chapter 1.

15. Quoted in Joyce Roodnat, "Ik heb niets tegen tranen/I've got nothing against tears" [Interview with Van Manen]," trans. Nicoline Gatehouse, in *Hans van Manen: Fotos-Feiten-Meningen/ Hans van Manen: Photographs-Facts-Opinions*, ed. Marc Jonkers, Pieter Kottman, Jhim Lamoree, and Divera Stavenuiter (Amsterdam: Nederlands Instituut voor de Dans, 1992), 20. Van Manen also notes that the relevant composer is also in his mind, although it is the composer's music—rather than the persona—that informs his choreographic process.

16. First comment cited in program notes for *Four Schumann Pieces*, performance by Rudolf Nureyev and members of the National Ballet of Canada, at the Metropolitan Opera House/ Lincoln Center for the Performing Arts, New York City, August 4, 1976, courtesy of the National Ballet of Canada Archives; also courtesy of the Jerome Robbins Dance Division, New York Public Library. Second comment cited in program notes for the London premiere on January 31, 1975, provided in Van Schaik, *Hans van Manen*, 372–73. Despite these clues, Van Manen, like Balanchine, has remained cryptic about more specific dance-music relationships.

17. Steve [last name anonymous], "For Shoemann Peaces [sic]," You Dance Funny, So Does Me Blog, entry posted January 31, 2011, http://youdancefunny.wordpress.com/2011/01/ (accessed August 6, 2022). On the original stage set, see Schmidt, *Der Zeitgenosse als Klassiker*, 76.

18. Sanjoy Roy, "Step-by-Step Guide to Dance: Hans van Manen," *The Guardian*, May 4, 2011, culture section, https://www.theguardian.com/stage/2011/may/04/hans-van-manen-dance (accessed July 22, 2023).

19. Quoted in Roodnat, "Ik heb niets tegen tranen/I've got nothing against tears," 25.

20. So too does Balanchine's cursory description of the ballet: a soloist who sometimes has "strength only to ignore" the others (sometimes by dancing independently, as in the tonally unstable sections of the first movement, or by not dancing at all despite being on stage, as in the middle part of the second movement); but who at other times summons the "courage... to join them" (perhaps by blending into the group, even synchronizing steps with them, as in the recapitulation of the first movement, the beginning and end of the second movement, and near the end of the finale). In the third movement, the soloist "dances with one of the girls [actually with two], then with one of the boys," and in the finale, largely seems to prefer "a lone splendour" (the C episode and subsequent refrain, along with the concluding measures of the movement). Balanchine and Mason, *Balanchine's Complete Stories of the Great Ballets*, 252.

21. Igor Stravinsky and Robert Craft, *Themes and Episodes* (New York: Alfred A. Knopf, 1966), 24.

22. Although analysis of formal music-dance relationships has long been part of scholarship by ethnomusicologists and early-music scholars, especially those studying Baroque music, such

"choreomusical" analysis has seen an upswing of interest in the twenty-first century. On this point, see Stephanie Jordan, "Choreomusicology and Dance Studies: From Beginning to End?," in *The Routledge Companion to Dance Studies*, ed. Helen Thomas and Stacey Prickett (Abingdon, UK, and New York: Routledge, 2020), 141–42; and Stephanie Jordan, "Introduction," *Journal of Music Theory* 65 (April 2021): 4–5. The latter opens a special issue devoted to close analysis of music-dance relationships in a variety of styles and musical traditions, albeit with particular emphasis on rhythmic-metric issues. For examples of methodological categories that may guide technical analysis of musical and balletic structures, see Paul Hodgins (who coined the term "choreomusical"), *Relationships between Score and Choreography in Twentieth-Century Dance: Music, Movement and Metaphor* (Lewiston, NY: Edwin Mellen Press, 1992). See also Jordan, *Moving Music*, especially chapter 2; for a summary of her approach, see her essay "Musical/Choreographic Discourse: Method, Music Theory, and Meaning," in *Moving Words: Re-writing Dance*, ed. Gay Morris (London and New York: Routledge, 1996), 15–28. For a recent overview of diverse approaches used in dance studies, including choreomusical analysis, see Helen Thomas and Stacey Prickett, eds., *The Routledge Companion to Dance Studies* (London and New York: Routledge, 2020).

23. Van Schaik, *Hans van Manen*, 373.
24. Quoted in Van Schaik, *Hans van Manen*, 373.
25. Van Schaik, *Hans van Manen*, 56–60.
26. Quoted in Van Schaik, *Hans van Manen*, 75. On the low prestige of dance in the Netherlands from the late nineteenth to mid-twentieth centuries, but also factors that led to its breakthrough ca. 1975–1985, including democratic principles in Dutch culture overall, see Anna Aalten and Mirjam van der Linden, "The Netherlands: The Dutch Don't Dance," in *Europe Dancing: Perspectives on Theatre Dance and Cultural Identity*, ed. Andrée Grau and Stephanie Jordan (New York: Routledge, 2000), 119–43. Van Manen has also noted, "In the pecking order of the arts, dance was at the bottom when I started," a low status that provided "a huge stimulus" for his work. Quoted in Van Schaik, *Hans van Manen*, 195.
27. Quoted in Roodnat, "Ik heb niets tegen tranen/I've got nothing against tears," 27. Given that *Four Schumann Pieces* was commissioned by the Royal Ballet (then a conservative dance company), it comes as no surprise that the costumes were more traditional, with women in simple, knee-length turquoise dresses and men in tights and loose blouses. Nevertheless, it is significant that the latter wear both pink (blouses) and blue (tights). Thus, the men's costumes appear to question the "binary structure of biological sex, as symbolized by the well-known 'pink-and-blue' syndrome"—a binary to which "the European and Anglophone world are deeply committed" and one frequently reinforced in classical ballet traditions. Jennifer Fisher and Anthony Shay, "Introduction," in *When Men Dance: Choreographing Masculinities across Borders*, ed. Jennifer Fisher and Anthony Shay (Oxford and New York: Oxford University Press, 2009), 8.
28. Horst Koegler, "Dancing in the Closet: The Coming Out of Ballet," *Dance Chronicle* 18, no. 2 (1995): 231–38. Scholars have posited various reasons for the "discretion" surrounding gay men and gay themes in the realm of dance. Fisher and Shay note the "very real fears of injurious discrimination" for homosexuals in the past, while also repeating Gay Morris's idea that the already low reputation of dance in the art world perhaps encouraged silence; Fisher and Shay, "Introduction," 5; Gay Morris, *Game for Dancers: Performing Modernism in the Postwar Years, 1945–1960* (Middletown, CT: Wesleyan University Press, 2006), 34. Peter Stoneley echoes the latter point while also suggesting that discrimination against ballet by proponents of modern dance has been a factor: "Ballet is seen to offer 'staid, old-fashioned images and ideas about gender' while modern dance is 'progressive, experimental, [and] avant-garde,'" a viewpoint that Stoneley contests; *A Queer History of the Ballet* (London and New York: Routledge, 2007), 2.
29. This company was one for which Van Manen danced (1961–1963), choreographed (even participating in their opening performance), and served as artistic director (1961–1971). In 1973, Van Manen joined the Dutch National Ballet, a company that performed classical repertory alongside new ballets, and one for which Van Manen worked for about fifteen years. During this latter period, his choreography made more pronounced use of academic technique, including greater use of *pointe* work; *Four Schumann Pieces*—though written for the London Royal Ballet—was written during this period.
30. Koegler, "Dancing in the Closet," 235–36.
31. Quoted in Roodnat, "Ik heb niets tegen tranen/I've got nothing against tears," 25.
32. Kottman, "Dat rokje, dat moest/That Skirt Was Essential," 35. Kottman also provides Van Manen's statement.

33. Koegler, "Dancing in the Closet," 235.
34. Ismene Brown, "On Their Toes! Birmingham Royal Ballet, Birminghan Hippodrome" [reviewing a performance of Van Manen's 1971 *Grosse Fuge*, among other works], *The Arts Desk*, online journalism website, theartsdesk.com, June 16, 2010, https://theartsdesk.com/dance/their-toes-birmingham-royal-ballet-birmingham-hippodrome (accessed July 22, 2023).
35. In this regard, the Adagio reveals a different strategy from the outer movements: there the main idea is largely kept intact, becoming re-colored only by undergoing numerous sequential repetitions. In the Adagio, however, the main idea itself undergoes constant evolution, a principle that also informs the other inner movement, a theme-and-variations that comprises the second movement. For a discussion of the first movement, see Brown, "Study, Copy, and Conquer," 393–407; for a brief survey of the finale, see Chapter 2, where I argue that this movement provided the point of departure for a more ambitious design in the finale of the piano quintet.
36. Daverio, *Robert Schumann*, 253; Gardner, "The Chamber Music," 209; Kohlhase, *Die Kammermusik Robert Schumanns*, vol. 2, 67; and Dickinson, "The Chamber Music," 149.
37. See for instance Chissell, *Schumann*, 160; Davies, "Schumann, Robert Alexander," 378; Roesner, "The Chamber Music," 131; and Thomas Synofzik, "Kunstreiche Verwebung der Viere: Zur Satztechnik in Schumanns Streichquartett op. 41/3," in *Das Streichquartett im Rheinland: Bericht über die Tagung der Arbeitsgemeinschaft für rheinische Musikgeschichte in Brauweiler Juni 2002*, ed. Robert von Zahn, Wolfram Ferber, and Klaus Pietschmann (Kassel: Merseburger, 2005), 58–61.
38. Hepokoski and Darcy, *Elements of Sonata Theory*, 322. On this point, see also William Caplin, *Classical Form: A Theory of Formal Functions for the Instrumental Music of Haydn, Mozart, and Beethoven* (New York and Oxford: Oxford University Press, 1998), 209.
39. The notion of infiltrating content has precedents in Schumann's earlier music. Sometimes it may occur on a local level (e.g. in *Carnaval*, the opening of "Coquette"—which rhetorically supplies the cadential gesture missing in the previous number, "Florestan"—further confuses musical boundaries by returning in the following number, "Replique"); sometimes such infiltration occurs on a larger level (represented by cyclic returns between more distantly numbered pieces, like the return of opening materials in the final numbers of *Carnaval* and *Papillons*; or by intertextual quotations, like the seeming reference to Beethoven's *An die ferne Geliebte* in the Op. 17 *Fantasie*, or quotations of Clara's music in the Op. 11 piano sonata or the final number of the Op. 21 *Novelletten*).
40. Avoidance of strong tonic downbeats permeates Schumann's earlier music, perhaps most famously in the opening of the Op. 17 *Fantasie*, which prolongs dominant harmony without ever resolving to the tonic. Another category involves works that open with closing gestures—*in medias res* beginnings found, for instance, in the first number of the Op. 21 *Novelletten*, and the fifteenth number of *Davidsbündlertänze*, the latter initially defining G minor before cadencing in B-flat major.
41. Weakened cadences also have precedents in Schumann's earlier output. For one such example, see the discussion of the fourth number from the Op. 4 *Intermezzi* near the beginning of chapter 2; for another example, see note 42. Although not unusual within Schumann's output, weak cadences in this Adagio also stand in relief against the outer movements, where an almost over-abundance of authentic cadences occurs, the partial result of main themes comprised of cadential ideas repeated multiple times. See note 35.
42. Seemingly misplaced cadences also occur in Schumann's earlier music. In "Eusebius" from *Carnaval*, for instance, the only authentic cadence occurs in the middle of the piece. This isolated appearance seems surprising since the main idea of "Eusebius" is itself a cadential idea; Schumann, however, repeatedly undermines the cadence by sustaining $\hat{5}$ in the bass when V resolves to I, a fitting way of representing the dreamy, head-in-the-clouds character.
43. An interesting nexus point occurs at m. 56 when the soloist joins his female partner on the floor after directing her there, as if anticipating his own floor work some twenty-eight measures later. (The 1975 performance features the soloist lying on top of his partner, rather than separately on the floor as happens in the later 1978 performance.)
44. Although the Adagio forefronts gender mixing between the sexes, additional examples occur elsewhere in the ballet. In the first "piece," for example, Van Manen suggests the soloist's growing recognition of the others by having him synchronize some steps with the women during the repetition of the exposition. In the second "piece" (a theme-and-variations movement), the soloist mimics the steps of female dancers during the first full statement of the theme. Commenting on

these and other instances, one dance blogger has commented that Van Manen's choreography "has very few gender biases." Steve [last name anonymous], "For Shoemann Peaces [sic]."

45. This same fully diminished chord surfaces in earlier appearances of the theme, particularly in its last phrase (see mm. 14 and 17 in A^1, and mm. 89 and 92 in A^3). There, however, the sonority occurs in anticipation of an implied PAC (even if non-materializing), not as a substitute for it, as happens in the coda. Plagal inflections serve important roles in other Leipzig chamber works, like the slow movement and finale of the Op. 44 piano quintet; see Chapter 2.

46. Karmen Mackendrick, "Embodying Transgression," in *Of the Presence of the Body: Essays on Dance and Performance Theory*, ed. André Lepecki (Middletown, CT: Wesleyan University Press, 2004), 140–41. In her writing on Alonzo King's San Francisco-based LINES—a company that explores how gender might be "undone, transversed, and reenacted"—Jill Nunes Jensen suggests similarly dynamic processes. For the dancers, "finding a way to work within ballet's rigidity and create movement that paradoxically suggests autonomy has proved a necessary part of the creative process. This very type of 'undoing' permits the dancers to interject their individual personalities, subsequently diversifying the vocabulary and making the act of doing ballet more meaningful." Jill Nunes Jensen, "Transcending Gender in Ballet's LINES," in *When Men Dance: Choreographing Masculinities across Borders*, ed. Jennifer Fisher and Anthony Shay (Oxford and New York: Oxford University Press, 2009), 123.

47. On formal ambiguity in the Op. 17 *Fantasie*, see Brown, "Higher Echoes of the Past," 519–22, which summarizes interpretations offered by various writers. For a discussion of the Op. 11 finale from a similar perspective, see Brown, "Schumann and the *style hongrois*," 273–79.

48. Van Manen, phone interview with the author, April 10, 2014.

49. Jordan, *Moving Music*, 89–102.

50. Kottman, "Dat rokje, dat moest/That Skirt Was Essential," 31; see also 32–33 on the importance of videography for Van Manen's output.

5

Listening in London

Robert Schumann's name seems to have first entered English periodical literature in 1838, although it was treated in passing and overshadowed by that of Clara Wieck. In a May 1838 issue of the London-based *Musical World*, the anonymous author surveyed Clara's career thus far, noting that lately she had been emphasizing "works of the old masters" along with "the less known compositions of Chopin, Henselt, and R. Schuman [*sic*]." Two weeks later, the same paper published, in translation, a fanciful piece of German criticism that contrasted the abilities of four pianists: Wieck, Liszt, Thalberg, and Henselt; only at the end did the author's name appear: "R. Schuman" [*sic*].[1] Not until 1840 did Robert receive focused attention when *The Musical Journal* published a single-page biographical sketch, one that highlighted Schumann's "amiable disposition and urbanity of manners," his "well written, witty, and impartial" criticism, and his recent honorary doctorate.[2] Translations of Schumann's writings continued to appear throughout the 1840s and beyond, but professional performances of his music in London did not begin until 1848. In March of that year, a "soirée" by Lindsey Sloper included two Schumann piano pieces. Shortly thereafter, the Musical Union presented the Op. 47 Piano Quartet in a concert, an event that marks the first institutional performance of Schumann's music in London.[3] Public performances gradually picked up frequency in the 1850s and beyond, though not without navigating difficult terrain for many years.

Despite auspicious beginnings in England, the figure of Schumann and his music would ultimately expose deep ideological divides, at first between English and modern German tastes, and later between conservative and progressive tastes within London itself. If public performances had begun sooner, the outcome might have differed. Occurring as they did from 1848 on, however, Schumann's music became entrenched in a polemic that pitted its composer against Felix Mendelssohn. The latter's ten visits to Britain (from 1827 to 1847) had made him a revered figure; indeed, Mendelssohn's music, as Janet Ritterman writes, was viewed by some as providing "the model for the establishment of a British 'school' of composition," a concept then gaining increasing support.[4] Mendelssohn's unexpected death in 1847 devastated his British adherents, while also strengthening their resolve to uphold his stature. This resolve led to a striking difference between English and German perceptions in the mid-nineteenth century. As discussed in Chapter 1, figures aligned with the New German School (Wagner, Liszt, and their supporters, including critics like Franz Brendel and later Theodor Uhlig) were redrawing Schumann—once a standard-bearer for musical progressivism—as a conservative because of his sustained interest in traditional instrumental genres and forms. Brendel even identified Schumann's "residence in classical Leipzig," where Mendelssohn had directed the Gewandhaus orchestra and under whose baton some of Schumann's music had premiered, as a source of influence.[5] In mid-century London, however, the situation was quite different: Schumann was cast as Mendelssohn's opposite, the dubious modernist to Mendelssohn the classicist, with Schumann eventually linked with "Brother Wagner" and the dangerous "music of the future." This Schumann-Mendelssohn polarity arose mainly through the colorful and opinionated writings of two of London's then most influential music critics: Henry F. Chorley, author of music books and critic for *The Athenaeum* from 1833 to 1868, and James W. Davison, the critic for *The Times* of London from 1846 to 1878, and editor of *The Musical World* from 1843 to 1885.[6] Both critics had personally known Mendelssohn and were deeply committed to maintaining the composer's stellar reputation in England. Any threat to that reputation, especially from abroad, was viewed with suspicion, even scorn. As Schumann's music gradually received more hearings, the two critics increasingly deprecated it, often by measuring it against Mendelssohn's output.

Drawing on extensive periodical literature and other primary sources, this chapter shows how Schumann's 1842 chamber music provides a significant and as yet unexplored lens through which to understand these perceptions. As noted earlier, the first performance of Schumann's music by a professional society occurred with a Leipzig chamber work, the Op. 47 piano quartet. A review of this performance also provides the first negative comparison of Schumann to Mendelssohn, a contrast that intensified in later years as London critics began associating Schumann with Wagner. In other words, in mid-century London, questions about whether the 1842 chamber music represented a more conservative or progressive mindset for Schumann centered less on the music's relationship to his earlier works and more on its contrast with the output of Felix Mendelssohn and the Classical tradition he was seen to uphold. The Leipzig chamber works also played a vital role in eventually moving the debate about Schumann's merits as a composer to the larger public. Where performances of his chamber works initially occurred in rarefied settings, eventually they began reaching larger and more diverse audiences, especially through the Monday Popular Concerts, a series devoted primarily to chamber music. Here the Op. 41 string quartets (especially the first of the set), the Op. 44 piano quintet, and the Op. 47 piano quartet found increasing favor with Popular audiences. Indeed, the quintet would become one of the most performed works in the series' history, and a work frequently held up by supporters as proof of Schumann's compositional talents. Equally important in this reception history was Clara Schumann, who as a widow toured London more than any other European capital, and who eventually made the Monday Popular Concerts her preferred venue. Clara's participation in performances of the piano quartet and, especially, the piano quintet garnered much acclaim and facilitated the growing acceptance of Robert's music by the greater public—what George Grove called "the larger tribunal" in the Schumann debate. Such acceptance led to a schism between popular and conservative critical opinion, which in turn elicited a variety of defensive responses from critics like Chorley and Davison. In all, the London reception of Schumann's Leipzig chamber works illustrates how critics, institutions, performers, and audiences may play decisive roles in shaping repertory formation and hence the place of a composer and their music "in the great stream of time."

First Performances and the Rise of the Schumann-Mendelssohn Polarity

Schumann's piano works, songs, and perhaps some chamber music, were likely performed in private, informal settings in England during the 1840s. Not until March 28, 1848, however, did the first institutional performance of his music in London occur. On this date, the Op. 47 piano quartet appeared on the program of a Musical Union concert, with the pianist Edward Röckel leading the performance. Founded by John Ella just three years prior, the Musical Union featured high-quality performances of chamber music played by top-notch performers, both native- and foreign-born. Ella fostered a conspicuously high-minded atmosphere. Expensive membership into the society—and Ella's approval—meant that his audiences comprised wealthier middle- and upper-class figures. Ella also desired earnestness from his listeners, insisting on silence during performances and educating his audience through program notes that he wrote for each performance, a new concept for the time. As Davison noted in his review of the 1848 concert, "Mr. Ella may be styled the musical Minerva of the aristocracy."[7]

Ella's programming focused on Classical chamber music (Christina Bashford has called the Musical Union a "heartland" for string quartets by Haydn, Mozart, and Beethoven),[8] but Ella was open to introducing newer works, including Schumann's piano quartet in 1848. For London's foremost critics, however, the work failed to make a positive impression. Chorley acknowledged Ella's effort "to bring a new composer to judgment," describing the piano quartet as "the first of [Schumann's] important compositions tried here." Nevertheless, Chorley asserted that if the work "be a fair specimen of Herr Schumann's talents as a thinker," then it only confirms his "second-rate" status: although the "German press" might proclaim works "of this order as something superfine," Schumann's "affections of originality [are] founded on pretension." Davison, for his part, appreciated the compositional effort behind the piano quartet but ultimately found it "devoid of any particular merit. The first three movements were listened to with indifference, and the last, from its nothingness, was hardly understood." For both critics, the performance of Mendelssohn's early String Quartet in E-flat Major (WoO) offered relief. Chorley stated that it "was like changing night-mare for repose," and for Davison, Mendelssohn's work—though composed "at the early age of fourteen"—showed "the impress of genius" throughout. And where Schumann's work was heard "with indifference," Mendelssohn's quartet "was listened to with the greatest attention, and appeared to afford the most unqualified delight to all present."[9]

By 1848, Chorley had already had occasion to appraise Schumann's music. His earlier Continental travels—which resulted in his 1841 book *Music and Manners in France and Germany*—led him to Leipzig, where he became acquainted with Schumann's *Kreisleriana* and other piano works. For Chorley, such works displayed "the very wildest strain of extravagant mysticism," prompting Chorley to label Schumann "the German Berlioz." Schumann's novelties stood in further relief against the musical activities of his Leipzig colleagues Mendelssohn and Ferdinand David, whom Chorley admired for their "consummate intelligence" (David) and "poetical genius" (Mendelssohn). Nevertheless, in a footnote, Chorley acknowledged Schumann's talent, even as he issued a warning: "Herr Schumann has too much talent and learning to lose himself forever in such mazes."[10] Predisposed toward suspicion, Chorley evidently saw no improvement in 1848 with Schumann's piano quartet, a stance that contrasted with German perceptions of the chamber repertory as marking a stylistic divide from his early output. Chorley's opinion remained unchanged in his 1854 publication *Modern German Music*, an expansion of his earlier book. Enlarging his original footnote commentary, Chorley asserted that although Schumann has since "produced largely," composing "Opera, Cantata, Symphony, Quartett, Sonata—all and each tell the same story, and display the same characteristics—the same skill ... of hiding an intrinsic poverty of invention, by grim or monotonous eccentricity."[11] An 1853 performance of Schumann's Op. 44 piano quintet at the Musical Union yielded similar comments: although others might describe the work "as his most intelligible and genial composition, ... we must give up Dr. Schumann if this Quintett *be* his most agreeable work." Chorley admitted that "[s]traightforward enough it is, and less freaked by uglinesses [sic] than is usual with him." However, "on the whole, unpleasing pretension hiding real poverty occurs to us as the general character of this Quintett."[12]

The younger Davison surely felt more curiosity, if not enthusiasm, going into the 1848 performance. Indeed, six years earlier, he had announced that "Dr. Robert Schumann has just published three violin quartets [Op. 41], which are highly spoken of." He also asserted that Robert's success in winning Clara's hand "seems to have inspired him with more than ordinary vigour; his last works (since his marriage has made him one of the happiest of men) display ten times the nerve and freshness of his earlier compositions."[13] No evidence exists that Davison had actually heard any of Schumann's "last works" (symphonies or chamber music, whether on the Continent or privately) at the time he wrote these words in late 1842. Thus he must have anticipated the 1848 Musical Union concert, and while disappointed with the piano quartet, Davison likely aimed his negative remarks as much at Ella as at Schumann. In writing his program notes, Ella typically adopted an ostentatious tone and sought to influence his audience's mindset toward the programmed works, a posturing that Davison saw as impinging on his own role as critic. For the 1848 concert, Ella wrote in his typical high-minded style:

> After a deliberate trial of new compositions, . . . a quartet for piano and string instruments by Doctor Schumann has been considered entitled to the suffrages of our members. This composer, the husband of the celebrated

pianist Clara Wieck, is highly esteemed for his literary, as well as musical, compositions; and the quartet here chosen has had success both in Leipzig and Dresden.

Ella admitted that he could not predict "whether it succeed or not in conciliating the unanimous approval of its hearers at a single performance," but he left no room for debate about certain merits of the work: "there can be no two opinions on its claim to great excellence in the beauty of its harmonies, the classical purity of its scoring, and orthodox development of its *motivi*."[14] In his review of the concert, Davison did not directly address Ella's comments, but the very traits he singled out in Mendelssohn's quartet seem like a rejoinder: "The quartet indicates, even at this boyish age, harmonious order [later he cites "glowing and natural" harmonies], transparent design, and masterly development."[15]

The contrasts drawn between Schumann and Mendelssohn would subsequently resonate in numerous reviews from the next few decades. While Chorley appeared more set in his opinions about Schumann, Davison evolved more gradually. In 1851, after reviewing an English edition of Schumann's *Waldszenen*, Op. 82, Davison announced his stance more clearly while giving room for further deliberation: "Our own opinion of Herr Schumann's music is so entirely opposed to that of his partisans, who place him on a level, and in many instances, above Mendelssohn, that we would rather be spared the task of criticism on the present occasion." The reason why? "So small an installment from one of the most prolific and plentiful writers of the day scarcely entitles us to form therefrom anything like a just estimate of his genius and acquirements."[16] In 1854, the Quartet Association performed Schumann's A-minor string quartet, the first of the Op. 41 set that Schumann dedicated to Mendelssohn. Davison acknowledged that this "special novelty" was "well written, and shows infinite care and elaboration, Herr Schumann seemingly being determined that his work should be worthy of the great composer to whom it is dedicated." However, despite being "played magnificently," the quartet "failed to excite the least interest." Compensation arrived in the form of Mendelssohn's Op. 12 string quartet, which for Davison bore "the stamp of his genius as any of the three great quartets in Op. 44," and (unlike Schumann's music) "each movement was received with delight." Davison nonetheless acknowledged that the directors "were justified in presenting to their subscribers an unknown work from a composer who has made so much stir in the musical world."[17]

In the early to mid-1850s, the Schumann-Mendelssohn polarity intensified as Davison and Chorley began linking Schumann with Wagner and the New German School. In 1852, *The Athenaeum* printed a series of essays titled "Notes on Music in Germany." The essays appeared under the label "Foreign Correspondence" but were almost surely written by Chorley, who was preparing his book *Modern German Music*, published shortly thereafter in 1854. (The tone and style of prose also point to Chorley.) The segment published in the December 18, 1852, issue focused entirely on Schumann and Wagner and launched an all-out attack on their music and "progressive" aesthetics. "Young Germany is in a fever which, should it last, will superinduce an epilepsy fatal to the life of music." Chorley begins by targeting Schumann—whom he saw as the movement's older representative—asserting that Schumann's supporters "set up the most threadbare screens of incompleteness." If listeners find the string quartets "dull, monotonous, in idea stale and trifling," his advocates will refer them to the piano music, and then the songs, and finally "take a last refuge in the symphonies; especially in a Symphony in B flat, described by them to be a master-work. This I heard at Leipsic, with less than little satisfaction." For Chorley, such posturing only revealed that Schumann was "the mystagogue who has no real mysteries to promulgate," hence belying assertions "put forth by Young Germany" that Schumann was "superior to Mendelssohn."[18] After hearing Clara perform *Carnaval* in 1856, Chorley again linked Schumann with Wagner and in a way that stated more clearly the detrimental effects on Mendelssohn:

> At the time when these poor and dreary trifles were written,—in criticism of contemporary German music and its direction,—there was still living and laboring in, *and for*, Germany, with all his heart and soul and strength, a certain man called Mendelssohn; "dry and empty" (to repeat the jargon of a sect) because his compositions, being pure music, stand in need of no historical or mystical explanation; and because, having studied his art as a science, he could not be other than "correct."[19]

The "sect" to which Chorley refers surely comprised Wagner and his followers.

Davison revealed a similar position, first subtly, then more explicitly. Just a week after Chorley's 1852 article appeared, Davison reprinted it in *The Musical World* but with a revealing new title attached: "Schumann and Wagner: The Two New (Rush) Lights to Lighten the Darkness of the Musical

Jesuits at Leipsic" (that is, David and other followers of Mendelssohn). Through his curious metaphor, Davison betrayed his own stance, for rush lights were weak-burning candles made of rush stems dipped in melted fat and used by impoverished people in the British Isles; in other words, Davison sarcastically refuted the supposed enlightenment that Schumann and Wagner could bring to the followers of Mendelssohn.[20] Four months later, Davison explicitly linked Schumann to Wagner in a lengthy essay that brought his harshest assessments of Schumann's music thus far. Davison began by asserting that Schumann and Wagner "are the representatives of what is styled the 'aesthetic' school in Germany," even as "the latter has written chiefly for the theatre, the former for the orchestra and the chamber." Davison continued:

> Of Schumann we have been compelled to speak frequently; and, as it has happened, never in terms of praise. So much has been said of this gentleman, and so highly has he been extolled by his admirers, that we who, born in England, are not necessarily acquainted with his genius, have been led to expect a new Beethoven, or, to say the least, a new Mendelssohn. Up to the present time, however, the trios, quartets, quintets, &c, which have been introduced by Mr. Ella, at the Musical Union, and by other adventurous explorers for other societies, have turned out to be the very opposite of good. An affectation of originality, a superficial knowledge of the art, an absence of true expression, and an infelicitous disdain for form have characterized every work of Robert Schumann hitherto introduced in this country.

These words were prompted by the first English performance of a Schumann orchestral work (the Op. 52 Overture, Scherzo, and Finale), the experience of which confirmed Davison's suspicions about the composer's weaknesses in larger forms. Davison proclaimed that "bad as we consider the chamber compositions ... we are forced to pronounce the present orchestral work still worse," the result of a "general style [that] betrays the patchiness and want of fluency of a tyro." Thus for Davison "the whole work is unworthy of analysis, since it has no merit whatever. ... And yet, Robert Schumann, according to some, is the composer who (in combination with Richard Wagner—'Brother Wagner,' be it understood) is to raise a new school of art, to extinguish Mendelssohn." For Davison, a Mendelssohn work again provided compensation during the concert: "As if in spite to Schumann, whenever one of his works has been played in England, something of Mendelssohn has been given on the same occasion. On Monday night the magnificent *finale* to the unfinished opera of *Lorely* [sic] was the most interesting feature of the evening."[21]

Although both Chorley and Davison linked Schumann with Wagner in the early to mid-1850s, they disagreed about who posed the greater threat. For Chorley, "Dr. Schumann is as clear as truth and as charming as grace themselves, if he be measured against the opera composer who has been set up by Young Germany, at the composer's own instigation, as the coming man of the stage: —I mean, of course, Herr Wagner."[22] Davison, however, found Schumann more dangerous, proclaiming in 1856 that "though Richard is more subtle, uncompromising, arrogant, and fearless, Robert is more specious. *His* music, at times, more nearly resembles music than the monstrous combination of *Tännhauser* and *Lohengrin*; yet, inasmuch as, in principle, it is just as vicious and bad, for that reason it is all the more dangerous." Davison's comments were prompted by the London premiere of Schumann's oratorio, *Paradise and the Peri*, which the Philharmonic Society had just performed and which Davison triumphantly claimed a failure:

> Robert Schumann has had his innings, and been bowled out—like Richard Wagner [who directed the Philharmonic the previous year and conducted some of his own overtures]. *Paradise and the Peri* has gone to the tomb of the *Lohengrins*. . . . How many times more shall we have to insist that the new school—the school of "the Future"—will never do in England?[23]

Taking the Case of Schumann's Music to the Larger Public

Schumann's music began finding greater acceptance when larger, more affordable concert venues became established in London, with directors who were sympathetic to modern music from the Continent. These establishments helped move the discussion about Schumann from the select environments of the Musical Union, Quartet Association, and Philharmonic Society to the larger public. In December 1855, August Manns conducted the first of his series of Saturday afternoon concerts at the Crystal Palace, which by the mid-1860s were hailed as "without parallel in this country and unsurpassed in any other."[24] Featuring high-quality orchestral concerts with tickets at affordable pricing, the Saturday concerts attracted thousands of people.

Indeed, the Concert Room where performances occurred (completed in its first stage in 1859 and expanded in 1868) eventually accommodated up to two thousand people. Manns, a German expatriate, sought to establish a Classical repertory while also introducing new works by modern composers. As Michael Musgrave—the foremost scholar on musical life at the Crystal Palace—has indicated, eventually "the range of the orchestral fare offered at the Palace, reflective of its educational ethos, eclipsed that of any other British concert-giving organization, with a unique record of new works by foreign composers given British first performances, and of new works by British composers likewise."[25] From the outset, Manns wished to introduce Schumann's orchestral music to the larger British public. On February 16, 1856, less than two months after his first Saturday Concert, Manns conducted the British premiere of the D-minor Symphony.[26] Schumann performances fell off in the next few years, then picked up from 1860 on. By the end of the 1866 season, some ten years after his premiere of the D-minor Symphony, Manns had given repeat performances of this symphony, the B-flat Major Symphony, and the A-minor Piano Concerto, along with single performances of the C-major and E-flat Major Symphonies, in addition to conducting a number of Schumann overtures. Manns's advocacy did not go unnoticed, as comments by Davison make clear: "Herr Manns seems determined to make Schumann popular" (1863); "a more devoted disciple than Herr Manns never preached the doctrine of a cherished teacher; and certainly, if the works of Schumann are to be generally accepted in England—popular, in the literal sense, they can never be—it will be in a great measure due to him" (1864); "Herr Manns goes on persistently in his crusade against the detractors of his favourite Robert Schumann" (1866).[27] Manns's mission was eventually furthered by George Grove, secretary of the Crystal Palace, whose writings began promoting Schumann's music in the mid- to late 1860s onward.[28]

Equally important were the Monday Popular Concerts, colloquially known as the Pops. Founded in 1859 by Arthur Chappell (of the well-known music publishing family), the Popular Concerts resembled those of the Musical Union by featuring high-quality performances of serious chamber music. As Therese Ellsworth has described, individual concerts typically featured two chamber works for strings only, and two works that featured a piano part or were for solo piano; vocal performances represented only "a diversion."[29] Unlike the exclusive Musical Union, however, the Popular Concerts catered to the larger public, with open ticketing offered at varied prices. As a result, Chappell's audiences represented a cross-section of English society, from members of the aristocracy and educated classes to working-class citizens. Indeed, Chappell attracted the latter population by offering unreserved seats in the gallery for just one shilling—a price equivalent to lunch in a local tavern.[30] Also important was Chappell's venue: St. James's Hall, recently completed in 1858 and a space that could accommodate over two thousand people. Davison—the figure who convinced Chappell to feature more serious chamber programming over lighter fare—praised the series' public outreach. As he noted shortly after the series' inception, "Till very recently, a string quartet, or a pianoforte sonata, played by first-class artists, was a luxury reserved for the enjoyment of a few exclusive circles, and regarded on the other hand, as something that must of necessity be *caviare* to the multitude."[31] Davison also expressed confidence about the public's ability to appreciate serious repertory. In February 1859, he wrote that thus far the concerts, in which "nothing but good music" had occurred, "proved eminently successful. . . . Quintets, quartets, and sonatas, not only pleased the multitude, but were heard with greater attention, and applauded with greater enthusiasm, than anything else." Davison claimed credit "for never having doubted the capability of the great public at least to appreciate the beautiful in art, and most especially in musical art."[32]

The Monday Popular Concerts were so successful that in 1865 Chappell instituted additional concerts on Saturday afternoons that featured separate programming. (Collectively the concerts were referred to in different ways, sometimes still as "Monday Popular Concerts" despite the addition of Saturday events, or more generally as the "Popular Concerts" or "Pops," the terms I favor hereafter.)[33] Given the series' longevity (forty years, with the final concerts occurring in the spring of 1899), the Popular Concerts proved quite influential in London's musical culture. In addition, concerts were so numerous that anniversary celebrations occurred frequently: the 100th concert was celebrated about four years after the series' founding (a sold-out performance, with almost 1,000 people refused entrance at the door), and the 500th concert occurred in January 1875, not even twelve years later. By way of comparison, Ellsworth notes that it took the Philharmonic Society—which only gave eight concerts per season—almost sixty-three years to reach their 500th anniversary concert.[34]

As director, Arthur Chappell programmed diverse repertory, from eighteenth-century works to recent compositions by British and Continental figures.[35] Schumann's Leipzig chamber music found an increasingly happy home in the Popular Concerts. As one sympathetic English writer wrote in the *Daily Telegraph* in 1874, these specific works constituted an "illustrious group of art creations" in Schumann's stylistic development, "represent[ing] the master at his best."[36] In the same year, even the *Musical World*—while expressing reservations about the A-major string quartet—identified this period as Schumann's "ripest and most productive."[37]

The remarks about Schumann's "illustrious group of art creations" were sparked by a performance of the A-minor string quartet, the first of the Op. 41 set and the quartet that proved especially beloved with Popular audiences. As described earlier, the 1854 British premiere of the work by the Quartet Association had apparently "failed to excite the least interest." At the Popular Concerts, however, the quartet's reception illustrates the rapidly growing public enthusiasm for Schumann's music. The work debuted in May 1865, and by 1866 the work was "played with such wonderful spirits, and so much to the gratification of the audience, that the scherzo was encored."[38] By 1872, the *Daily Telegraph* remarked that the quartet was "a composition already popular enough to have been played six times at these concerts." Four years later, the same paper noted that the work "is now an established favourite, and, since its production eleven years ago, has done as much for Schumann's fame amongst us as anything else from his pen." An 1877 performance prompted the same paper to describe the quartet as "one of the most familiar in the popular repertory," a work "so characteristic of [its] tender and thoughtful genius" that it "holds a place in the affection of amateurs."[39] By 1884, the *Musical World* acknowledged that the A-minor quartet was "a great favourite with Mr. Chappell's public, who have now heard it eighteen times, and are quite ready, we fully believe, to hear it eighteen times more, so soon as may be."[40]

The chamber works with piano also experienced a notable growth in popularity at the Popular Concerts. Indeed, the first performance of a Schumann work at the Pops occurred with the Op. 44 piano quintet, which premiered on December 1, 1862. The pianist was Ernst Pauer, and he must have anticipated resistance from the audience because his program note offered a gentle defense of Schumann, while also speculating about English resistance to his music:

> The English have adopted Mendelssohn, but in Germany an equal rank is accorded to Schumann. It may arise from affection for Mendelssohn that the English deny Schumann's claims, fearing that the recognition of them

may interfere with the justly deserved reputation of their favorite; but, be this as it may, a comparison should not be instituted between them.[41]

As Davison sarcastically noted in his review, which reprinted parts of Pauer's note: "Herr Pauer immediately proceeds to institute a comparison (the first, we believe, that *ever was* instituted), and in that comparison satisfactorily shows why Schumann does not and cannot attain the same popularity as Mendelssohn" (whose "magnificent *Ottetto*" formed, in Davison's opinion, "the feature of the concert"). As for Pauer, differences in the composers' personality also explained English hesitations about Schumann, for "apart from his not having the natural gifts of Mendelssohn, [Schumann] was unable by the use of his talents or his manners to make himself popular" and that "if he did not treat popular opinion with contempt, he would not consult it."[42]

Two weeks later, on January 20, 1863, Chappell decided to reprogram the Op. 44 quintet with Pauer again at the piano. We do not know whether this performance occurred because of Chappell and Pauer's desire to shape audience taste, or because the audience reaction had been so positive the first time around. Critics, however, remained unconvinced: a piece in the *Saturday Review* claimed that the first performance left an "unfavourable impression," and Davison subsequently pronounced: "A second hearing did not engender a very strong desire for the third."[43] For his part, Chorley waited until the second performance to unleash his criticism: whatever Schumann's aspirations, "in his best works, he was deficient in fancy, and audacious, not only in taking, but also in making, those liberties, which can but be pardoned in consideration of consummate genius" (which, for Chorley, Schumann clearly lacked). In addition to an "immodesty of eccentricity," Schumann's "taste in harmony is, throughout, impure—showing a perverse leaning" toward "extreme chords and suspenses [*sic*]."[44]

In his review of the first concert, Davison urged Pauer to use "his fingers" rather than "his pen" in advocating for Schumann: "the best means he can employ to render Schumann's music popular is not to write about it but to play it."[45] Perhaps unwittingly, Davison pinpointed the very means by which Schumann's chamber music became popular, namely, through high-quality performances by Schumann advocates. Joseph Joachim represents one such advocate. He performed in the first 1859 Monday Popular Concert and remained a regular visitor in the series up until its end. Over the course of forty years, he played a remarkably wide repertory, including numerous performances of Schumann's chamber music. As a writer remarked in 1887 after a Pops performance of the A-minor string quartet, Joachim had long served as "an exponent and fervent advocate of Schumann's genius" who was "instrumental in introducing repeated performances of that master's chamber music at these concerts."[46] To fully understand the growing public acclaim for Schumann's chamber works with piano, however, we must turn to Clara Schumann, for she eventually made the Popular Concerts her most preferred venue during her London tours.

Clara's Role in Robert's London Reception: The First Ten Years

Clara's first British tour occurred in the spring of 1856, three years before the Popular Concerts began and just months before Robert died. As Janet Ritterman and more recently Alexander Stefaniak have shown, Clara's visit was remarkably ambitious. In less than twelve weeks, she gave twenty-two performances in London alone and in a variety of venues: two concerts with the Philharmonic Society, four with Ella's Musical Union, one with the New Philharmonic (an ensemble begun just four years prior), a private concert in Buckingham Palace, three of her own recitals, and eleven concerts sponsored by other individuals or smaller societies. Her repertory also spanned an impressive range: almost fifty works by thirteen composers, including herself.[47] Not surprisingly, Robert's music received particular focus. Clara played twelve works in all, from his A-minor Piano Concerto to various chamber works and solo piano pieces. Nevertheless, Clara—aware of the controversy surrounding Robert's music—was judicious in how she aligned repertory with venues. With the more conservative Philharmonic Society, she performed only familiar works by Beethoven (the "Emperor" Concerto) and Mendelssohn (the D-minor Piano Concerto and the *Variations sérieuse*). Robert's music she reserved for (1) institutions open to newer music from the Continent (the Musical Union, where she performed four times, and the New Philharmonic, with which she played the A-minor Piano Concerto); and (2) smaller events comprising her own recitals and concerts sponsored by other individuals or more minor societies.

Given that most of Robert's music appeared in less prominent venues, press notice was limited. Comments that survive, however, show critical resistance to his works. In a *Musical World* review of the New Philharmonic concert, Davison praised Clara's performance "of her husband's concerto [as] admirable, full of enthusiasm. Of the music itself we would rather not speak." In his *Times* review, however, Davison elaborated: the concerto was "too laboured and ambitious," with an unacceptable number of "utterly extravagant" virtuosic passages.[48] In Chorley's review of Clara's second recital, at which she played *Carnaval*, Chorley complained that "she seems determined to offer Dr. Schumann's music in all the fullness of its eccentricity to the public"; the pieces therein seemed "uncouth, faded, and wanting in clearness."[49] As for Davison, he noted that *Carnaval* "was interesting chiefly because Madame Schumann interpreted them," a sentiment echoed in his other reviews. After hearing an excerpt from the Op. 12 *Phantasiestücke* at Clara's first Musical Union concert, for instance, Davison asserted that Robert's music "represents a school that runs counter to our ideas of musical propriety," yet he also acknowledged that "[i]f anything could make Schumann's music popular it would be the playing of Clara Wieck."[50] Critical resistance to Robert's music clearly exasperated Clara: "They are terribly backwards or rather one-sided; they do not want to accept any modern composers except for Mendelssohn, who is their God!"[51]

As Ritterman has observed, Clara's 1856 tour drew mixed impressions as it came to an end. Davison suggested that "[t]he reception accorded to this accomplished lady on her first coming to England will no doubt encourage her to repeat her visit." Chorley, however, offered only faint praise and ended by recommending the opposite: "That this Lady is among the greatest female players who have ever been heard has been universally admitted. That she is past her prime, may be now added without discourtesy, when we take leave of her; nor do we fancy that she would do wisely to adventure a second visit to England."[52] Nevertheless, Clara did return in 1857 and again in 1859. Although playing less of Robert's music, she still struggled in these two tours. For one, Clara found it harder to get engagements. Two weeks into her 1857 tour, she wrote in a letter: "The season has been very bad thus far, and if it doesn't improve in June ... then I will return [home]. ... This month I've only had 2 engagements. If things go well and I get two more, then I'll have just enough to cover my living expenses. ... Everything here always moves so slowly."[53] Despite staying for two and a half months, Clara performed only eight concerts in London; the 1859 tour did not fare much better, bringing only nine such concerts. For another, Clara received less press notice, and what attention she did receive contained more pointed criticisms. In 1857, several reviews criticized her freedom with tempos and overly enthusiastic interpretations. For instance, after hearing Clara play Beethoven's "Appassionata" Sonata at a Musical Union concert, Davison griped about the first movement, which "was too much tormented—stretched as it were on the wheel," and while admiring the "fire imparted to the *finale*," the coda "was indistinct, and the abuse of the *pedal* was very remarkable throughout." A later performance of the Archduke Trio, he said, "did not go well."[54] After Clara's final concert of the 1857 tour, Chorley suggested that Clara's "pre-eminence among women" perhaps leads her "to overlook clearness and certainty of execution," which he found "wanting" in her performance of Beethoven's Kreutzer Sonata.[55]

Given the above, it comes as no surprise that six years elapsed before Clara came back to England. Upon her return, she noticed a considerable change in reception, both for her and for Robert's music. To Brahms she wrote in May 1865: "I have played three times in public, with very great success," and "I am approached from all sides to play Robert Schumann's works." In her diary she indicated that "I've found a remarkable change from five years ago [it had actually been six], in the disposition towards Robert. To my great astonishment, I now find a large number of Schumann followers."[56] Of course, three of the most prominent followers were August Manns and George Grove at the Crystal Palace, and Arthur Chappell at the Popular Concerts. Clara met all three during her 1865 tour. Of Manns she noted that he was "an industrious man, who gives a hearing to anything new of importance." As for Grove, Clara noted that among the "Schumann followers," he was "one of the most zealous," and someone "I prefer more and more [and] with whom I feel quite comfortable."[57]

Clara not only met these figures in 1865, she gave her first performances with their institutions. At the Crystal Palace, Clara played in a "Grand Extra Concert" that Grove arranged for the first of June because "he so wished me to play Robert's Concerto, and the regular concerts always take place before the start of the London season. I played and was well accompanied under Manns' direction.... I also gave an encore. The applause was great and I was quite moved."[58] Clara also made her début at the Monday Popular Concerts, performing in St. James's Hall on May 15, 1865. Joseph Joachim had already briefed Clara about this newer series. In an 1862 letter, he indicated that "only the best chamber music is performed" and that the series' name derived from its availability of shilling seats, which drew larger audiences: "2000 or more listeners, where Apollo freely spills his golden rays."[59] For Clara's first Pops concert, Chappell arranged an all-Schumann program in her honor.

Joachim was also present, and together he and Clara played the Op. 73 *Fantasiestücke* and led a performance of the Op. 47 piano quartet. In addition, the A-minor string quartet was played, several Schumann Lieder were sung, and Clara performed the Op. 13 *Etudes symphoniques*. The audience reaction was overwhelmingly positive, as Clara's diary reveals:

> The 15th (of May) was a red-letter evening in my heart, for such a reception must truly delight one deeply.... [It was] warmer than I have ever experienced, and I was really overcome. It took a long time before I could sit at the piano. Ah, if Robert had experienced it, he probably never would have thought that he (for the greater part of the applause was for him, after all) would ever get such recognition in England.[60]

In his *Musical World* review, Davison confirmed this positive reception while also referencing—though sidestepping (for the moment)—the debate about Robert's music:

> Space will not permit, at this busy time, of our discussing the merits of so many works of importance from the pen of a composer, the question of whose claims to consideration still divides the opinions of thinkers on music. But the reception awarded to every effort of Madame Schumann, who stood valiantly forward as the champion of her regretted husband, and played from beginning to end with an enthusiasm that never flagged, was according to her deserts. She was applauded wherever applause could find a vent, and several times called forward.[61]

Clara thought the positive reception that she and Robert's music had received in 1865, while pleasant, might be short-lived. After returning home from England, Clara wrote to a friend that "it went extraordinarily well there for me. While the revenues weren't significant, my reception was quite enthusiastic, and the recognition given to my Robert's compositions, as you can imagine, was very gratifying." However, Clara qualified her remarks by saying that "in England much is merely fashion" and that "the enthusiasm for these compositions" comes mainly "from a little group of friends, and the receptivity of the public was, in any event, stimulating for the moment."[62] Although Clara could not have foreseen the enormous growth in public acclaim for her and for Robert's music, she must have sensed a notable degree of change, for she planned to return the following year. Although an 1866 tour did not materialize, she did return in 1867, and ultimately spent more time as a widow concertizing in London than in any other European capital, visiting nineteen times between 1856 and 1888.[63]

The 1865 tour served as a turning point in other ways. Indeed, it seems that this tour prompted Clara to reconsider the venues in which she played, and to take the case of Robert's music to the larger public. Although she continued her association with the select Philharmonic Society—even premiering Robert's A-minor Piano Concerto with that orchestra in 1865— she began disassociating herself from the exclusive Musical Union. While Clara admired Ella's "industriousness" and the quality and seriousness that underlay his concerts, she disliked his patronizing manner. During her 1856 tour, she confided to her diary:

> His audiences are his children, they obey his every word. He speaks loudly to them, gets them to be quiet whenever they're noisy, and doesn't begin until no one is speaking.... Still, he's a man for whom this is all serious, and he doesn't spare either himself or the audience.[64]

During her 1865 tour, Clara wrote that "Ella is an eccentric, a ridiculous figure . . . but his concerts, and the Popular Concerts of Chappell have the most cultivated audiences." After a Musical Union concert on June 20, 1865, she wrote: "I played at Ella's for the last time.... The man's industriousness is unbelievable; thus, he had placed my photograph in a frame on the stage, and passed it among the ladies sitting nearby. He constantly gushes to me in in tender *billets-doux*."[65] The three concerts that Clara gave in 1865, while well-received, were the last that she gave with the Musical Union.

Cultivating the Greater London Public: Performances of Robert's Chamber Music with Piano

After 1865, Clara emphasized London institutions that featured not only top-notch performances and regular doses of modern music, but ones that also sought the larger public. Hence began a sustained relationship with the Crystal Palace, at which Clara performed a total of eleven times from 1865 through 1877. Robert's A-minor Piano Concerto became the work she performed most with Manns's orchestra.[66] Even more important for Clara were the Popular Concerts. Chappell's decision in 1865 to add regular

Saturday concerts in addition to Monday events surely spoke volumes to Clara about the burgeoning success of the series. For her next fifteen tours, Clara favored the Popular Concerts more than any other series, with anywhere from three, four, five, or more engagements filling out her schedule. Indeed, during her 1881 tour she played at eleven Pops concerts, and by her last English tour in 1888, she had performed in more than one hundred such events. Clara's diary and letters indicate the growing enthusiasm with which she was received by Popular audiences. An 1869 letter to a friend indicates that "I only wish that you had heard my reception on [two such] occasions; it was truly enthusiastic; friendly faces everywhere smiled at me." After giving her opening Pops concerts in 1871, she wrote to Brahms, "My reception here is again extraordinary—they really greet me like a darling." For her debut concert in 1873, Clara wrote: "On the 10th, my reception at the first Popular was enormous; for a long time I couldn't seat myself at the piano because the applause wouldn't stop."[67] Because of severe rheumatic attacks in her arms and hands from 1874 to 1875, Clara became more discriminating about where she played, writing in 1877: "I had to refuse a number of engagements; I look for those places where I enjoy playing."[68] Her London tour of this year would be followed by six more, with the Popular Concerts increasingly becoming the focus. In 1881—the tour in which she played at eleven Pops concerts—her first performance received a "tremendous reception—I was really moved by the enthusiasm of the people; they received me as if I were a darling." For her tenth Pops, "It was so full again that Mr. Burnand [a close friend] says hundreds of people were turned away, and that's how it has always been whenever I played." And for her eleventh concert, Clara witnessed "a very tremendous reception.... I was very moved, my knees shook."[69] Clara's diary also indicates how beloved she became with the "shilling" portion of the audience. After her first Pops concert during her 1884 tour, she remarked:

> When I was called back, a veritable shower of flowers came from the shilling seats and the gallery.... It is said that no flowers have ever been thrown to an artist before.... The loyalty of the English is truly touching—most of these tokens came from poorer people.[70]

At the Popular Concerts, Clara played solo piano works by Robert and other composers, but because the series specialized in chamber music, Clara also emphasized Robert's chamber works with piano. Although she gave occasional hearings of the Piano Trio in D Minor (Op. 63) and character pieces for chamber ensemble (like the Op. 88 *Phantasiestücke*, the Op. 94 *Drei Romanzen*, and the Op. 102 *Fünf Stücke im Volkston*—often playing only excerpts), the Op. 44 piano quintet and Op. 47 piano quartet were far and away the works she favored most. (The quintet especially held a close place in her heart, a work that Robert dedicated to her and that, as Nancy Reich notes, "became the cornerstone of her repertoire almost immediately after its composition.")[71] Under her hands, the piano quintet and eventually the piano quartet became much beloved by Popular audiences. Her first performance of Op. 44 occurred in February 1867 at a Saturday Popular Concert. A *Pall Mall Gazette* review explained how Clara "enraptured all hearers in her husband's quintet," a piece that "with other players has more than once fallen dead, but into which she infuses extraordinary life." Disappointment with the other performers then led to this surprising remark: "It is a pity that Schumann was not an Oriental. He could then have had five wives; and supposing (which is natural enough) each an enthusiast for his music, the other instruments might have been handled with the same enthusiasm."[72] Two years later, a *Musical World* review asserted that the quintet "is always a treat to hear when Schumann's widow is at the piano. How she interprets this cherished work, with Herr Joachim, prince of violinists, and Signor Piatti, prince of cellists, at her side, need hardly be told." An 1872 review remarked, "Every part of this quintet ... exhibited her at her best," and "no wonder that the applause at the conclusion was general, ending in a loud call for the performer. We are sometimes tempted to think that no one should meddle with the music of Schumann except Schumann's wife."[73] By 1876, a *Times* review remarked that Op. 44 was now "a favourite alike with amateurs and musicians. No performer, however, can enter heart and soul into this music like Mdme Schumann." It was played "*con amore.*" An 1881 review described how Schumann's "admirers" and "amateurs in general" enjoy the quintet, a work in which "the accomplished lady shines alone, her whole heart being thrown into the task."[74]

On April 4, 1887, the piano quintet appeared in an event that the *Times* called "all but unprecedented in the history of music," namely, the 1,000th Popular Concert, which occurred during Clara's second-to-last English tour.[75] In her diary, Clara explained that Chappell arranged this extra concert "so that the last of this season would be the 1,000th." She also praised him by saying:

> he has always offered the best to the public, and consequently added greatly to the whole of music education. A stranger who first came here, like I did,

some 20–25 years ago [it had been more than 30], can best judge how far the Popular public has advanced; it comprises the elite of the musical world, teachers, and true lovers of music, though a few go because it is the fashion. However, even among these few, a small, good seed falls and propagates itself.[76]

The front cover of the weekly newspaper *The Graphic* featured an engraving that showed Chappell receiving an award after the concert; visible just behind Chappell are Clara and Joseph Joachim, both of whom participated in the concert (see Figure 5.1). Although the review in *The Graphic* found the programming "of little interest," the author singled out "one item" as an exception because of its electrifying performance: "the exception we have made is in favour of Schumann's pianoforte quintet, which was played by Mesdames Schumann and Néruda, Dr. Joachim, Messrs. Straus and Piatti in a manner such as the present generation are not likely to hear again."[77] Clara's diary referred to the "immensely animated audience," and described how when she "came out and wanted to get in the

Figure 5.1 Front cover of *The Graphic*, April 16, 1887. "Presentation to Mr. Arthur Chappell, at St. James's Hall, after the Thousandth Popular Concert."

carriage—it was 11 o'clock—a bunch of the audience waited for me, waved their handkerchiefs, and yelled 'Come back again Frau Schumann!' That was lovely."[78]

Out of Schumann's chamber music, the Op. 44 quintet received the most admiration from critics (sometimes begrudgingly) and audiences alike. In an 1871 review of a Pops concert, the *Daily Telegraph* noted that the work provides "an effective testimony to [Robert's] singular independence," one "adapted to excite the admiration of his sympathizers."[79] In 1872 the *Musical World* pinpointed the quintet as "perhaps the most brilliant and effective among the chamber compositions of Robert Schumann, and by its colouring throughout . . . just suited to the impulsive style, emphatic accentuation, and restless energy of his gifted widow"; later that year the paper stated that the quintet "will remain as Schumann's worthiest representative in the department of chamber music, and as a proof that, in his happiest moments, the composer whom aesthetic Germany prefers before Mendelssohn could do great things."[80] Similar comments crop up in later years: it is "one of Schumann's most deeply-imagined and elaborately worked out chamber pieces" (1876); "assuredly *his* finest composition for the chamber" (1879); a "*pièce de resistance*" and "a masterpiece" (1885).[81]

So admired was the quintet by critics and especially Popular audiences that it became one of the most favored works in the series' repertory. In studying the compositions played at the Pops during 1859–1889, Ellsworth has identified the ten most-performed works; where Beethoven pieces occupy the first three positions, the fourth spot is held by Schumann's Op. 44 quintet, which received a total of thirty-six performances.[82] Although different pianists participated in the work's performances throughout the years, including Ernst Pauer, Wilhelmine Clauss-Szarvady, Franklin Taylor (who for a time studied with Clara), Kate Roberts, and Agnes Zimmermann, Clara's performances garnered the most attention by far. Ellsworth has also charted the rise and fall of various composers at the Pops during the forty decades of its existence. In the 1860s, Schumann's music was just making inroads at the Pops; works by Beethoven (358 performances) and Mendelssohn (141 performances) held sway. In the 1870s, however, Schumann became the fourth most performed composer at the Pops (125 performances), trailing behind Beethoven, Mendelssohn, and J. S. Bach. In the 1880s, Beethoven was still the most performed composer by far, but Schumann now displaced Mendelssohn in the second position, with 206 performances compared to 150 for Mendelssohn.[83] Clara's participation in the Popular Concerts surely helps to explain this meteoric rise in Robert's popularity. Indeed, in certain ways, Clara's presence fulfilled a prophecy laid out by Joachim years before. In an 1864 letter to Clara, he had explained that for the "larger public in England, Schumann is too exclusively of a German-romantic spirit. He will penetrate the masses only through individuals."[84] Clara proved to be one of these defining individuals.

The Op. 47 piano quartet gained critical acceptance more slowly than the piano quintet, even though the former represents the first Schumann work to receive an institutional performance in London. For Clara, the quartet was significant enough to perform during two important early tours: her first of 1856—with the work appearing on the second of two concerts sponsored by the Re-Union des Arts society—and her "turning-point-year" of 1865, where the quartet occurred as part of Clara's first Popular Concert. Both events drew admiration for her playing but without specific remarks on the work itself. In general, though, the piano quartet gave critics more pause for thought. Such skepticism became especially noticeable in the 1860s onward as the work gained favor with Schumann lovers, whether practicing musicians or audience members. According to Bashford, Schumann's chamber works began appearing more frequently in Musical Union programs from circa 1860 on, "largely at player's behests." Where the piano quartet "had been hurriedly abandoned by Ella" in 1848 after its lackluster reception, it "returned at [Edward] Dannreuther's suggestion in 1863," with the pianist leading the performance.[85] If Chorley's remarks on the work had seemed severe in 1848, they appear mild compared to those prompted by this concert: "This is no music for us; nor shall we ever become reconciled to the hardihood of ugliness which is therein paraded by way of originality." The "uncouthness of the work" was one on which Dannreuther's "labour was wasted," and thus Chorley recommended that he "eschew Schumann's music, for that has as small chance of establishing itself in England as it had in 1848, when this very quartett was introduced by Herr Edward Röckel."[86] Despite such a warning, other musicians alongside Clara took up the cause of Robert's chamber music, whether at the Musical Union, Popular Concerts, or other venues. In 1868, for instance, Adolph Schloesser gave a series of four "Schumann evenings" devoted to the music of a composer "of whom Herr Schloesser is a warm admirer," as the more favorable *Illustrated London News* indicated. Performances occurred before an "expressly exclusive" audience (the *Musical World* identified them as "a very select audience of amateurs and professors" in one review, and "a full assemblage of

Schumannites" in another).[87] In the first concert, the "heartiness of their applause [showed] how fully they agreed with M. Schloesser in their estimate of Schumann's merit as a composer." While some songs and piano works were programmed, the emphasis lay on chamber music. The piano quartet appeared in the first concert and pleased listeners enough that it reappeared on the third concert "by desire."[88]

At the Popular Concerts, performances of the Op. 47 piano quartet by Clara and other musicians especially threw into relief the differences between public and critical opinion, the result of audiences accepting the work rather quickly. After Clara performed the work in 1870, Davison asserted a divide in opinion about its merits. "Most amateurs have, by this time, made up their minds about it, and while some reverence the work as an inspiration, others regard it as simply pretentious."[89] After a performance two years later, the *Musical World* insisted that "we have no desire to join the fray" even as it offered a more judgmental, if indirect opinion:

> Schumann's Quartet is a work not yet thoroughly accepted [presumably by listeners like Davison] for reasons which may lie within itself, or with the prejudice and false taste of the public.... In time, perhaps, when we quite clearly see what the music means, and recognize the purpose of a good deal that now seems purposeless, we may entertain a definite notion.

As if to further drive home his doubts, Davison framed his comments with praise of string quartets by Mendelssohn and Haydn: music by the former displays "polish resulting from consummate art," and in the latter "there is no laziness" nor any "points to be excused by the elastic plea of progress." The Haydn quartet "ended the concert delightfully," so that "even those whom Schumann had fretted the most" were "sent away in good humor."[90]

Even papers less partisan than the *Times, Musical World*, and *Athenaeum* offered limited praise for the Op. 47 piano quartet, suggesting that the work, if not wholly successful, at least demonstrated Schumann's earnestness and original voice. Although the *Daily Telegraph* was generally disposed toward Schumann's music, an 1873 Pops performance of the work led the paper to qualify its praise via a lengthy overview of Schumann's stylistic development. In his early period, "an unquestionable genius" was allowed "to run wild" when Schumann should have spent time "in severe self-discipline" acquiring "technical knowledge." As a result, when "soberer ideas prevailed" in the second period (to which Op. 47 "belongs"), Schumann "saw an arduous and weary travel between him and his goal." To his credit, he:

> faced his task with characteristic earnestness, and gallantly strove to redeem the past. But self-discipline at thirty is difficult; and by taking no amount of thought could Schumann make up for precious time lost in the pursuit of phantoms. [Nevertheless, while] a critic may not admire Schumann, as represented, say, by the quartet performed on Monday, . . . it is impossible to despise him.[91]

Five years later, a performance of the piano quartet prompted additional qualified praise from the same paper: the work serves as a "representative composition," and "anything characteristic in a special sense of a man like Schumann must always command attention even from those who do not extend to him their fullest confidence." Still, the author had to admit that "Schumann's quartet gave, it is scarcely necessary to say, very great pleasure to the master's admirers."[92]

By the 1880s, the piano quartet enjoyed more wholehearted praise, even finding equal footing with the piano quintet in its appeal. After Clara performed the latter in an 1881 Popular Concert, one review noted that the quintet "divides with the pianoforte quartet in the same key the preference of Schumann's many admirers, and in fact of amateurs in general." A review of an 1883 Pops performance described the piano quartet as "a very old favourite at these concerts," noting that the performers "did justice to music of rare beauty and significance."[93] In these later years, the piano quartet even seemed to hold its own with chamber works by other acknowledged masters. During her penultimate tour of 1887, Clara played the work in a Pops concert that also featured string quartets by Beethoven and Haydn; instead of coming up short, the Op. 47 quartet now served as one of "three large concerted [i.e., chamber] works" that produced a concert "conspicuous for quantity as well as excellence of quality in its instrumental portion."[94] In a Pops performance in 1889 (the last year of the series), the piano quartet was played alongside a Mendelssohn string quartet; not only did this linkage draw no comment from the *Musical World*, the author also praised the performance of "Schumann's glorious quartet."[95] A number of other performances in the 1880s drew no direct comments about Op. 47 at all, another sign of its acceptance into the repertory.[96]

Critical Reactions to the Rise in Popularity of Schumann's Music

In the late 1840s and 1850s, Davison and Chorley had sometimes cited apathetic audience reactions as partial evidence of Schumann's compositional weaknesses. As larger venues assumed importance, however, these critics and their like-minded peers found themselves increasingly at odds with audience opinion. The reception of the piano quartet in the 1860s and 1870s, sketched above, illustrates this growing divide between public and critical opinion, as do other examples. After Clara's first Popular Concert in 1865, for instance, Davison implied that any positive audience reaction was due not to Robert's music (which filled the entire program) but to Clara's "valiant" efforts to "champion" the music "of her regretted husband."[97] As noted earlier, Clara modestly asserted the opposite, writing that the "greater part of the applause" occurred for Robert. Her opinion was echoed by *The Musical Times*, a paper under the fairly new editorship of Henry C. Lunn, who was more sympathetic to Schumann: "The music of Schumann—so often spoken of and so little heard—was listened to with intense enjoyment by a crowded audience." Indeed, as if in rebuttal to conservative critics, the author encouraged more independent thinking for listeners: "to those pioneers of progress who take the liberty of judging for themselves, such a concert may speak more forcibly than all the 'notices' for or against a man who is at least original enough to provoke controversy."[98] An 1872 Pops performance of the A-minor string quartet provides another instance of clashing opinions: while the *Daily Telegraph* stated that the work is "already popular enough to have been played six times at these concerts," Davison asserted in the *Musical World* that "[w]e doubt, however, if the work really progresses in public esteem."[99]

For Davison in particular, the growing admiration for Schumann among Pops audiences placed him in a difficult position. From the time of the series' inception, Davison had proclaimed his faith in "the capability of the great public" to value "the beautiful ... in musical art."[100] As the years passed, however, the taste of Popular audiences began diverging from that of Davison and other conservative critics, who must have found it ever more challenging to influence public opinion. Occasionally, jabs at positive audience reactions appear in their reviews. For example, after finding Clara's playing lacking in two 1867 Pops Concerts, a writer for the *Saturday Review* (possibly Davison) described "the applause bestowed indiscriminately on her every effort."[101]

In an 1872 review of a concert where the A-minor string quartet appeared, Davison referenced "the anxiety of a Monday Popular audience to believe well of everything Mr. Chappell presents."[102] In the same year, as mentioned earlier, a review of a Pops performance of the Op. 47 piano quartet suggested that the "prejudice and false taste of the public" could partly explain why (presumably more discerning) listeners had "not yet thoroughly accepted the work."[103]

Of course, Davison would have risked alienating his readers had such audience jabs occurred too frequently. Hence, he and like-minded peers offered other explanations for why Schumann's music was supposedly capturing the public imagination. First, they suggested that Clara's powerful interpretations were difficult to resist. Three different reviews of Pops performances where the Op. 44 quintet appeared may illustrate. In 1867, a writer for the *Pall Mall Gazette* (possibly Davison) wrote:

> Madame Schumann has come, to rejoice the hearts of the Schumannites. And really to hear this famous pianist play the music of her late husband, whom some people want us to believe is a second Beethoven, or, still more, a continuer of Beethoven, is enough to make any one a Schumannite. Talk of enthusiasm! Here is more than enthusiasm. No wife could be more completely her husband's better half. Madame Schumann, the pianist, is the better half of Robert Schumann's music.[104]

For her debut performance of the 1869 tour, Davison remarked that Clara "is playing with all that fine energy and earnest sympathy ... by which she forces her hearers to share her own enthusiasm."[105] For Clara's first Pops performance in 1872, Davison wrote that she brings to music an "enthusiasm which is the salient characteristic of her playing, and, with a vast number of amateurs, the secret in a great measure of her popularity."[106] Critics also suggested a second reason for Clara's success in promoting Robert's music: namely, that audiences could not help but sympathize with her as a widow advocating on behalf of her husband. Numerous reviews describe Clara in this role, and sometimes critics suggested that performances of Robert's music occurred not by audience demand but in deference to her. For instance, in February 1868, Chorley wrote that the recent appearance of the Op. 44 quintet at a Pops concert occurred "rather in propitiation of Madame Schumann (we suspect) than because the composition has really taken root here. Dislike for this music must be separated from the thorough sympathy every generous person feels for the devotion of a widow to the memory of the husband in whom she believed." A few weeks later, he observed that the repertory of Popular Concerts "consist[s] of works which have been accepted, excepting the music of Schumann, introduced by his devoted wife, and rather tolerated out of respect to her generous enthusiasm ... than enjoyed or growing in general favour."[107]

Conservative critics also targeted the efforts of prominent "Schumannites" for explaining the rise in the composer's popularity. In 1866, Davison acknowledged the sincerity of Schumann's "devoted and uncompromising army of followers" even as he questioned the validity of their position: "By their persistent, specious and often eloquent (because rarely disingenuous) preaching, these followers have widened the circle of [Schumann's] appreciators and driven much of his music into the hearts of amateurs, as well as musicians."[108] August Manns advocated primarily from the podium, but from the mid-1860s onward George Grove increasingly advocated with his pen, which drew swift attention, even deprecation, from Davison. A lightning rod around which Grove and Davison began a public debate was the second London performance of *Paradise and the Peri* in March 1866, a decade after its premiere there. Davison's lengthy review provided the above gripe about Schumann's "army of followers" while also presenting a litany of complaints.[109] In his response (published a day later), Grove not only defended the oratorio, he proclaimed that "Schumannites ... are as much Beethovenites and Mendelssohnites," and he asserted that the debate about Schumann's merits was reaching its end in the public eye: "We do not deprecate criticism; but, while critics wrangle and hesitate, we believe that the matter is being fast decided in Schumann's favour by the 'larger tribunal' of the public."[110] The latter statement proved especially galling to Davison; indeed, his response shows an even stronger distrust of public taste than the audience jabs found above:

> Criticism has other duties; and, among the rest, to prevent ... this same "larger tribunal" from sinking into a state of lethargy, and viewing every artistic production through a mist of apathetic indulgence for the mere want of vigour to protest. To this condition the public would assuredly be brought (were "criticism" to "stand aside") by the writers of the dilettante-sentimental school [like Grove].[111]

As the reception of Schumann's chamber music (among other works) shows, Grove proved more prophetic.

The influence of "Schumannites" made itself personally felt on Davison when one of his own followers shifted position. Joseph Bennett met Davison in 1866, and beginning in 1868 Bennett served as sub-editor of the *Musical World* for several years. In his memoirs, Bennett wrote that because of his youth "I looked to Davison as my master and teacher. He easily influenced me against Schumann's music. At that point, however, I did not long remain. Schumann's music began to grow upon me, and continued growing. I soon recognized its beauty and felt its charm."[112] In November 1868, Bennett published an essay in the *Pall Mall Gazette* that acknowledged Schumann's growing popularity ("It is evident that Schumann has been making not a few English friends of late"), and the worthiness of Schumann's music, especially that written in the composer's "second period," which for Bennett began with the composition of the first symphony. Singling out the symphonies, piano concerto, oratorio, and "the quintet in E flat" for particular notice, Bennett asserted that "room should be made for one who comes with such independent thought and original expression.... His speech may be strange, but that of itself is no reason for rejection or even doubt." Bennett remained diplomatic. He acknowledged that long-standing reservations about Schumann's music had merit for people who were "sticklers for form," also noting that "[w]e charge nobody with unfairness or prejudice in this matter." Furthermore, Bennett tried smoothing the Mendelssohn-Schumann divide by suggesting that the success of the latter's second period arose partly when "the charm of Mendelssohn's purity and sweetness began to work upon [Schumann's] mind."[113] Davison nevertheless took Bennett's change in stance personally. As the latter noted in his memoirs, "Davison was hurt at what he looked upon as my defection from a cause to which he had committed himself." To his credit, Davison reprinted the article in the *Musical World* and remained on friendly terms with Bennett.[114] Grove, for his part, enthusiastically wrote to Bennett that "your article makes an epoch in English musical criticism."[115] Bennett subsequently became the music critic at the *Daily Telegraph, Sunday Times*, and the *Graphic*, and his more open-minded writings, along with those of Lunn at the *Musical Times*, created additional networks of support for Schumann's music in England.[116] Less than half a year after Bennett's article appeared, the Irish composer Charles Stanford published his own statement of support. Defending Schumann more vigorously than Bennett, Stanford highlighted the Op. 44 piano quintet more pointedly than any other work as evidence of Schumann's talents: "It is clear and sparkling" and "one of the most beautiful of the composer's concerted pieces."[117]

Once started, the growing wave of enthusiasm for Schumann seemed difficult to counter, and conservative critics dealt with it in different ways. Even in his last year as a critic (1868), Chorley resisted acknowledging any public appeal of Schumann's music, as the above comments about sympathy for Clara-the-widow demonstrate. In addition, Chorley had no qualms about continuing to denounce most of Schumann's output in the strongest terms, even asserting its unhealthy qualities: "[T]here will be always a small congregation of people who worship an oracle in proportion as he is misty and unintelligible. Of course, too, there are people who cannot resist unwholesome influences."[118] A month earlier, Chorley had similarly stated:

[T]hough besieged people in time of famine have been constrained to content themselves with strange aliments in place of the honest food of healthier days, such fact does not imply that the meat is not diseased. Schumann's music of pretension, to our apprehension, smacks of unwholesome decay. There is no life in it, no idea, no beauty.[119]

Chorley also continued to associate Schumann with Wagner, another source of unwholesomeness. Indeed, as Robert Bledsoe describes, so concerned was Chorley about the "serious threat of disease and decay" to musical culture in the 1860s that "antipathy towards the 'music of the future'—chiefly the music of Schumann and Wagner—thus permeated much of Chorley's writing during his final years."[120] A particularly lengthy attack occurred in 1864 with Chorley's two-part article "Old, New, and No Music," which drew a line of pernicious influence from Beethoven to Schumann, Liszt, and Wagner. The "flaws and specks" found particularly in Beethoven's late music became the "starting-point for the movement," with Schumann representing "the first name among those moderns who have helped in German music to confound good and evil." Schumann's "instinct for Beauty seems to have been extra-ordinarily weak" and "very little of the mass of music bearing [his] name has any real value." Followers like Wagner and Liszt took up "the work of musical destruction, consciously or unconsciously begun by Schumann."[121] So dogmatic did Chorley remain that, according to Charles Graves, he "made it a point to the end of his life to walk out of the concert-room at the beginning of the second movement of Schumann's Quintet, to mark, it is said, his high disapproval of a certain chord in the eighth bar!" Whether true or not, this anecdote parallels similar stories told by others, which together indicate Chorley's consistent opposition to Schumann's music throughout his career.[122]

Davison proved a more complex figure than Chorley in the London reception of Schumann, partly because he wavered about the association with Wagner. In August 1853, just months after first asserting this linkage, Davison published a satirical piece that loosened Schumann's association with the New German School. Adopting a mock-biblical tone, Davison satirized Liszt, the seer of new geniuses:

> Liszt discovered Robert Schumann, and did him. He . . . held him up, in the face of the worshippers of Mendelssohn, as the real idol to be adored. . . . The peoples listened, and were edified. . . . And the peoples became Schumannites. . . . Liszt was content; he had done Schumann. But now to undo him! Liszt pondered. . . . He dragged out from darkness one Wagner, and blew a trumpet on his behalf. . . . Thus Liszt discovered Richard Wagner, and did him. As for Robert Schumann, he undid him.[123]

Subsequent events must have further problematized the Schumann-Wagner link in Davison's mind. First, as the memoirs compiled by Davison's son indicate, "not a note of Schumann was heard" during Wagner's directorship of the Philharmonic Society in 1855; such an absence must have been "strange, surely, to those who regarded the two as companions in arms." Second, a series of "Reactionary Letters" by Eduard Sobolewski—reprinted in 1855 in *The Musical World*—likely prompted Davison to adapt his thinking, for Sobolewski (who had known the composer and written for his journal) laments the treatment of Schumann at the hands of Wagnerians: "For Wagner's sake, Schumann is abused almost as much as Meyerbeer," for Wagner and his supporters care "nothing about the interest of music" but only "for their own interest. Yet Schumann is the only composer of the present day who attaches himself more and more to the old classical masters."[124] Such comments surely proved thought-provoking for Davison. It is true that he reasserted the Schumann-Wagner link after hearing the 1856 London premiere of *Paradise and the Peri*, proclaiming that "Robert Schumann has had his innings, and been bowled out—like Richard Wagner."[125] Yet two months later, Davison reprinted a critique of himself and

Chorley for this very linkage, one published in the Boston-based *Dwight's Journal of Music*:

> But the most striking folly and injustice of this partisan warfare [perpetuated by critics at the *Athenaeum* and *Times*] is the absurd way in which it confounds together composers who are most essentially unlike.... For Schumann is no more like Wagner, than Mendelssohn is like Wagner. Their adventurousness, their Beethoven-like unwillingness to be mere copyists, is about all they have in common.[126]

Even though Davison never saw Schumann on the same level as Mendelssohn, a year later he seemed to agree, albeit subtly. In October 1857, he reprinted excerpts from a travel diary by William Saar, in which the latter described how the "harshest dissonances" in the music of Schumann and Wagner produced "a monstrous, shudderingly sweet, mystical impression on me." To Schumann's name, Davison (as editor) appended a footnote, asking: "Why couple Schumann with Wagner?—Ed."[127]

Davison also holds interest because his career as a critic lasted until his death in 1885; as a result, he witnessed the full sea change in reception for Schumann's music. Continuing to denounce it inflexibly—as Chorley had done until his retirement in 1868—would have undermined Davison's own credibility as a critic, especially in the face of increasing support for Schumann from other critics, musicians, and audiences. Indeed, after his 1866 debate with Grove, Davison seems to have tread more lightly, adopting various approaches to make his criticism seem less partisan. Easiest was to praise those works Davison considered most successful in Schumann's chamber output: namely, the A-minor string quartet ("his first and, on the whole, perhaps his best"—1866), and the Op. 44 piano quintet ("Schumann's worthiest representative in the department of chamber music"—1872).[128] Elsewhere pains are taken to balance praise with fault-finding. After a Pops performance of the A-major string quartet in 1874, the *Musical World* indicated that "while containing many and estimable beauties," the work "is on the whole the least evenly balanced" of the three quartets; especially problematic was the "monotonous, if not wearisome" finale, which nevertheless "exhibits a mastery of detail, a determined will, and an incontestably original way of thinking peculiar to the author."[129] For other works he considered problematic, Davison might "beg off" from discussing them or reference vague "others" as a way to de-emphasize his own voice while suggesting that other people had doubts as well. For instance, in his review of Clara's first Pops concert (the all-Schumann program), Davison wrote that Schumann's "claims to consideration still divide the opinions of thinkers on music." Similarly, an 1870 review of the piano quartet suggests that while "some reverence the quartet, others regard it as simply pretentious."[130] The premiere of the F-major string quartet at the Pops in 1867 brought further disappointment. Yet Davison deflected by beginning his review with reference to Schumann's "opponents": the quartet "cannot fail to reopen the discussion upon the artistic *status* of its author, because it cannot fail to strengthen the hands of his opponents." In addition (and rather shamelessly), Davison states: "we have never cared to enter" into the "vexed question of the merits, absolute and comparative of Robert Schumann," and thus "we belong ... neither to the Schumannites nor to the anti-Schumannites, but occupy neutral ground; equally free to praise or to censure as circumstances may demand." And censure he does, asserting that the quartet is "bad" and a "failure" (which Davison calls a "fact"). In a balancing act, however, Davison suggests that while "Schumann scores a loss" in this quartet, "it by no means determined the game" and that Schumann "will occupy no mean place in the roll of composers." Davison, however, could not help but revert to a comparison with Mendelssohn: "but between him and Mendelssohn there was just the difference to be found between first-rate talent [Schumann] and absolute genius [Mendelssohn]. So much, at least, the Quartet in F helped to establish, if it did not point towards something yet more unfavourable to its composer."[131]

In such a review—written just one year after his public feud with Grove—Davison struggles to remain even-handed in his comments. As the years passed, however, the expression of doubts in strong terms gradually became rarer in his writings. Joseph Bennett, who worked at the *Musical World* from 1868 to circa 1873, surely exercised influence. Indeed, even after he left, Bennett's voice retained a prominent place in the journal, for Davison—a man entering his sixties—increasingly relied on reprinting reviews from the *Daily Telegraph* (where Bennett served as music critic) in place of writing his own. These reprints, along with Davison's own ever-less partisan writings, speak to the influence of growing public support for Schumann, whose Leizpzig chamber music became largely ensconced in the English musical canon by the time of Davison's death in 1885.[132] A primary incubator for this development was the Popular Concerts series. By 1874, the *Musical World* had to concede as much, writing: "Mr. Arthur Chappell, it must be admitted, has done for the chamber-music of Robert Schumann, at St. James's Hall, quite as much as Messrs. G. Grove and Manns have been enabled to do for his orchestral music at the Saturday performances at the Crystal Palace." Acknowledging that Chappell "has derived no little aid" from both Clara Schumann and Joachim in popularizing the chamber works, the *Musical World* also acknowledged the importance of the larger public:

> but Mr. Chappell, at any rate, was the first to test the value of the amiable Leipsic musical philosopher's quartets and other chamber pieces before large, mixed audiences—before a general public, in short, combined of various elements, from the wealthiest and most conspicuous patrons of the art down to its humblest though equally earnest followers.[133]

Public sentiments could not wholly change Davison's opinion, however. In an 1882 letter to an acquaintance, he expressed feelings not unlike those found in his first concert review of Schumann's music in 1848: "How you can regard Schumann and Mendelssohn as equals is altogether beyond my comprehension."[134] Others, however, breathed a sigh of relief that partisanship seemed to have waned. In his 1885 *Musical History*, the composer Sir George Macfarren asserted that Schumann had "suffered through the persistence of his partisans in comparing him with another, instead of displaying and extolling his own merit." Hearing Schumann on his own terms allowed "the grace, the deep feeling, [and] the ingenuity... that mark his symphonic and chamber music" to come more fully into view.[135]

Notes

1. "Clara Wieck, the Celebrated Pianist," *The Musical World* (hereafter *MW*), May 3, 1838, 7; and "Characteristic Peculiarities of Four Great Pianoforte Players," *MW*, May 17, 1838, 47–48. Although Clara would not visit England until 1856, she had already received multiple notices in London papers by 1838. The earliest instance I have found occurred in 1831, in a "Foreign Musical Report" by a Leipzig correspondent about the girl "only in her eleventh year"; *The Harmonicon*, February 1831, 47.
2. J. H., "Biographical Sketches.—No. II. Dr. Robert Schumann," *The Musical Journal*, September 8, 1840, 149.
3. For reviews of these two concerts, see *MW*, March 11, 1848, 168–69, which indicates that Sloper performed Schumann's "Arabesque" (Op. 18) and a "Nocturne" (likely one of the Op. 23 *Nachtstücke*), but with no further comments; and *MW*, April 1, 1848, 221–22; I discuss this latter review in more detail below.
4. Janet Ritterman, "Schumann and the English Critics: A Study in Nineteenth-Century Musical Reception," in *Musical Dimensions: A Festschrift for Doreen Bridges*, ed. Martin Comte (Melbourne: Australian Scholarly Publishing, 2009), 202. Ritterman traces the general contours

of Schumann's reception in England; taking a cue from Reinhard Kapp, she also explores how the unconventional "cut" of Schumann-the-musician hindered ready acceptance of his music: he was a composer who, instead of promoting his music through his own performances (as Mendelssohn so often did), established an academic career as a writer and critic. This path made it easier for critics to fault what they saw as amateurish deficiencies in his music. For a detailed account of Mendelssohn's time in England, see Colin Timothy Eatock, *Mendelssohn and Victorian England* (Aldershot, UK, and Burlington, VT: Ashgate, 2009).

5. Quoted in Thym, "Schumann in Brendel's *Neue Zeitschrift für Musik* from 1845–1856," 33.
6. For an account of Chorley's life and career, see Robert Terrell Bledsoe, *Henry Fothergill Chorley: Victorian Journalist* (Aldershot, UK: Ashgate, 1998). Regarding Davison's life and career, see the insightful and fairly balanced memoir compiled by his son Henry Davison, *From Mendelssohn to Wagner: Being the Memoirs of J. W. Davison, Forty Years Music Critic of "The Times"* (London: William Reeves, 1912). See also Charles Reid, *The Music Monster: A Biography of James William Davison, Music Critic of* The Times *of London, 1846–78* (London: Quartet Books, 1984). On the role of both writers in the reception of native English composers, see Meirion Hughes, *The English Musical Renaissance and the Press 1850–1914: Watchmen of Music* (London and New York: Routledge, 2002). Davison's writings for *The Musical World* are more colorful and prone to exaggeration, humor, and satire than those he wrote for *The Times*. At different periods of his life, Davison also contributed pieces to other papers, including the *Pall Mall Gazette*, *Saturday Review*, and *The Graphic*. Because critics generally published anonymously in Victorian England, determining authorship for pieces outside of the main papers for which critics wrote can be difficult. However, Davison's idiosyncratic writing style generally makes it easier to discern his pen in these other papers; when uncertain, I will only reference an anonymous author or the name of the journal in which a piece of writing appears.
7. *MW*, April 1, 1848, 221. For a thorough discussion of Ella and the Musical Union, see Christina Bashford, *The Pursuit of High Culture: John Ella and Chamber Music in Victorian England* (Woodbridge, Suffolk, UK: Boydell Press, 2007). For a shorter discussion, see Bashford, "John Ella and the Musical Union," in *Music and British Culture, 1785–1984: Essays in Honour of Cyril Ehrlich*, ed. Christina Bashford and Leanne Langley (Oxford: Oxford University Press, 2000), 193–214. Bashford's 1996 dissertation discusses the growing popularity of chamber-music concerts in London during 1835–1850, and hence provides historical context for understanding how Ella's society could successfully take root; Bashford, "Public Chamber-Music Concerts in London, 1835–50: Aspects of History, Repertory and Reception," 2 vols. (PhD diss., University of London, King's College, 1996).
8. Bashford, *The Pursuit of High Culture*, 1.
9. *Athenaeum*, April 1, 1848, 344–45; *MW*, April 1, 1848, 221.
10. Henry Fothergill Chorley, *Music and Manners in France and Germany: A Series of Travelling Sketches of Art and Society* (1841), repr. (Cambridge: Cambridge University Press, 2009), vol. 3, 126, 95–98, and 126, asterisk footnote.
11. Henry Fothergill Chorley, *Modern German Music: Recollections and Criticisms* (1854), repr. (Cambridge: Cambridge University Press, 2009), vol. 2, 52, asterisk footnote.
12. *The Athenaeum*, March 26, 1853, 391; emphasis original.
13. *The Musical Examiner*, December 3, 1842; quoted in Davison, *From Mendelssohn to Wagner*, 44.
14. Quoted in F[rederick] G[eorge] E[dwards], "Schumann's Music in England [Part I]," *The Musical Times* 46, no. 753 (November 1, 1905): 716–17. See also Bashford, *The Pursuit of High Culture*, 131, which describes how Ella subsequently reversed his opinion about the work, "flattering his audience about their powers of discrimination and taste for more classical composition"; 131, note 57.
15. *MW*, April 1, 1848, 221. On Davison's dislike of Ella "undertak[ing] the task of criticism himself," and his deteriorating relationship with Ella as the years progressed, see Davison, *From Mendelssohn to Wagner*, 232–34.
16. *MW*, September 27, 1851, 619. The review labels the *Waldszenen* as "Seven Pieces for the Pianoforte."
17. *MW*, May 6, 1854, 295. Like the Musical Union, the Quartet Association also cultivated a higher-class audience. As Davison remarked in his review of this concert, "already it has laid hold on the sympathies of the upper classes, to whom chiefly it must look for support."
18. "Notes on Music in Germany," *Athenaeum*, December 18, 1852, 1398–99.
19. *Athenaeum*, June 21, 1856, 786; emphasis original.

20. "Schumann and Wagner: The Two New (Rush) Lights to Lighten the Darkness of the Musical Jesuits at Leipsic (from *The Athenaeum*)," *MW*, December 25, 1852, 820–22.
21. *MW*, April 9, 1853, 225–26.
22. "Notes on Music in Germany," *Athenaeum*, December 18, 1852, 1399.
23. *MW*, June 28, 1856, 408. For an overview of the British reception of *Paradise and the Peri* and how it reflects the larger debate about Schumann, see Nicholas Marston, "'The most significant musical question of the day': Schumann's Music in Britain in the Later Nineteenth Century," in *Robert und Clara Schuman und die Nationalen Musikkulturen des 19. Jahrhunderts: Bericht über das 7. Internationales Schumann-Symposium am 20. und 21. Juni 2000 im Rahmen des 7. Schumann-Festes, Düsseldorf*, ed. Matthias Wendt (Düsseldorf. Mainz: Schott Musik International, 2005), 153–65.
24. *The Times*, commenting on the conclusion of the 1866–1867 season; quoted in Michael Musgrave, *The Musical Life of the Crystal Palace* (Cambridge and New York: Cambridge University Press, 1995), 69. For the latter's discussion of Manns and the Saturday Concerts, see ibid., 67–132.
25. Musgrave, *The Musical Life of the Crystal Palace*, 84.
26. In his review of this concert, Davison complained: "We did not find [Schumann's symphony] so superior to that of Mendelssohn as to entitle it to the honour of being performed entire, while Mendelssohn's (the 'Italian') was shorn of its first and most elaborate movement." *MW*, February 23, 1856, 122.
27. *MW*, reviews of April 11, 1863, 230; November 26, 1864, 760; and March 3, 1866, 134.
28. An 1866 letter to the editor of the *Pall Mall Gazette* brought Grove directly into the Schumann debate with Davison, a polemic I discuss further below. As the 1860s unfolded, Grove gradually became more active in authoring the program notes for Crystal Palace concerts; those he wrote for Schumann works occurred from 1869 on. On Grove as a program annotator for the Palace concerts, see Musgrave, *The Musical Life of the Crystal Palace*, 113–14; and Christina Bashford, "Not Just G: Towards a History of the Programme Note," in *George Grove: Music and Victorian Culture*, ed. Michael Musgrave (Basingstoke, UK: Macmillan, 2003; New York: Palgrave Macmillan, 2003), 115–42, especially 119–24; Appendix 2 of the book anthology in which Bashford's chapter appears cites the years for which Grove, Manns, and others wrote program notes for various Schumann works.
29. Therese Ellsworth, "'*Caviare* to the Multitude': Instrumental Music at the Monday Popular Concerts, London," in *Instrumental Music and the Industrial Revolution*, ed. Roberto Illiano and Luca Sala, Ad Parnassum Studies 5 (Bologna: UT Orpheus, 2010), 126; Ellsworth provides a fine overview of the series in terms of its history, programming, and featured performers, among other matters.
30. Ibid., 128.
31. Preface to the program for February 14, 1859; cited in Ellsworth, "'*Caviare* to the Multitude,'" 124.
32. *MW*, February 26, 1859, 136.
33. A February 16, 1867, piece in *The Musical World* remarked on this terminological flexibility: "The Popular Concerts held on Saturdays in the afternoon are so like those to which the London public is accustomed on Monday nights, that no one thinks of questioning the exact propriety of their title, and Saturday is cheerfully accepted for Monday by zealous amateurs of quartets, sonatas, and trios" (106).
34. Ellsworth, "'*Caviare* to the Multitude,'" 127.
35. The music of Continental composers—whether current or past—dominated programs by far, although British composers like William S. Bennett, George Macfarren, and Alexander Mackenzie received occasional hearings of their works. For a table of living composers whose music was performed, see Ellsworth, "'*Caviare* to the Multitude,'" 137. On the preference given to Continental composers over British-born ones, see also William Everett, *British Piano Trios, Quartets, and Quintets, 1850–1950: A Checklist* (Warren, MI: Harmonie Park Press, 2000), 20; Everett also discusses how the People's Concert Society at South Place (founded 1878) provided a correction by typically having "each season . . . include at least one concert devoted to native music" (22).
36. *Daily Telegraph* review of a Monday Popular concert, likely by Joseph Bennett, who became critic at this paper in 1870; reprinted in *MW*, November 21, 1874. Bennett began working for Davison at the *MW* in 1868, but in the same year published a defense of Schumann, likely

explaining the more open-minded attitudes found in the *Daily Telegraph*. I discuss Bennett's shift in stance further below.
37. *MW*, January 17, 1874, review of a Monday Popular concert, 35.
38. *MW*, June 30, 1866, 409. This enthusiasm for the scherzo echoes that of Continental admirers, as discussed in Chapter 3.
39. *Daily Telegraph* reviews, reprinted in *MW*, November 30, 1872, 770; February 12, 1876, 125; and November 24, 1877, 783.
40. *MW*, January 19, 1884, 36.
41. Pauer's comments were subsequently echoed in a *Saturday Review* piece that reviewed recent Popular Concerts. After noting Chappell's programming of "new and unfamiliar music," including "a quintet by Schumann," the author continued: "We are in England, perhaps, too little 'given to new things' in music. Our steady attachment to those who please us renders us almost jealous of the attempt of any newcomer, and, with rare exceptions (Mendelssohn being one), he has to knock long and loudly at our ears before we give him a hearing." *Saturday Review*, December 12, 1862; reprinted in the *MW*, January 10, 1863, 21.
42. Pauer program note; excerpts reprinted in the *MW*, December 6, 1862, 774, with additional commentary by Davison; emphasis original.
43. *Saturday Review*, December 12, 1862; reprinted in the *MW*, January 10, 1863, 21. Davison's review of the second concert appeared in the *MW*, January 24, 1863, 55.
44. *Athenaeum*, January 24, 1863, 123–24.
45. *MW*, December 6, 1862, 774.
46. *MW*, April 2, 1887, 774; this review was perhaps written by Francis Hueffer, who edited the journal during 1886–1888. (Davison had died two years earlier.) On Joachim's more general role in this concert series, see Ellsworth, "'Music Was Poured by Perfect Ministrants': Joseph Joachim at the Monday Popular Concerts, London," in *The Creative Worlds of Joseph Joachim*, ed. Valerie Woodring Goertzen and Robert Whitehouse Eshbach (Woodbridge, UK: Boydell Press, 2021), 129–44. In this same collection of essays, Michael Musgrave summarizes the violinist's activities at the Crystal Palace ("Joachim at the Crystal Palace," 118–28), and Ian Maxwell surveys Joachim's place in British music culture more generally ("'Thou That Hast Been in England Many a Year': The British Joachim," 104–117).
47. Janet Ritterman, "'Gegensätze, Ecken und sharfe Kanten': Clara Schumanns Besuche in England, 1856–1888," in *Clara Schumann 1819–1896: Katalog zur Ausstellung*, ed. Ingrid Bodsch and Gerd Nauhaus (Bonn: Bonn Stadtmuseum, 1996), 234–61. Ritterman provided the first in-depth overview of Clara's British tours, with a particularly rich discussion of the 1856 tour and tables indicating Clara's repertory and the venues in which they were performed. Alexander Stefaniak has since offered an updated survey of this repertory and concert year; see Stefaniak, *Becoming Clara Schumann*, 222–34. In addition to the concerts listed in Ritterman's Table 1 and Stefaniak's Table 5.4, the *Musical World* also noted that Clara performed in "Signor and Madame Ferrari's Annual Concert," playing Beethoven's "Moonlight" Sonata, a "notturno" by Chopin, and "one of Mendelssohn's songs without words." *MW*, May 17, 1856, 315. Clara's 1856 repertory reflects the shift in her programming that began in the mid-1840s, with Clara dropping opera-based fantasies and variations in favor of "historicist repertoire and lied-style miniatures"; for more on this point, see Stefaniak, *Schumann's Virtuosity*, 198–199, and Stefaniak, *Becoming Clara Schumann*, 56–58. As for her own compositions, Clara only played one during her 1856 tour: the Op. 20 Variations on a Theme of Robert Schumann, featured in one of her London recitals. On how this work reflects upon the course of her career and pianistic strategies, see Alexander Stefaniak, "Clara Schumann's Interiorities and the Cutting Edge of Popular Pianism," *Journal of the American Musicological Society* 70, no. 3 (Fall 2017): 752–61.
48. *MW*, May 17, 1856, 315; and *The Times*, May 15, 1856, 6.
49. *Athenaeum*, June 21, 1856, 786.
50. *MW*, June 21, 1856, 395; and *The Times*, April 17, 1856, 9.
51. Quoted in Litzmann, *CS*, vol. 2, 409.
52. *MW*, July 5, 1856, 424; and *Athenaeum*, July 5, 1856, 843.
53. Quoted in Litzmann, *CS*, vol. 2, 18.
54. *MW*, May 9, 1857, 295; and June 13, 1857, 380.
55. *Athenaeum*; reprinted in *Punch* and subsequently reprinted in the *MW*, July 11, 1857, 439. So limited was the attention to Clara's 1857 and 1859 tours that subsequent writers describing her English reception seemed unaware of them. For instance, in his dictionary entry on Clara, George Grove wrote that "her reception in this conservative country" in 1856 "was hardly such

as to encourage her to repeat her visit, and many years passed before she returned." *A Dictionary of Music and Musicians* (London: Macmillan, 1879–1890), vol. 3, 422. An 1890 biographical sketch of Clara noted, "In England the popularity of Madame Schumann was of somewhat late growth, for though she appeared here in 1856, and again in 1865, it was not till a few years after that that she took her place in the first rank of popular favourites." Supplement to the *MW*, September 6, 1890, 711.

56. Letter to Brahms of May 1, 1865, *Briefedition* II/3.2, 986; and diary entry of early May (date unspecified), quoted in Litzmann, *CS*, vol. 2, 179–80.
57. Diary entries of April 29 and early May 1865; quoted in Litzmann, *CS*, 179–80. As Janet Ritterman indicates, Joachim had previously told Clara of Grove's enthusiasm for Robert's music, and a letter dated August 26, 1864, from Clara to Grove indicated that the latter's support had helped drive her decision to return to England in 1865; Ritterman, "'Gegensätze, Ecken und sharfe Kanten,'" 246; on this letter, see also Charles L. Graves, *The Life and Letters of Sir George Grove* (London: Macmillan, 1903), 113.
58. Diary entry of early June (date unspecified), quoted in Litzmann, *CS*, vol. 2, 180–181. Despite the warm reception, Clara indicated that the Concert Hall "is a dreadful place for music making" because of less-than-ideal acoustics and distractions from visitors "constantly passing by" (181). On the broadening of bourgeois experience offered by the Crystal Palace and other institutions—both British and German—and Clara's response to such a development, see Klassen, *Clara Schumann: Musik und Öffentlichkeit*, 298–315. On the educational role of music within British exhibitions overall, including those in Scotland and Australia, see Sarah Kirby, *Exhibitions, Music, and the British Empire* (Woodbridge, UK: Boydell Press, 2022), 109–27.
59. Letter of April 1, 1862; Joseph Joachim, *Briefe von und an Joseph Joachim*, ed. Johannes Joachim and Andreas Moser (Berlin: Julius Bard, 1911–1913), vol. 2, 189–90; also quoted in Ritterman, "'Gegensätze, Ecken und sharfe Kanten,'" 249.
60. Diary entry of May 15, 1865; quoted in Litzmann, *CS*, vol. 2, 180.
61. *MW*, May 20, 1865, 303. In a May 1, 1865, letter to Brahms, Clara remarked on more favorable press coverage: "The highest praise occurs in all of the papers (which here are sent to one publishing house)"; *Briefedition*, II/3.2, 986. Clara likely intended *The Musical World*, which frequently reprinted reviews found in other papers. It does seem that Davison tempered his criticism during her 1865 tour, perhaps in deference to her after a six-year absence. The very next year, however, the Schumann debate would only grow more heated with a performance of *Paradise and the Peri* (ten years after its English premiere), a debate in which Grove actively rallied with Davison, as I discuss below.
62. Letter to Elisabeth Werner of September 10, 1865; quoted in Litzmann, *CS*, vol. 2, 239–40.
63. For the years of Clara's visits, see Ritterman, "'Gegensätze, Ecken und sharfe Kanten,'" 257, Table 3. For a study that situates the British tours within the context of Clara's other tours via statistical analysis of her programs, see Reinhard Kopiez, Andreas Lehmann, and Janina Klassen, "Clara Schumann's Collection of Playbills: A Historiometric Analysis of Life-Span Development, Mobility, and Repertoire Canonization," *Poetics* 37 (2009): 50–73.
64. Diary entry of May 11, 1856; quoted in Litzmann, *CS*, vol. 2, 407–408.
65. Diary entries of April 25 and June 20, 1865; quoted in ibid., vol. 3, 179 and 181. On how Ella lost not just Clara but also (eventually) Joachim, the cellist Alfredo Piatti, and the pianist Charles Hallé, see Bashford, *The Pursuit of High Culture*, 238–41.
66. For a list of Clara's Crystal Palace performances and the repertory played, see Ritterman, "'Gegensätze, Ecken und sharfe Kanten,'" 258, Table 5.
67. Letters of February 3, 1869, and February 5, 1871, and diary entry for February/March 1873; quoted in Litzmann, *CS*, vol. 3, 227, 254, and 286.
68. Letter to Hermann Levi of September 24, 1877; quoted in ibid., vol. 3, 363; and *Briefedition*, II/5, 748.
69. Diary entries of February 28, April 9, and April 11, 1881; quoted in Litzmann, *CS*, vol. 3, 417–18.
70. Diary entry of March 3, 1884; quoted in ibid., vol. 3, 452.
71. Reich, *Clara Schumann*, 231. Even before the quintet was completed, Clara wrote in the marriage diary that the "almost completed" work "seems glorious to me—a work filled with strength and freshness!" *Tb*, vol. 2, 249.
72. *Pall Mall Gazette* review; reprinted in *MW*, February 23, 1867, 116.
73. *MW*, reviews of February 13, 1869, 102; and February 10, 1872, 83.
74. *Times* review; reprinted in *MW*, April 1, 1876, 236. *MW* review, March 26, 1881, 193.

75. *Times*, April 5, 1887, 8; quoted in Ellsworth, "'*Caviare* to the Multitude,'" 127. Clara had missed earlier anniversary concerts: the 100th concert in July of 1862 and the 500th concert in January 1875—both non-tour years for Clara.
76. Diary entry of April 1, 1887; quoted in Litzmann, *CS*, vol. 3, 487.
77. *The Graphic*, April 16, 1887, 378.
78. Diary entry of April 4, 1887; quoted in Litzmann, *CS*, vol. 3, 487.
79. *Daily Telegraph*, January 11, 1871; reprinted in *MW*, January 14, 1871, 22.
80. *MW*, reviews of February 10, 1872, 83, and December 14, 1872, 797.
81. *Times* review; reprinted in *MW*, April 1, 1876, 236; and *MW* reviews of April 12, 1879, 224 (emphasis original) and December 19, 1885, 805.
82. Beethoven's "Kreutzer" Sonata, Op. 47, Septet in E-flat Major, Op, 20, and String Quintet in C Major, Op. 29, hold the top three spots; see Ellsworth, "'*Caviare* to the Multitude,'" 135, Table III.
83. Ibid., 133–35, especially Table II.
84. Letter of August 24, 1864; Joachim, *Briefe*, vol. 2, 347.
85. Bashford, *The Pursuit of High Culture*, 231; see also note 51, which indicates that according to Ella's 1864 *Record of the Musical Union*, the piano quartet and quintet were always "the choice of one or other of our principal executants," whether they be Clara, Dannreuther, Alfred Jaëll, Nikolay Rubinstein, or Theodor Leschetizky. Regarding how Ella in 1848 reversed his initially positive opinion of the Piano Quartet, see note 14 above.
86. *Athenaeum*, June 20, 1860, 817.
87. *Illustrated London News*, March 21, 1868, 287; *MW*, reviews of March 7, 1868, 164, and April 11, 1868, 254.
88. *Illustrated London News*, March 21, 1868, 287; and *MW*, April 11, 1868, 254.
89. *MW*, April 9, 1870, 248.
90. *MW*, March 16, 1872, 169.
91. *Daily Telegraph*; reprinted in *MW*, January 25, 1873, 48. Such a review—likely written by Joseph Bennett—illustrates an unusual instance of viewing Schumann's work of the 1840s not against Mendelssohn's output—as had long been the case—but against his earlier output. This reframing first occurred in an essay that Bennett published in 1868 proclaiming support for Schumann; I discuss this essay in more detail below.
92. *Daily Telegraph*; reprinted in *MW*, May 11, 1878, 317.
93. *MW*, reviews of March 26, 1881, 193; and January 20, 1883, 43.
94. *MW* March 26, 1887, 236, likely written by Francis Hueffer, the editor from 1886 to 1888. A follower of Wagnerian ideals, Hueffer did not lump Schumann with the "Music of the Future" but nonetheless seems to have respected his and others' legacies. In an 1889 book, Hueffer—after expressing disappointment in the lack of a notable English school of composition—wrote: "It seems as if Nature, after her effort in creating such men as Schumann, Mendelssohn, Liszt, Wagner, Berlioz, and Verdi, had for a time relapsed into a passive stage." Hueffer, *Half a Century of Music in England, 1837–1887: Essays towards a History* (London: Chapman and Hall, 1889), 27.
95. *MW*, February 23, 1889, 123.
96. For instance, see the *MW* reviews of July 2, 1881, 420; June 21, 1884, 389 (which only notes the performance of "Schumann's favourite pianoforte quartet"); November 13, 1886, 731; and December 15, 1888, 942.
97. *MW*, May 20, 1865, 303; cf. note 61.
98. *The Musical Times*, June 1, 1865, 73.
99. *Daily Telegraph* review; reprinted in *MW*, November 30, 1872, 770; and *MW*, review of December 7, 1872, 783.
100. *MW* February 26, 1859, 136; cf. note 32.
101. *Saturday Review*, March 9, 1867; reprinted in *MW*, March 16, 1867, 159.
102. *MW*, December 7, 1872, 783.
103. *MW*, March 16, 1872, 169; cf. note 90.
104. *Pall Mall Gazette* review; reprinted in *MW*, February 23, 1867, 115. The seeming praise sets up a backhanded comparison with Joachim: while Clara "makes her hearers think of nothing but Schumann" when she performs his music, "she hardly enters with the same loving self-denial" when playing works by other composers. Joachim, however, was a "model artist" who resists "obtrud[ing] his own individuality" into his interpretations. A review the following month similarly remarked that while Clara's performances "are beyond compare in the music

of Schumann," her playing was apparently "open to question in that of other composers" because "her enthusiasm runs away with her." *Saturday Review*, March 9, 1867; reprinted in *MW*, March 16, 1867, 159. The latter criticism occurs with some frequency in reviews of Clara's concerts and hence provides a counterpoint to the Continental—especially Germanic—view of Clara as a "true priest" (Hanslick) who devotes herself to an "objective interpretation of art" (Liszt). On this latter idealization of Clara (and Joachim) as virtuosi devoted to the *Werktreue* concept, and their collaborations with Robert in this regard, see Stefaniak, *Schumann's Virtuosity*, 195–238.

105. *MW*, February 13, 1869, 102.
106. *MW*, February 10, 1872, 83.
107. *Athenaeum*, reviews of February 8, 1868, 221; and March 7, 1868, 364.
108. *Pall Mall Gazette*, March 19, 1866, 897. The review was only signed "Z"—identified as Davison in the memoirs compiled by his son; *From Mendelssohn to Wagner*, 489–96, which reprinted this review. By "Z" Davison likely meant that his commentary was the last word on the matter.
109. Davison cites the oratorio's form, which "does not hang together"; a melodic treatment that "does not flow on in a continuous stream"; and "queer progressions of harmony," among other gripes. *Pall Mall Gazette*, March 19, 1866, 897. For more on Davison's review and related responses, see Marston, "'The most significant musical question of the day,'" 158–60.
110. *Pall Mall Gazette*, letter to the editor dated "Sydenham [where Grove had a residence], March 20, 1866." In response to Davison, Grove humorously signed his letter "A"!
111. Davison must have seen Grove's letter in advance since these remarks conclude his initial review of the oratorio; *Pall Mall Gazette*, March 19, 1866, 898. A few days later, he reprinted Grove's letter in the *Musical World* only to mock it ("A mild thunderbolt!") and to contradict the claim that Schumann's music was growing in popularity; *MW*, April 7, 1866, 223–24. Moreover, instead of divulging his identity as "Z," Davison posed as an outside voice, writing as "Dishleii Petersii," one of several fanciful pseudonyms he began cultivating in the early 1860s; on these aliases, see Davison, *From Mendelssohn to Wagner*, 263–69; Joseph Bennett, *Forty Years of Music: 1865–1905* (London: Methuen, 1908), 222–25; and Reid, *The Music Monster*, 97–99.
112. Bennett, *Forty Years of Music*, 21, 222, and 109.
113. "Robert Schumann," *Pall Mall Gazette*, November 30, 1868, 1751. Bennett also acknowledged "the influence of a gifted wife" for "the manifest difference between [Robert's] first and second periods." For a later instance of Bennett framing the works of the early 1840s against Schumann's earlier period (rather than contrasting them with Mendelssohn's output), see note 91.
114. Bennett, *Forty Years of Music*, 109. Davison's reprinting (slightly abridged) appeared in the *MW*, December 5, 1868, 826.
115. For Grove's response, see Bennett, *Forty Years of Music*, 109–10. According to Frederick George Edwards, Grove "was so taken with the article that he reprinted it in the Crystal Palace programme of December 12, 1868." Edwards, "Schumann's Music in England [Part I]," 718.
116. The papers for which Bennett wrote are described in his *Forty Years of Music*, 27 and 214–32.
117. *The Express* (a Dublin newspaper), May 2, 1869; Edwards reprinted Stanford's piece in his article, "Schumann's Music in England [Part II]," 786–87.
118. *Athenaeum*, March 7, 1868, 364.
119. *Athenaeum*, February 1, 1868, 179.
120. Bledsoe, *Henry Fothergill Chorley*, 272.
121. "Old, New, and No Music," *All the Year Round*, October 22, 1864, 262. The second part of the article appeared in the issue dated November 5, 1864.
122. Graves, *Life and Letters of Sir George Grove*, 170, note 1. For Bledsoe, this anecdote is likely apocryphal, and the reference to the "eighth bar" does stretch credulity; see Bledsoe, *Henry Fothergill Chorley*, 310, note 42. Nevertheless, other people related similar anecdotes. A letter from Ernest G. de Glehn to Henry Saxe Wyndham recalled Chorley's response to Franklin Taylor's desire to play "some new works of Schumann." Chorley apparently "burst out that nothing would induce him to listen to Schumann, and when the rest of those there insisted, he went out and sat in the hall while Taylor played." Quoted in Henry Saxe Wyndham, *Arthur Seymour Sullivan: 1842–1900* (London: Kegan Paul, 1923), 240. Beginning in April 1887, *The Musical World* published a series of "Recollections of Musical Vienna, Forty Years Ago," by "Rip van Winkle, redivius." The installment dated June 11, 1887, focused on Jenny Lind's reception not only in Vienna but also in London, where she participated in the 1856 London

premiere of *Paradise and the Peri* "in the teeth of a desperately hostile press." The author continues by noting that "Henry Chorley took to his heels before any composition by Robert Schumann, so that Joachim (as he told me) once asked him at least to stay and take the trouble and listen before criticizing" (451).
123. *MW*, August 6, 1853, 491.
124. E[duard] Sobolewski, "Reactionary Letters," collected from the *Ostpreussische Zeitung* and reprinted in the *MW*, beginning on January 13 and ending March 31, 1855. The above comment appeared in the issue dated February 24, 1855, 114.
125. *MW*, June 28, 1856, 408; cf. note 23 above.
126. "Musical Party Warfare," from *Dwight's Journal of Music*; reprinted in the *MW*, August 23, 1856, 541.
127. "Liszt and His Followers: Extracts from the Diary of William Saar," *Dwight's Journal of Music*; reprinted in the *MW*, October 17, 1857, 666. While de-emphasizing the Schumann-Wagner link in subsequent years, Davison could not but help imply it again in his 1866 tirade against *Paradise and the Peri*: Schumann's "rambling from one key to another [is] in the style of that redoubtable enemy of keys, Herr Wagner," and when Schumann died, so too did "the hopes of 'Young Germany.'" *Pall Mall Gazette*, March 19, 1866, 897.
128. *MW* reviews of June 30, 1866, 409; and December 14, 1872, 797.
129. *MW*, January 17, 1874, 35. An 1875 Pops performance of the work prompted similar sentiments: "It is a beautiful, though somewhat unequal work"; and if it did not completely please Davison, at least "the lovers of Schumann were treated" to it. *MW*, November 27, 1875, 812.
130. *MW*, reviews of May 20, 1865, 303, and April 9, 1870, 248; cf. notes 61 and 89.
131. *MW*, March 2, 1867, 138.
132. The A-major string quartet represents a notable exception. Even as late as 1885, a writer for the *MW* indicated that it was "seldom played." *MW*, review of March 7, 1885, 154.
133. *MW*, January 17, 1874, 35.
134. Letter to "Herleus le Berbius," January 16, 1882; quoted in Davison, *From Mendelssohn to Wagner*, 340.
135. G[eorge] A. Macfarren, *Musical History Briefly Narrated and Technically Discussed, with a Roll of the Names of Musicians and the Times and Places of their Births and Deaths* (Edinburgh: Adam and Charles Black, 1885), 116.

6
Epilogue

In June 2011, the first movement of Schumann's A-major String Quartet was played in a most unusual space: in the Grand Canyon, near the banks of the Colorado River. This performance occurred as part of a multi-day, music-themed river-rafting trip that was organized by a professional company based in my city of residence, Flagstaff, Arizona.[1] The string quartet consisted of musicians of varying age and experience, from a violinist in the Seattle Symphony (Stephen Bryant), to a free-lance musician and teacher (SueJane Bryant, who played viola), a younger cellist with a recently completed degree from Peabody Conservatory (Hannah Pressley), and an amateur musician (David Koerner, on second violin) who held a professorship in astronomy at my academic institution, Northern Arizona University. The practicalities of such a performance are challenging. Instruments must be carefully packed in multiple layers, from dry bags to a larger airtight cooler, to an even larger box on the "quartet raft." Depending on the time of year, temperatures at the bottom of the canyon can be intense. Since the 2011 trip occurred before the arrival of annual monsoon rains, temperatures soared as high as 110 degrees—an extreme that produced a literally sizzling performance of the Brahms's C-minor string quartet. So dry were the conditions that a crack in the viola was discovered during a layover at Red Wall Cavern, a huge natural amphitheater carved by the Colorado into fossil-laden limestone at river mile 33.3. The amphitheater's size allows multiple expeditions to stop there, one of which had a client who happened to be a luthier from the Midwest; his recommendation to use Gorilla Glue saved the day, and future performances by the ensemble.[2]

If such a trip sounds astonishing, it nonetheless follows a long tradition of music meeting nature in and around the Canyon. John Wesley Powell, who in 1869 became the first person of European descent to successfully navigate and survey the Colorado River system, at times resorted to musical imagery to convey the splendor of the place. "The Grand Canyon is a land of song," he famously declared, a song he located primarily in its sources of water. "Mountains of music swell in the rivers, hills of music billow in the creeks, and meadows of music murmur in the rills that ripple over the rocks. Altogether it is a symphony of multitudinous melodies."[3] Contemporary writers, too, draw on musical metaphors to facilitate appreciation of the canyon and its waterways. Kevin Fedarko has compared the low and narrow Granite Gorge—with its ancient black walls of Vishnu schist (up to two billion years old)—as presenting "nocturnes of deep time." The "pool and drop" nature of the Colorado River meant that earlier generations of river runners had to adopt a "staccato" process whereby long, calm floats were punctuated by scouting episodes to determine how best to traverse rapids of "unholy chaos."[4] The Grand Canyon has also long served as a space for music making itself, with Indigenous songs and more recently the music of other traditions echoing on its rims and below, sometimes in more comfortable relationships, other times less so. In a 2016 performance that coincided with the centennial of the U.S. National Park Service, *Puhutawi*, or "new traditional songs," by Hopi musicians served, as Trevor Reed has recently argued, not merely as aesthetic objects but also as a "source of sonic sovereignty" over ancestral lands now controlled by the Park Service and by others.[5] This performance was itself sponsored by the Grand Canyon Music Festival, an institution that brings together musicians locally and from around the world, while also sponsoring outreach programs, including the Native American Composer Apprentice Project (NACAP). (Diné composer Raven Chacon—a Pulitzer Prize winner and recent awardee of the MacArthur Fellowship—is one of several teachers there.)[6] The origin of the Music Festival itself has roots in a common form of music making in and around the canyon: impromptu performances, including in spaces that offer new acoustical experiences. On a five day, rim-to-rim-and-back trip in 1983, one of the Festival's would-be founders was discovered by a park ranger playing her flute "in the washed out trunk of a tree," and was asked if she and her partner (who played harmonica) would give a concert that night in a campground below the north rim.[7] Tom Sheeley—a recently deceased colleague of mine and a decades-long guitarist and teacher, formidable hiker, and lover of the canyon (including experience as a river runner)—described striking acoustical properties inside the Grand Canyon. "There is a [side] canyon about 20 miles downriver" (and a "painstaking" one-mile hike upward), "that has the most remarkable acoustics I have ever experienced. The sound actually goes up and swirls and does not so much reverberate as it actually seems to get louder." He also noted that "the acoustics are better in the sandstones [than in] limestone [where] the sound is hard and tight and sharp."[8]

Sheeley told me that he was on the "ground floor" of themed river trips when they began in the mid-1970s, some arising from unofficial trips he had made with his "gee-tar" in the few years prior. Now one could take a trip with various "consultants" who would enlighten clients about the history of the Southwest in general, and the river and canyon in particular, and—for music-themed trips—provide information about compositions performed.[9] Such experiences often meld the familiar with the unfamiliar for all participants, though what is new versus old is fluid, including on trips that are specifically music-themed. As described by Hunter Noack—founder of the series "In a Landscape: Classical Music in the Wild," replacing the concert hall with stunning outdoor spaces can get "classical music lovers" to explore landscapes "they otherwise might not," while for hikers, campers, hunters, and other outdoor enthusiasts, Classical music may provide a new lens through which to experience familiar outdoor haunts.[10] For the 2011 rafting trip, Koerner remembers the quartet performances as especially "transformative" for the seasoned river runners: "by the time it's over, they all go back home and start listening to classical music, . . . and they compete to be able to do this trip again." If a get-together occurs before a planned new trip—with musicians rehearsing their music—the runners "listen intently" and "make requests, based on what they've heard on prior trips." Koerner also remembers earlier quartet trips organized by Steve Bryant as so impressing one of the river guides—who also worked for the company—that she subsequently got her own son involved in cello lessons; he is now pursuing a music major in performance. As for Koerner himself, the expedition proved life changing. A mild heart attack just months before prompted a new set of priorities, with the river trip helping to "kickstart my return to music." (As a youth, he studied piano intensively—even participating in prestigious piano competitions—while also studying violin with the same teacher who taught his friend, violinist Steve Bryant.) Approaching retirement age, Koerner began studying viola, subsequently earning a master's degree in violin/viola performance, establishing his own string quartet, and pursuing more intensive piano studies and performance. In such stories, the river—and the musical experiences it enabled—provided a pathway not only for bringing together diverse people, but also for reframing life experiences, with new contact points made between past, present, and future.[11]

The performance of a Schumann string quartet on the banks of the Colorado River is attractive for various reasons, not least because it provides an alternative framework in which to hear Schumann's music—a broad theme of this book. As previous chapters have shown, Schumann's own music productively accommodates reframing, whether by hearing the chamber works against the models of his forebears or against the output of his youth, or by approaching these works from new lenses, be they historical, cultural, biographical, literary, and the like. The squaring of new against old, of the familiar with the unfamiliar—so central to Schumann's view of history—may even play out within musical processes themselves, as we have seen. For instance, in the finales of the A-major quartet and piano quintet, thematic familiarity (arising from appearances of the refrain) resides within ever-changing harmonic landscapes (the result of non-tonic returns amid a sojourn through numerous keys)—a situation that, when aligned with the *verbunkos* idiom, evokes the Gypsy wanderer trope. As described at the end of Chapter 2, an August 1842 anecdote provides an analogous image of Schumann himself as romantic wanderer—a composer-centric perspective that is turned inside-out in the Grand Canyon performance. After Robert and Clara hiked two small mountains in two days—the second notably higher than the first—Robert used the experience of gazing down on the day's previous summit as a metaphor for a composer's artistic development. (In a sense, this anecdote provides a topological realization of a comment he made as a youth, namely, that the "future should be a higher echo of the past.")[12] The 2011 Grand Canyon performance provides a compelling inversional image. For one, it replaces the notion of mountainous ascent with canyon descent. Indeed, the performance of the A-major quartet—a work itself reflecting various layered histories—quite literally presented lower "echoes of the past" as it resonated against rock strata of far older geologic ages. In a way, the Colorado River—which facilitated this quartet performance—itself serves as a "great stream of time," sometimes progressing into ever-older basement rocks at certain points of the trip, but also encountering newer layers at other points.[13] In knitting together different points of time, the river thus makes a fitting—if surprising—vehicle for performances that bring together the music of "old" composers with newer audiences in the present day. For another, hearing Schuman in such an unusual setting inevitably highlights diverse, listener-centric experiences: those of the performers (amateur or otherwise), clients (including "accidental" listeners along with paying clients), and river guides, some of whom used their experience of the musical and natural environments to create new ways forward—another bridging of different time spans. We've already seen how figures in other artistic disciplines have found inspiration in listening to Schumann, including a modern-day Dutch choreographer who used the same string quartet as a vehicle for embodying his rethinking of balletic norms. We've also heard from many other listeners, whether in Schumann's day or beyond, and collectively their perspectives have in turn provided me fruitful points of reference for developing my own aural frameworks for the Leipzig chamber repertory. And isn't the ability to accommodate new and flexible perspectives—which, for me, Schumann's music especially facilitates—a mechanism for allowing musical works to achieve some degree of continuity in that "great" but human-scaled "stream of time"? (Schumann also found meaning in water imagery.) In his criticism, Schumann frequently offered imaginative interpretations of others' music, and his 1849 exchange with Franz Liszt made clear not only the "variety of views" reflected within his own works, but also the importance of listeners who adopt a generous and creative mindset toward them. The coursing of time will yet draw us into ever more diverse contexts in which to re-hear the music of past composers.[14]

Notes

1. Canyon Explorations, now Canyon Explorations/Expeditions: Grand Canyon Oar and Paddle Trips. For information on string-quartet expeditions and other themed trips, see "Specialty Trips," https://canyonexplorations.com/trip-types/#specialtytrips (accessed July 22, 2023).
2. My heartfelt thanks to David Koerner for sharing details of this trip.
3. John Wesley Powell, *Report on the Exploration of the Colorado River of the West and Its Tributaries*, 1875; reprinted as *The Exploration of the Colorado River and Its Canyons* (New York: Penguin, 1987), 394.
4. Kevin Fedarko, *The Emerald Mile: The Epic Story of the Fastest Ride in History through the Heart of the Grand Canyon* (New York: Scribner, 2014), 26 and 104–7.
5. Trevor Reed, "Sonic Sovereignty: Performing Hopi Authority in Öngtupqa," *Journal of the Society for American Music* 13 (2019): 1.
6. "Native American Composer Apprentice Project," Grand Canyon Music Festival Official Website, https://grandcanyonmusicfest.org/native-american-composer-apprentice-project/ (accessed July 22, 2023).
7. "History," Grand Canyon Music Festival Official Website, https://grandcanyonmusicfest.org/history/ (accessed July 22, 2023).
8. Sheeley, personal communication, February 2014. Sheeley was the guitar instructor at Northern Arizona University for more than 45 years.
9. Ibid. According to Sheeley, after about two or three years of less formal river trips, Pat Conley—the owner of a now-defunct company, Wilderness World—"started putting themes together with various 'consultants'—David Lavender on river history; Edward Abbey on Southwest history in general; Ann Zwinger on literature and history; me on music. By the time I got the courage to row in Grand Canyon, my first training trip had a string quartet from the LA Phil along. [Conley's company also] had started a regular 'music trip.'"
10. "Classical Pianist Reimagines Concert Hall by Taking Music to the Great Outdoors," aired on *CBS This Morning*, August 19, 2021. Available on YouTube, https://www.youtube.com/watch?v=rctC0MkSg2Y (accessed July 22, 2023). Noack comments at 2:47–3:08.
11. Guided trips on the Colorado River seem to have provided somewhat analogous experiences for present-day Hopi people. As described by Trevor Reed (whose ancestry stems from both

Hopi and settler worlds), the Hopi had long performed "overland pilgrimages" that involved "walk[ing] the seventy-plus miles from the Hopi village of Orayvi through the desert to Öngtupqa" (the Hopi name for the Grand Canyon, which they view as their place of origin). Such walking pilgrimages "ended in the 1920s" when the federal government began settling Diné people on the Hopi Reservation (established in 1882), ultimately granting the Navajo Nation sovereign status over lands on which Hopi pilgrimages had occurred. Recently, however, some Hopi people have taken advantage of professionally guided river trips "to re-embody our territories and re-establish relations with actors within these territories, and with one another." For more, see Reed, "Sonic Sovereignty: Performing Hopi Authority in Öngtupqa," 514–15, note 32; 517–19; and 521–22. Indigenous-owned river-rafting companies have also appeared in recent years. See "Colorado River Rafting" by the Hualapai River Runners, Grand Canyon West, https://grandcanyonwest.com/things-to-do/colorado-river-rafting/ (accessed January 16, 2024), and "Ancient Wayves River and Hiking Adventures," https://www.tourancientwayves.com/ (accessed August 10, 2023).
12. Entry of June 5–6, 1834. *Tb*, vol. 1, 304.
13. River-level rocks vary between a few hundred million years old (e.g., the Kaibab Limestone at Lees Ferry, where river trips put in) to 1.2 to 2 billion years old (e.g., the non-layered igneous and metamorphic basement rocks near Phantom Ranch).
14. On the 1849 episode, see the conclusion of Chapter 1.

Bibliography

Nineteenth-Century Journals and Newspapers

Allgemeine musikalische Zeitung
All the Year Round
The Athenaeum
Caecilia
The Daily Telegraph
Dwight's Journal of Music
The Express
The Graphic
The Harmonicon
The Illustrated London News
The Musical Examiner
The Musical Journal
The Musical Times
The Musical World
Neue Berliner Musikzeitung
Neue Zeitschrift für Musik
Ostpreussische Zeitung
Pall Mall Gazette
Repertorium für Musik
Saturday Review
The Times (London)

Video Recordings and Websites

Ancient Wayves River and Hiking Adventures. Official website of Indigenous-owned company providing guided trips for the San Juan River and Bears Ears National Monument. https://www.tourancientwayves.com/. Accessed August 10, 2023.

Anthony Dowell: All the Superlatives. Videorecording, 2 cassettes. *BBC* documentary directed by Colin Nears and produced by Barrie Gavin. Made for the Omnibus series and first broadcast on October 21, 1976, on *BBC One London*.

"Classical Pianist Reimagines Concert Hall by Taking Music to the Great Outdoors." Aired on *CBS This Morning*, August 19, 2021. Available on YouTube. https://www.youtube.com/watch?v=rctC0MkSg2Y. Accessed July 22, 2023.

"Colorado River Rafting." Official website for the Hualapai River Runners, who provide shorter guided trips on the Colorado River. Grand Canyon West. https://grandcanyonwest.com/things-to-do/colorado-river-rafting/. Accessed January 16, 2024.

"Four Schumann Pieces." Performance Database, Royal Opera House: Collections Online. https://www.rohcollections.org.uk/work.aspx?work = 156&row = 40&letter = F&genre = All&.Accessed July 22, 2023.

Grand Canyon Music Festival. Official website. https://grandcanyonmusicfest.org/. Accessed July 22, 2023.

Hans van Manen. DVD, 2 discs containing dances by and interviews with Hans van Manen (English subtitles available). Performances by Het National Ballet and Nederlands Dans Theater. [Leipzig]: Arthaus Musik, 2007.

Hans van Manen Festival: Dutch National Ballet and Guests. DVD containing dances by Van Manen and interviews with him and performers (portions in English and subtitles available). Produced, directed, and edited by Altin Kaftira, Adrienne Liron, and Jeff Tudor. West Long Branch, NJ: Kultur, 2007, 2008.

Hans van Manen Foundation. Official website maintained by the Dutch National Opera and Ballet. Presents a survey of Van Manen's career, and an updated catalogue of his ballets with related photographs and videos, among other items. Available in both Dutch and English. https://www.operaballet.nl/ballet/hans-van-manen-foundation. Accessed July 22, 2023.

Hans van Manen: Master of Movement. DVD, 6 discs, containing dances by and interviews with Hans van Manen. Compiled and distributed by the Stichting Hans van Manen. [IJsselstein, Netherlands]: Cobra Records, 2007.

"Publications/Releases." *The Schumann Network.* Information on finding Schumann-related publications since 1856, including published writings, musical editions, film and stage productions, recordings, and image-related content. Funded by the German Federal Government Commissioner for Culture and Media. https://www.schumann-portal.de/veroeffentlichungen-en.html. Accessed July 22, 2023.

"Robert Schumann, Soundtrack." *Internet Movie Database (IMDb).* https://www.imdb.com/filmosearch/?sort=year&explore=title_type&role=nm0006281&ref_=nmbio_ql_flmg_1.Accessed September 20, 2022.

The Royal Ballet Salutes the USA. July 22, 1978, broadcast of a Royal Ballet performance, hosted by Gene Kelly, telecast live by satellite on WNEW-TV/Channel 5, New York. Videorecording, 3 cassettes. Directed by Colin Nears, Bob Lockyer, and Brian Large, and produced by Brian Large. *BBC* production made in association with *Metromedia Television*, New York, 1978.

Six Ballets: The Art of Hans van Manen. DVD, 2 discs, containing dances by and interviews with Hans van Manen (English subtitles available). Directed by Wilbert Bank and Jellie Dekker. Performances by the Nederlands Dans Theater and Het Nationale Ballet. Halle: Arthaus, 2016.

Steve [last name anonymous]. "For Shoemann Peaces [sic]." *You Dance Funny, So Does Me.* Blog entry, posted January 31, 2011. http://youdancefunny.wordpress.com/2011/01/. Accessed August 6, 2022.

Primary and Secondary Writings

Aalten, Anna, and Mirjam van der Linden. "The Netherlands: The Dutch Don't Dance." In *Europe Dancing: Perspectives on Theatre Dance and Cultural Identity*, edited by Andrée Grau and Stephanie Jordan, 119–43. New York: Routledge, 2000.

Abraham, Gerald. "Robert Schumann." In *The New Grove's Dictionary of Music and Musicians*, edited by Stanley Sadie, vol. 16, 831–70. London: Macmillan, 1980.

Ambros, August Wilhelm. "Die neu-romantische Musik." In *Culturhistorische Bilder aus dem Musikleben der Gegenwart*, 51–104. 2nd ed. Leipzig: H. Matthes, 1865.

Applegate, Celia. "How German Is It? Nationalism and the Idea of Serious Music in the Early Nineteenth Century." *19th-Century Music* 21 (1998): 274–96.

Auzolle, Cécile. "Quand les Ballets Russes rêvent l'Allemagne romantique: *Carnaval* op. 9 de Schumann à Fokine." *Ostinato rigore: Revue international d'études musicales* 22 (2004): 203–18.

Balanchine, George, and Francis Mason. *Balanchine's Complete Stories of the Great Ballets.* Rev. ed. Garden City, NY: Doubleday, 1977.

Barham, Jeremy. "Recurring Dreams and Moving Images: The Cinematic Appropriation of Schumann's Op. 15, No. 7." *19th-Century Music* 34 (Spring 2011): 271–301.

Barthes, Roland. "Loving Schumann." In Barthes, *The Responsibility of Forms: Critical Essays on Music, Art, and Representation*, 293–98. Translated by Richard Howard. New York: Hill & Wang, 1985.

Bashford, Christina. "John Ella and the Musical Union." In *Music and British Culture, 1785–1984: Essays in Honour of Cyril Ehrlich*, edited by Christina Bashford and Leanne Langley, 193–214. Oxford: Oxford University Press, 2000.

Bashford, Christina. "Not Just G: Towards a History of the Programme Note." In *George Grove: Music and Victorian Culture*, edited by Michael Musgrave, 115–42. Basingstoke, UK: Macmillan, 2003; New York: Palgrave Macmillan, 2003.

Bashford, Christina. "Public Chamber-Music Concerts in London, 1835–50: Aspects of History, Repertory and Reception." 2 vols. PhD diss., University of London, King's College, 1996.

Bashford, Christina. *The Pursuit of High Culture: John Ella and Chamber Music in Victorian England*. Woodbridge, UK: Boydell Press, 2007.

Beaumont, Cyril. *Complete Book of Ballets: A Guide to the Principal Ballets of the Nineteenth and Twentieth Centuries*. Garden City, NY: Garden City Publishing, 1941.

Bellman, Jonathan. "The Hungarian Gypsies and the Poetics of Exclusion." In *The Exotic in Western Music*, edited by Jonathan Bellman, 74–103. Boston: Northeastern University Press, 1998.

Bellman, Jonathan. *The* style hongrois *in the Music of Western Europe*. Boston: Northeastern University Press, 1993.

Bennett, Joseph. *Forty Years of Music: 1865–1905*. London: Methuen, 1908.

Berger, Melvin. *Guide to Chamber Music*. New York: Dodd, Mead, 1985.

Bischoff, Bodo. *Monument für Beethoven: Die Entwicklung der Beethoven-Rezeption Robert Schumanns*. Cologne: Dohr, 1994.

Biss, Jonathan. *A Pianist under the Influence*. E-book [2012]; reissued 2018. Available at Amazon.com. https://www.amazon.com/Pianist-Under-Influence-Jonathan-Biss-ebook/dp/B07BZRB5RL/ref = sr_1_1?keywords = Jonathan+Biss+a + pianist+under + the+ influence&qid = 1639763359&sr = 8–1. Accessed July 22, 2023.

Bledsoe, Robert Terrell. *Henry Fothergill Chorley: Victorian Journalist*. Aldershot, UK: Ashgate, 1998.

Braunschweig, Michelle Elizabeth Yael. "Biographical Listening: Intimacy, Madness, and the Music of Robert Schumann." PhD diss., University of California, Berkeley, 2013.

Brendel, Franz. "Robert Schumann, with Reference to Mendelssohn-Bartholdy and the Development of Modern Music in General (1845)." Translated by Jürgen Thym. In *Schumann and His World*, edited by R. Larry Todd, 317–37. Princeton, NJ: Princeton University Press, 1994.

Brittan, Francesca. "Fairyology, Entomology, and the *Scherzo fantastique*." In Brittan, *Music and Fantasy in the Age of Berlioz*, 268–325. Cambridge and New York: Cambridge University Press, 2017.

Brown, Ismene. "On Their Toes! Birmingham Royal Ballet, Birminghan Hippodrome [reviewing a performance of Van Manen's 1971 *Grosse Fuge*, among other works]." *The Arts Desk*, online journalism website, theartsdesk.com, June 16, 2010. https://theartsdesk.com/dance/their-toes-birmingham-royal-ballet-birmingham-hippodrome. Accessed July 22, 2023.

Brown, Julie Hedges. "'A Higher Echo of the Past': Schumann's 1842 Chamber Music and the Rethinking of Classical Form." PhD diss., Yale University, 2000.

Brown, Julie Hedges. "Higher Echoes of the Past in the Finale of Schumann's 1842 Piano Quartet." *Journal of the American Musicological Society* 57 (2004): 511–64.

Brown, Julie Hedges. "Schumann and the *style hongrois*." In *Rethinking Schumann*, edited by Roe-Min Kok and Laura Tunbridge, 265–99. Oxford: Oxford University Press, 2011.

Brown, Julie Hedges. "Study, Copy, and Conquer: Schumann's 1842 Chamber Music and the Recasting of Classical Sonata Form." *Journal of Musicology* 30 (2013): 369–423.

Brown, Kathy H. *Lotte Lehmann in America: Her Legacy as Artist Teacher, with Commentaries from Her Master Classes.* Missoula, MT: College Music Society, 2012.

Caplin, William. *Classical Form: A Theory of Formal Functions for the Instrumental Music of Haydn, Mozart, and Beethoven.* New York and Oxford: Oxford University Press, 1998.

Carner, Mosco. "Some Observations on Schumann's Sonata Form." *Musical Times* 76 (1935): 884–86.

Carner, Mosco. "Studien zur Sonatenform." PhD diss., University of Vienna, 1928.

Chissell, Joan. *Schumann.* 2nd ed. London: Dent, 1967.

Chorley, Henry Fothergill. *Modern German Music: Recollections and Criticisms.* 1854. Reprint, 2 vols. Cambridge: Cambridge University Press, 2009.

Chorley, Henry Fothergill. *Music and Manners in France and Germany: A Series of Travelling Sketches of Art and Society.* 1841. Reprint, 3 vols. Cambridge: Cambridge University Press, 2009.

Cooper, Michael. *Mendelssohn, Goethe, and the Walpurgis Night: The Heathen Muse in European Culture, 1700–1850.* Rochester, NY: University of Rochester Press, 2007.

Dahlhaus, Carl. *Nineteenth-Century Music.* Translated by J. Bradford Robinson. Berkeley: University of California Press, 1989.

Daverio, John. "'Beautiful and Abstruse Conversations': The Chamber Music of Robert Schumann." In *Nineteenth-Century Chamber Music*, edited by Stephen E. Hefling, 208–41. New York: Schirmer, 1998.

Daverio, John. *Crossing Paths: Schubert, Schumann, and Brahms.* Oxford and New York: Oxford University Press, 2002.

Daverio, John. *Nineteenth-Century Music and the German Romantic Ideology.* New York: Macmillan, 1993.

Daverio, John. *Robert Schumann, Herald of a "New Poetic Age."* Oxford and New York: Oxford University Press, 1997.

Davies, Fanny. "Schumann, Robert Alexander." In *Cobbett's Cyclopedic Survey of Chamber Music*, edited by Walter Wilson Cobbett, 368–94. London: Oxford University Press, 1930.

Davison, Henry. *From Mendelssohn to Wagner: Being the Memoirs of J. W. Davison, Forty Years Music Critic of "The Times."* London: William Reeves, 1912.

Desai, Boman. *Trio: A Novel Biography of the Schumanns and Brahms.* Bloomington, IN: AuthorHouse, 2015.

Dickinson, A. E. F. "The Chamber Music." In *Schumann: A Symposium*, edited by Gerald Abraham, 138–75. London: Oxford University Press, 1952.

Dorfmüller, Kurt, Norbert Gertsch, and Julia Ronge. *Ludwig van Beethoven: Thematisch-bibliographisches Werkverzeichnis.* 2 vols. Munich: G. Henle Verlag, 2014.

Druick, Douglas, and Michel Hoog, eds. *Fantin-Latour: Exhibition.* Ottowa: National Gallery of Canada; National Museums of Canada, 1983.

Eatock, Colin Timothy. *Mendelssohn and Victorian England.* Aldershot, UK, and Burlington, VT: Ashgate, 2009.

E[dwards], F[rederick] G[eorge]. "Schumann's Music in England [Parts I and II]." *The Musical Times* 46, no. 753 (November 1, 1905): 716–18; and 46, no. 754 (December 1, 1905): 786–87.

Ellsworth, Therese. "'Caviare to the Multitude': Instrumental Music at the Monday Popular Concerts, London." In *Instrumental Music and the Industrial Revolution*, edited by Roberto Illiano and Luca Sala, 121–42. Ad Parnassum Studies 5. Bologna: UT Orpheus, 2010.

Ellsworth, Therese. "'Music Was Poured by Perfect Ministrants': Joseph Joachim at the Monday Popular Concerts, London." In *The Creative Worlds of Joseph Joachim*, edited by Valerie Woodring Goertzen and Robert Whitehouse Eshbach, 129–44. Woodbridge, UK: Boydell Press, 2021.

Everett, William. *British Piano Trios, Quartets, and Quintets, 1850–1950: A Checklist.* Warren, MI: Harmonie Park Press, 2000.

Fedarko, Kevin. *The Emerald Mile: The Epic Story of the Fastest Ride in History through the Heart of the Grand Canyon*. New York: Scribner, 2014.
Ferris, David. "The Fictional Lives of the Schumanns." In *Rethinking Schumann*, edited by Roe-Min Kok and Laura Tunbridge, 357–94. Oxford and New York: Oxford University Press, 2011.
Ferris, David. "Schumann and the Myth of Madness." *Nineteenth-Century Music Review* 18, no. 3 (2021): 389–426.
Finson, Jon. *Robert Schumann and the Study of Orchestral Composition: The Genesis of the First Symphony, Op. 38*. Oxford: Clarendon Press, 1989.
Fisher, Jennifer, and Anthony Shay, eds. "Introduction." In *When Men Dance: Choreographing Masculinities across Borders*, edited by Jennifer Fisher and Anthony Shay, 3–27. Oxford and New York: Oxford University Press, 2009.
Froidefond, Marik. "'C'est encore du roman, ça': Fonctions des citations schumanniennes dans *Mademoiselle Else* d'Arthur Schnitzler." In *Musique et roman*, edited by Aude Locatelli and Yves Landerouin, 153–69. Paris: Le Manuscrit, 2008.
Fuller-Maitland, J. A. *Schumann's Concerted Chamber Music*. London: Oxford University Press, Humphrey Milford, 1929.
Funke, Klaus. *Am Ende war alles Musik*. Leipzig: Faber & Faber, 2005.
Galloway, Janice. *Clara*. London: Jonathan Cape, 2002.
Garafola, Lynn. "Reconfiguring the Sexes." In *The Ballet Russes and Its World*, edited by Lynn Garafola and Nancy Van Norman Baer, 245–68. New Haven, CT: Yale University Press, 1999.
Gardner, John. "The Chamber Music." In *Robert Schumann: The Man and His Music*, edited by Alan Walker, 200–40. London: Barrie and Jenkins, 1972.
Gingerich, John M. *Schubert's Beethoven Project*. Cambridge: Cambridge University Press, 2014.
Goehr, Lydia. *The Imaginary Museum of Musical Works: An Essay in the Philosophy of Music*. Rev. ed. Oxford and New York: Oxford University Press, 2007.
Gramit, David. *Cultivating Music: The Aspirations, Interests, and Limits of German Musical Culture, 1770–1848*. Berkeley: University of California Press, 2002.
Gramit, David. "Schubert's Wanderers and the Autonomous Lied." *Journal of Musicological Research* 14 (1995): 147–68.
Graves, Charles L. *The Life and Letters of Sir George Grove*. London: Macmillan, 1903.
Grieg, Edvard. "Robert Schumann (1893)." In *Edvard Grieg: Diaries, Articles, Speeches*, edited and translated by Finn Benestad and William H. Halverson, 255–74. Columbus, OH: Peer Gynt Press, 2001.
Grimes, Nicole. "Formal Innovation and Virtuosity in Clara Schumann's Piano Trio in G Minor, Op. 17." In *Clara Schumann Studies*, edited by Joe Davies, 139–64. Cambridge: Cambridge University Press, 2022.
Grosse, Karl. *Geschichte der Stadt Leipzig, von der ältesten bis auf die neueste Zeit*. 2 vols. Leipzig: Verlag von C. B. Polet, 1839–1842.
Grove, George. *A Dictionary of Music and Musicians*. 4 vols. London: Macmillan, 1879–1890.
Gruen, John. "Antoinette Sibley and Anthony Dowell." In *The Private World of Ballet*, 117–24. New York: Viking Press, 1975.
Gülke, Peter. "Mutmaßungen über waghalsiges Komponieren: Robert Schumanns Streichquartette op. 41." In *Ereignis und Exegese: Musikalische Interpretation—Interpretation der Musik*, edited by Camilla Bork, 412–19. Schliengen: Edition Argus, 2012.
Hanslick, Eduard. "Dr. Robert Schumann [1846]." In *Sämtliche Schriften: Historisch-kritische Ausgabe*, edited by Dietmar Strauss, vol. 1, no. 1, *Aufsätze und Rezensionen, 1844–1848*, 104–6. Vienna: Bohlau, 1993.
Hanslick, Eduard. "Robert Schumann in Endenich (1899)." Translated by Susan Gillespie. In *Schumann and His World*, edited by R. Larry Todd, 268–87. Princeton, NJ: Princeton University Press, 1994.

Härtling, Peter. *Schumanns Schatten: Variation über mehrere Personen*. Cologne: Kiepenheuer & Witsch, 1996.
Heisler, Wayne. "Choreographing Schumann." In *Rethinking Schumann*, edited by Roe-Min Kok and Laura Tunbridge, 329–56. Oxford and New York: Oxford University Press, 2011.
Heller, Berndt. "Spiel beim Abschied leise Schumann: Zur Musik der Stummfilmzeit." In *Einblicke, Ausblicke: Gedanken, Erinnerungen, Deutungen zu musikalischen Phänomenen*, edited by Axel Michael Sallowsky, 37–41. Berlin: Robert Lienau, 1985.
Hepokoski, James, and Warren Darcy. *Elements of Sonata Theory: Norms, Types, and Deformations in the Late-Eighteenth-Century Sonata*. Oxford and New York: Oxford University Press, 2006.
Hodgins, Paul. *Relationships between Score and Choreography in Twentieth-Century Dance: Music, Movement and Metaphor*. Lewiston, NY: Edwin Mellen Press, 1992.
Hoeckner, Berthold. *Programming the Absolute: Nineteenth-Century German Music and the Hermeneutics of the Moment*. Princeton, NJ: Princeton University Press, 2002.
Hoeckner, Berthold. "Schumann and Romantic Distance." *Journal of the American Musicological Society* 50 (Spring 1997): 55–132.
Hueffer, Francis. *Half a Century of Music in England, 1837–1887: Essays towards a History*. London: Chapman and Hall, 1889.
Hughes, Meirion. *The English Musical Renaissance and the Press, 1850–1914: Watchmen of Music*. London and New York: Routledge, 2002.
Irving, John. "The Invention of Tradition." In *The Cambridge History of Nineteenth-Century Music*, edited by Jim Samson, 178–212. Cambridge: Cambridge University Press, 2002.
Jensen, Eric. *Schumann*. The Master Musicians. Oxford and New York: Oxford University Press, 2001.
Jensen, Jill Nunes. "Transcending Gender in Ballet's LINES." In *When Men Dance: Choreographing Masculinities across Borders*, edited by Jennifer Fisher and Anthony Shay, 118–45. Oxford and New York: Oxford University Press, 2009.
Joachim, Joseph. *Briefe von und an Joseph Joachim*. 3 vols. Edited by Johannes Joachim and Andreas Moser. Berlin: Julius Bard, 1911–1913.
Jonkers, Marc, Pieter Kottman, Jhim Lamoree, and Divera Stavenuiter, eds. *Hans van Manen: Fotos-Feiten-Meningen/Hans van Manen: Photographs-Facts-Opinions*. Amsterdam: Nederlands Instituut voor de Dans, 1992.
Jordan, Stephanie. "Choreomusicology and Dance Studies: From Beginning to End?" In *The Routledge Companion to Dance Studies*, edited by Helen Thomas and Stacey Prickett, 141–56. Abingdon, UK, and New York City: Routledge, 2020.
Jordan, Stephanie. "Introduction." Special issue devoted to dance-music analysis. *Journal of Music Theory* 65 (April 2021): 3–9.
Jordan, Stephanie. *Moving Music: Dialogues with Music in Twentieth-Century Ballet*. London: Dance Books, 2000.
Jordan, Stephanie. "Musical/Choreographic Discourse: Method, Music Theory, and Meaning." In *Moving Words: Re-writing Dance*, edited by Gay Morris, 15–28. London and New York: Routledge, 1996.
Kaminsky, Peter. "Aspects of Harmony, Rhythm, and Form in Schumann's 'Papillons,' 'Carnaval,' and 'Davidsbundlertänze.'" PhD diss., University of Rochester, Eastman School of Music, 1990.
Kerman, Joseph. *The Beethoven Quartets*. New York and London: Norton, 1979.
Kirby, Sarah. *Exhibitions, Music and the British Empire*. Woodbridge, UK: Boydell Press, 2022.
Klassen, Janina. *Clara Schumann: Musik und Öffentlichkeit*. Cologne: Böhlau Verlag, 2009.
Koegler, Horst. "Dancing in the Closet: The Coming Out of Ballet." *Dance Chronicle* 18, no. 2 (1995): 231–38.
Kohlhase, Hans. *Die Kammermusik Robert Schumanns. Stilistische Untersuchungen*. 3 vols. PhD diss., University of Hamburg, 1978; published as no. 19 in the series Hamburger Beiträge zur Musikwissenschaft, edited by Constantin Floros. Hamburg: Verlag der Musikalienhandlung Wagner, 1979.

Kohlhase, Hans. "Kritischer Bericht/Critical Report." In *Three Quartets for Two Violins, Viola and Violoncello op. 41*, edited by Hans Kohlhase, 131–301. Series II, Group I, Vol. 1 of *Robert Schumann: New Edition of the Complete Works*. Mainz: Schott, 2006.

Kohlhase, Hans. "Robert Schumanns Klavierquintett op. 44: Eine semantische Studie." In *Musik-Konzepte Sonderband: Robert Schumann, I, November 1981*, edited by Heinz-Klaus Metzger and Rainer Riehn, 148–73. Munich: Johannesdruck Hans Pribil, 1981.

Komar, Arthur, ed. *Dichterliebe: An Authoritative Score, Historical Background, Essays in Analysis, Views and Comments*. Norton Critical Scores. New York: W. W. Norton, 1971.

Kopiez, Reinhard, Andreas Lehmann, and Janina Klassen. "Clara Schumann's Collection of Playbills: A Historiometric Analysis of Life-Span Development, Mobility, and Repertoire Canonization." *Poetics* 37 (2009): 50–73.

Koßmaly, Carl. "On Robert Schumann's Piano Compositions (1844)." Translated by Susan Gillespie. In *Schumann and His World*, edited by R. Larry Todd, 303–16. Princeton, NJ: Princeton University Press, 1994.

Kottman, Pieter. "Dat rokje, dat moest/That Skirt Was Essential." In *Hans van Manen: Fotos-Feiten-Meningen/Hans van Manen: Photographs-Facts-Opinions*, edited by Marc Jonkers, Pieter Kottman, Jhim Lamoree, and Divera Stavenuiter, 31–41. Amsterdam: Nederlands Instituut voor de Dans, 1992.

Krebs, Harald. *Fantasy Pieces: Metrical Dissonance in the Music of Robert Schumann*. New York and Oxford: Oxford University Press, 1999.

Krummacher, Friedhelm. "Reception and Analysis: On the Brahms Quartets, Op. 51, Nos. 1 and 2." *19th-Century Music* 18 (1994): 24–45.

Landis, J. D. *Longing*. New York: Harcourt, 2000.

Lester, Joel. "Robert Schumann and Sonata Forms." *19th-Century Music* 18 (1995): 189–210.

Liszt, Franz. *Franz Liszt: Selected Letters*. Translated and edited by Adrian Williams. Oxford: Clarendon Press, 1998.

Litzmann, Berthold. *Clara Schumann: Ein Künstlerleben nach Tagebüchern und Briefen*. 3 vols. Leipzig: Breitkopf & Härtel, 1902–1908.

Lockwood, Lewis. *Beethoven: Studies in the Creative Process*. Cambridge, MA: Harvard University Press, 1992.

Lockwood, Lewis. "Beethoven's Emergence from Crisis: The Cello Sonatas of Op. 102 (1815)." *Journal of Musicology* 16 (1998): 301–22.

Lott, Marie Sumner. *The Social Worlds of Nineteenth-Century Chamber Music: Composers, Consumers, Communities*. Urbana: University of Illinois Press, 2015.

Loya, Shay. *Liszt's Transcultural Modernism and the Hungarian-Gypsy Tradition*. Rochester, NY: University of Rochester Press, 2011.

Loya, Shay. "The *Verbunkos* Idiom in Liszt's Music of the Future: Historical Issues of Reception and New Cultural and Analytical Perspectives." PhD diss., King's College, 2006.

Macfarren, G[eorge] A. *Musical History Briefly Narrated and Technically Discussed, with a Roll of the Names of Musicians and the Times and Places of their Births and Deaths*. Edinburgh, UK: Adam and Charles Black, 1885.

Mackendrick, Karmen. "Embodying Transgression." In *Of the Presence of the Body: Essays on Dance and Performance Theory*, edited by André Lepecki, 140–56. Middletown, CT: Wesleyan University Press, 2004.

Marston, Nicholas. "'The most significant musical question of the day': Schumann's Music in Britain in the Later Nineteenth Century." In *Robert und Clara Schuman und die nationalen Musikkulturen des 19. Jahrhunderts: Bericht über das 7. Internationales Schumann-Symposium am 20. und 21. Juni 2000 im Rahmen des 7. Schumann-Festes, Düsseldorf*, edited by Matthias Wendt, 153–65. Düsseldorf, Mainz: Schott Musik International, 2005.

Marston, Nicholas. "Schumann's Heroes: Schubert, Beethoven, Bach." In *The Cambridge Companion to Schumann*, edited by Beate Perrey, 48–61. Cambridge: Cambridge University Press, 2007.

Martin-Plesske, Hans. "Robert und Clara im Roman und in der Novelle." *Sammelbände der Robert-Schumann-Gesellschaft* 2 (1967): 87–98.

Maxwell, Ian. "'Thou That Hast Been in England Many a Year': The British Joachim." In *The Creative Worlds of Joseph Joachim*, edited by Valerie Woodring Goertzen and Robert Whitehouse Eshbach, 104–17. Woodbridge, UK: Boydell Press, 2021.

Mayes, Catherine. "Turkish and Hungarian-Gypsy Styles." In *The Oxford Handbook of Topic Theory*, edited by Danuta Mirka, 214–37. New York: Oxford University Press, 2014.

McCorkle, Margit L. *Robert Schumann: Thematisch-Bibliographisches Werkverzeichnis.* Munich: G. Henle Verlag, 2003.

Morris, Gay. *Game for Dancers: Performing Modernism in the Postwar Years, 1945–1960.* Middletown, CT: Wesleyan University Press, 2006.

Musgrave, Michael. "Joachim at the Crystal Palace." In *The Creative Worlds of Joseph Joachim*, edited by Valerie Woodring Goertzen and Robert Whitehouse Eshbach, 118–28. Woodbridge, UK: Boydell Press, 2021.

Musgrave, Michael. *The Musical Life of the Crystal Palace.* Cambridge and New York: Cambridge University Press, 1995.

Musgrave, Michael, ed. *George Grove: Music and Victorian Culture.* Basingstoke, UK: Macmillan, 2003; New York: Palgrave Macmillan, 2003.

Muxfeldt, Kristina. *Vanishing Sensibilities: Schubert, Beethoven, Schumann.* Oxford and New York: Oxford University Press, 2012.

Newcomb, Anthony. "Schumann and Late Eighteenth-Century Narrative Strategies." *19th-Century Music* 11 (1987): 164–74.

Newcomb, Anthony. "Schumann and the Marketplace: From Butterflies to Hausmusik." In *Nineteenth-Century Piano Music*, edited by R. Larry Todd, 258–315. New York: Schirmer, 1990.

Oberhaus, Lars. "Spurensuche: Variationen zu Peter Härtlings Roman *Schumanns Schatten*." *Musik & Bildung: Praxis Musikunterricht* 36, no. 3 (2004): 10–19.

Ostwald, Peter. *Schumann: The Inner Voices of a Musical Genius.* Boston: Northeastern University Press, 1985.

Payk, Theo R. *Robert Schumann: Lebenslust und Leidenszeit.* Bonn: Bouvier Verlag, 2006.

Perrey, Beate Julia. *Schumann's Dichterliebe and Early Romantic Poetics: Fragmentation of Desire.* Cambridge: Cambridge University Press, 2002.

Pfatteicher, Philip H. *New Book of Festivals and Commemorations: A Proposed Common Calendar of Saints.* Minneapolis: Fortress Press, 2008.

Pinsker, Adam. "*Davidsbündlertänze*." *Ballet Review* 30, no. 3 (Fall 2002): 79–93.

Piotrowska, Anna G. *Gypsy Music in European Culture from the Late Eighteenth to the Early Twentieth Centuries.* Translated by Guy R. Torr. Boston: Northeastern University Press, 2013.

Plantinga, Leon. *Schumann as Critic.* New Haven, CT: Yale University Press, 1967.

Pohl, Richard. "Reminiscences of Robert Schumann (1878)." Translated by John Michael Cooper. In *Schumann and His World*, edited by R. Larry Todd, 233–67. Princeton, NJ: Princeton University Press, 1994.

Powell, John Wesley. *Report on the Exploration of the Colorado River of the West and Its Tributaries*, 1875; reprinted as *The Exploration of the Colorado River and Its Canyons.* New York: Penguin, 1987.

Reed, Trevor. "Sonic Sovereignty: Performing Hopi Authority in Öngtupqa." *Journal of the Society for American Music* 13 (2019): 508–30.

Reich, Nancy. *Clara Schumann: The Artist and the Woman.* Rev. ed. Ithaca, NY: Cornell University Press, 2001.

Reid, Charles. *The Music Monster: A Biography of James William Davison, Music Critic of* The Times *of London, 1846–78.* London: Quartet Books, 1984.

Reiman, Erika. *Schumann's Piano Cycles and the Novels of Jean Paul.* Rochester, NY: University of Rochester, 2004.

Reininghaus, Frieder. "Zwischen Historismus und Poesie: Über die Notwendigkeit umfassender Musikanalyse und ihre Erprobung an Klavierkammermusik von Felix Mendelssohn Bartholdy und Robert Schumann, (2. Teil)." *Zeitschrift für Musiktheorie* 4, no. 2 (1973): 22–29; and 5, no. 1 (1974): 34–44.

Ritterman, Janet. "'Gegensätze, Ecken und sharfe Kanten': Clara Schumanns Besuche in England, 1856–1888." In *Clara Schumann 1819–1896: Katalog zur Ausstellung*, edited by Ingrid Bodsch and Gerd Nauhaus, 234–61. Bonn: Bonn Stadtmuseum, 1996.

Ritterman, Janet. "Schumann and the English Critics: A Study in Nineteenth Century Musical Reception." In *Musical Dimensions: A Festschrift for Doreen Bridges*, edited by Martin Comte, 192–211. Melbourne: Australian Scholarly Publishing, 2009.

Roesner, Linda Correll. "The Chamber Music." In *The Cambridge Companion to Schumann*, edited by Beate Perrey, 123–47. Cambridge: Cambridge University Press, 2007.

Roesner, Linda Correll. "Schumann's 'Parallel' Forms." *19th-Century Music* 14 (1991): 265–78.

Roesner, Linda Correll. "Studies in Schumann Manuscripts: With Particular Reference to Sources Transmitting Instrumental Works in the Large Forms." PhD diss., New York University, 1973.

Roodnat, Joyce. "Ik heb niets tegen tranen/I've got nothing against tears [Interview with van Manen]." Translated by Nicoline Gatehouse. In *Hans van Manen: Fotos-Feiten-Meningen/ Hans van Manen: Photographs-Facts-Opinions*, edited by Marc Jonkers, Pieter Kottman, Jhim Lamoree, and Divera Stavenuiter, 13–30. Amsterdam: Nederlands Instituut voor de Dans, 1992.

Rosen, Charles. *The Romantic Generation*. Cambridge, MA: Harvard University Press, 1995.

Rosen, Charles. *Sonata Forms*. Rev. ed. New York: W. W. Norton, 1988.

Rosen, Lillie F. *Anthony Dowell*. Photographs by Anthony Crickmay. Dance Horizons Spotlight Series. [Brooklyn, NY]: Dance Horizons, 1976.

Roy, Sanjoy. "Step-by-Step Guide to Dance: Hans van Manen." *The Guardian*, May 4, 2011. Culture section. https://www.theguardian.com/stage/2011/may/04/hans-van-manen-dance. Accessed July 22, 2023.

Samson, Jim. "The Great Composer." In *The Cambridge History of Nineteenth-Century Music*, edited by Jim Samson, 259–84. Cambridge: Cambridge University Press, 2002.

Schaik, Eva van. *Hans van Manen: Leven & Werk*. Amsterdam: Arena, 1997.

Schmidt, Jochen. *Der Zeitgenosse als Klassiker: Über den holländischen Choreographen Hans van Manen*. Cologne: Ballett-Bühnen-Verlag, 1987.

Schumann, Clara, and Robert Schumann. *Briefedition*. Edited by the Robert-Schumann-Haus, Zwickau, the Institute für Musikwissenschaft der Hochschule für Musik Carl Marie von Weber, Dresden, and the Robert-Schumann-Forschungsstelle, Düsseldorf, with direction from Thomas Synofzik and Michael Heinemann. Cologne: Dohr, 2008–.

Schumann, Clara, and Robert Schumann. *The Complete Correspondence of Clara and Robert Schumann*. Edited by Eva Weissweiler with Susanna Ludwig. Translated by Hildegard Fritsch and Ronald L. Crawford. 3 vols. New York: Peter Lang, 1994–1996.

Schumann, Clara, and Robert Schumann. *Tagebücher*. 3 vols. Edited by Georg Eismann and Gerd Nauhaus. Leipzig: VEB Deutscher Verlag für Musik, 1971–1982.

Schumann, Robert. "Aufzeichnungen über Mendelssohn." In *Felix Mendelssohn Bartholdy*, edited by Heinz-Klaus Metzger und Rainer Riehn, 97–122. Musik-Konzepte series, vol. 14–15. Munich: Dieter Vollendorf, 1980.

Schumann, Robert. *Briefe, Neue Folge*. 2nd ed. Edited by F. Gustav Jansen. Leipzig: Breitkopf & Härtel, 1904.

Schumann, Robert. *Gesammelte Schriften über Musik und Musiker*. 5th ed. Edited by Martin Kreisig. 2 vols. Leipzig: Breitkopf & Härtel, 1914.

Schwarz, Werner. "Eine Musikerfreundschaft des 19. Jahrhunderts: Unveröffentlichte Briefe von Ferdinand David an Robert Schumann." In *Zum 70. Geburtstag von Joseph Müller-Blattau*, edited by Christoph-Hellmut Mahling, 282–303. Kassel: Bärenreiter, 1966.

Smallman, Basil. *The Piano Quartet and Quintet: Style, Structure, and Scoring.* Oxford: Clarendon Press, 1994.
Smith, Peter. "Harmonies Heard from Afar: Tonal Pairing, Formal Design, and Cyclical Integration in Schumann's A-minor Violin Sonata, op. 105." *Theory and Practice* 34 (2009): 47–86.
Smith, Peter. "Schumann's Continuous Expositions and the Classical Tradition." *Journal of Music Theory* 58 (2014): 25–56.
Smith, Peter. "Tonal Pairing and Monotonality in Instrumental Forms of Beethoven, Schubert, Schumann, and Brahms." *Music Theory Spectrum* 35 (2013): 77–102.
Spitta, Philipp. "Robert Schumann." In *A Dictionary of Music and Musicians*, edited by George Grove, vol. 3, 384–421. London: Macmillan, 1883.
Stefaniak, Alexander. *Becoming Clara Schumann: Performance Strategies and Aesthetics in the Culture of the Musical Canon.* Bloomington: Indiana University Press, 2021.
Stefaniak, Alexander. "Clara Schumann's Interiorities and the Cutting Edge of Popular Pianism." *Journal of the American Musicological Society* 70, no. 3 (Fall 2017): 697–765.
Stefaniak, Alexander. *Schumann's Virtuosity: Criticism, Composition, and Performance in Nineteenth-Century Germany.* Bloomington and Indianapolis: Indiana University Press, 2016.
Stoneley, Peter. *A Queer History of the Ballet.* London and New York: Routledge, 2007.
Stravinsky, Igor, and Robert Craft. *Themes and Episodes.* New York: Alfred A. Knopf, 1966.
Suurpää, Lauri. "The Undivided *Ursatz* and the Omission of the Tonic *Stufe* at the Beginning of the Recapitulation." *Journal of Schenkerian Studies* 1 (2005): 66–91.
Synofzik, Thomas. "Kunstreiche Verwebung der Viere: Zur Satztechnik in Schumanns Streichquartett op. 41/3." In *Das Streichquartett im Rheinland: Bericht über die Tagung der Arbeitsgemeinschaft für rheinische Musikgeschichte in Brauweiler Juni 2002*, edited by Robert von Zahn, Wolfram Ferber, and Klaus Pietschmann, 42–65. Kassel: Merseburger, 2005.
Talbot, Michael. *The Finale in Western Instrumental Music.* Oxford and New York: Oxford University Press, 2001.
Taylor, Benedict. *Mendelssohn, Time, and Memory: The Romantic Conception of Cyclic Form.* Cambridge: Cambridge University Press, 2011.
Taylor, Benedict. *Music, Subjectivity, and Schumann.* Cambridge and New York: Cambridge University Press, 2022.
Thomas, Helen, and Stacey Prickett, eds. *The Routledge Companion to Dance Studies.* London and New York: Routledge, 2020.
Thym, Jürgen. "Schumann in Brendel's *Neue Zeitschrift für Musik* from 1845 to 1856." In *Mendelssohn and Schumann: Essays on Their Music and Its Context*, edited by Jon W. Finson and R. Larry Todd, 21–36. Durham, NC: Duke University Press, 1984.
Todd, R. Larry. "The Chamber Music of Mendelssohn." In *Nineteenth-Century Chamber Music*, edited by Stephen Hefling, 170–207. New York: Schirmer; London: Prentice Hall, 1998.
Todd, R. Larry. "Familiar and Unfamiliar Aspects of Mendelssohn's Octet." In *Mendelssohn Essays*, 171–79. New York: Routledge, 2008.
Todd, R. Larry. *Mendelssohn: A Life in Music.* New York and Oxford: Oxford University Press, 2003.
Tovey, Donald Francis. *Essays in Musical Analysis.* 7 vols. London: Oxford University Press, 1944.
Tunbridge, Laura. "Deserted Chambers of the Mind (Schumann Memories)." In *Rethinking Schumann*, edited by Roe-Min Kok and Laura Tunbridge, 396–99. Oxford and New York: Oxford University Press, 2011.
Tunbridge, Laura. "Schumann as Manfred." *Musical Quarterly* 87 (Fall 2004): 546–69.
Tunbridge, Laura. *Schumann's Late Style.* 2007. Reprint, Cambridge: Cambridge University Press, 2009.
Verrier, Michelle. *Fantin-Latour.* New York: Harmony Books, 1978.
Vetter, Eddie. "Déja vu?" Liner notes to *Hans van Manen*, English translation, 10–15. DVD containing dances by and interviews with Hans van Manen, 2 discs. Performances by Het National Ballet and Nederlands Dans Theater. [Leipzig]: Arthaus Musik, 2007.

Vetter, Eddie. "Nooit te wijs om te leren. Een interview." In *Hans van Manen: Meer dan een halve eeuw dans*, edited by Bram van Baal, 7–30. Amsterdam and Antwerp: Arbeiderspers, 2007.
Wadsworth, Benjamin. "Directional Tonality in Schumann's Early Works." *Music Theory Online* 18 (December 2012): article 7.
Wagner, Richard. "Judaism in Music [1869 version]. In *Richard Wagner's Prose Works*, translated by William Ashton Ellis, vol. 3, *The Theatre*, 101–22. London: Routledge and Kegan Paul, 1894; reprint, New York: Broude Brothers, 1966.
Waldura, Markus. *Monomotivik, Sequenz und Sonatenform im Werk Robert Schumanns*. Saarbrücken: Saarbrücker Druckerei & Verlag, 1990.
Wasielewski, Josef W[ilhelm] von. *Robert Schumann: Eine Biographie*. Dresden: Verlagsbuchhandlung von Rudolf Kunze, 1858.
Weber, William. *The Great Transformation of Musical Taste: Concert Programming from Haydn to Brahms*. Cambridge and New York: Cambridge University Press, 2008.
Weber, William. "Musical Canons." In *The Oxford Handbook of Music and Intellectual Culture in the Nineteenth Century*, edited by Paul Watt, Sarah Collins, and Michael Allis, 319–42. New York: Oxford University Press, 2020.
Weichlein, Siegfried. "Bonifatius als politischer Heiliger im 19. und 20. Jahrhundert." In *Bonifatius: Vom angelsächsischen Missionar zum Apostel der Deutschen*, edited by Michael Imhof and Gregor K. Stasch, 219–34. Petersberg: Michael Imhof Verlag, 2004.
Weingartner, Felix. "On Schumann as Symphonist [1897; English translation from 1904]." In *Schumann and His World*, edited by R. Larry Todd, 375–84. Princeton, NJ: Princeton University Press, 1994.
Wyndham, Henry Saxe. *Arthur Seymour Sullivan: 1842–1900*. London: Kegan Paul, 1923.
Young, Percy M. *Tragic Muse: The Life and Works of Robert Schumann*. London: Hutchinson, 1957.

Index

For the benefit of digital users, indexed terms that span two pages (e.g., 52–53) may, on occasion, appear on only one of those pages.

Abraham, Gerald, 13–15
Athenaeum. See Chorley, Henry

Bach, Johann Sebastian, 1–2, 11, 16–17, 101, 163–64
Balanchine, George, 20, 106–12
Bashford, Christina, 145, 164–65, 176n.14
Beethoven, Ludwig van
   allusions to his music, 16–18, 34, 47–49, 90–93, 100
   in canon formation, 1–2, 8, 9–13, 14–15
   Cello Sonata in C Major, Op. 102, No. 1, 17–18, 47–49
   chamber works, 7–8, 9–10, 145, 165 (string quartets generally); 156–57, 175–76n.4, 180n.82 (other works)
   English reception, 145, 149, 155, 156–57, 163–64, 166, 168, 169, 171–72, 173
   late works, 9–10, 11–13, 171–72
   movement confusion, 48–49
   piano concertos, 16–17, 155
   piano sonatas, 9–10, 156–57, 178n.47
   piano trios, 10–11, 156–57
   String Quartet in E-flat Major, Op. 127, 17–18, 25n.30, 90–93, 100, 101
   String Quartet in A Minor, Op. 132, 47–48
   symphonies, 16–17, 47
Bellman, Jonathan, 34–35, 68n.32
Bennett, Joseph, 170–71, 174–75, 177–78n.36, 180n.91
Berlioz, Hector, 74–76, 104n.44, 145–46, 180n.94
Bledsoe, Robert, 171–72
Bohrer, Anton, 10–11
Boniface, St., 83–85
Brahms, Johannes, 8, 14–15, 25n.27, 157, 159–60, 183
Brendel, Franz, 11–13, 22–23, 142–43
Bryant, Stephen and SueJane, 183, 185
Buckingham Palace, 155

canon formation, 1–2, 8, 9–11, 142–75

Carner, Mosco, 13–14
Chacon, Raven, 183–84
chamber music (general)
   with piano part, 10–11
   social uses of, 8–9, 10–11
   string quartet genre and history, 7–10
Chappell, Arthur, 151–53, 154, 157–58, 159–60, 161–63, 167–68, 174–75. *See also* Popular Concerts.
Chissell, Joan, 13–14
Chopin, Frédéric, 2–3, 6–7, 10–11, 142, 178n.47
Chorley, Henry F.
   on Clara's performances/advocacy of Robert's music, 148, 155–57, 168–69
   as critic and book author, 142–43, 145–46
   defensive strategies in Schumann debate, 143–44, 171–72
   praise of Mendelssohn, 142–43, 145–46, 148
   on Schumann and New German School, 142–43, 148, 150, 171–72
   on Schumann's Leipzig chamber music, 145–46, 148 (string quartets); 145–46, 164–65 (piano quartet); 145–46, 154, 168–69, 172 (piano quintet)
   on Schumann's orchestral music, 145–46, 148, 155–56
   on Schumann's piano music, 145–46, 148, 155–56
   on unhealthy qualities of Schumann's music, 171
Clauss-Szarvady, Wilhelmine, 163–64
Colorado River (U.S.). *See* Grand Canyon
Cooper, Michael, 84–87
Crystal Palace (London), 150–51, 157–58, 159–60, 174–75

Dahlhaus, Carl, 8, 26–27n.60
dances/ballets inspired by Schumann, 20, 106–7
Dannreuther, Edward, 164–65
Darcy, Warren, 120–21
Daverio, John, 14–15, 47, 80–82, 89–93, 97, 120

David, Ferdinand, 4–6, 7–8, 145–46, 148–49
Davison, James W.
  Clara's performances/advocacy of Robert's music, 146, 155–57, 158, 163, 167–69, 173–75
  as critic of newspapers/journals, 142–43
  defensive strategies in Schumann debate, 167–70, 173–75
  John Ella, 144–45, 146–47, 149
  at odds with public opinion, 167, 171, 173–74
  Popular Concerts, 151–52, 154–55
  praise of Mendelssohn, 142–43, 145, 147, 148–50, 154, 165, 173–74, 175
  Schumann acolytes in England, 150–51, 154–55, 164–65, 169–71
  Schumann and New German School, 142–43, 148–50, 163, 172–73
  Schumann's chamber music, 149–50, 163 (general); 145, 146–47, 165 (piano quartet); 154, 163 (piano quintet); 147 (string quartets)
  Schumann's orchestral music, 149–50
  Schumann's piano music, 147
Dickinson, A. E. F., 120–21
"domestic string style," 8–9
Dorn, Heinrich, 6–7
Dowell, Anthony, 107–10, 134–35
Dvořák, Antonin, 8

Ella, John:
  Clara Schumann's association with, 155, 159
  founding, audience, and concerts of Musical Union, 142, 144–45, 146–47, 149, 150–51
  as perceived by John Davison, 146–47
  response to Schumann's piano quartet, 146–47, 164–65
Ellsworth, Therese, 151–53, 163–64

fantastic style, 17–18, 70–89
Fedarko, Kevin, 183–84
Finson, Jon, 14–15
formal cyclicism, 48–49, 55, 59–61
formalism (in dance), 20, 108–12
Four Schumann Pieces (ballet). *See* Van Manen, Hans
Friese, Robert, 70
fugal writing. *See* Schumann, Robert, contrapuntal writing

Gardner, John, 47–48, 120
gender protocols (and disruption thereof) in dance. *See* Van Manen, Hans
Glasstone, Richard, 112–14

Goethe, Johann Wolfgang von
  correspondence with Karl Friedrich Zelter, 86–87
  "Die erste Walpurgisnacht" (ballad), 19–20, 85–87, 88–89
  Faust, 19–20, 74–76, 77, 80–82, 85
  influence on Schumann, 19–20, 69–70, 74–76, 80–82, 87, 105n.62
  in relation to Felix Mendelssohn, 19–20, 77–78, 80–82, 85–87
Grand Canyon, 183–85
Grand Canyon Music Festival, 183–84
Grieg, Edvard, 2–3
Grosse, Karl, 83–84
Grove, George, 143–44, 150–51, 157, 169–71, 173–75, 178–79n.55. *See also* Crystal Palace
Gypsy stereotypes. *See verbunkos* idiom

Handel, Georg Frideric, 85
Haydn, Franz Joseph, 1–2, 8, 9–11, 145, 165, 166
Heisler, Wayne, 107–8
Heller, Stephen, 88–89
Hensel, Fanny Mendelssohn, 77–78, 86
Hepokoski, James, 120–21
Hetsch, Louis, 16–17
Hirschbach, Hermann, 9–10, 15–16
Hopi tribe (U.S.), 183–84, 187–88n.11
Hueffer, Francis, 178n.46, 180n.94
Hummel, Johann Nepomuk, 2–3
Hungarian-Roma music. *See verbunkos* idiom

Indigenous music making, 183–84, 187–88n.11

Jean Paul, 19–20, 69, 80–82, 89–93, 97–100
Jensen, Eric, 13–14
Joachim, Joseph, 25n.27, 154–55, 157–58, 160–61, 162–64, 174–75, 179n.57, 180–81n.104
Jordan, Stephanie, 133–34

Kerman, Joseph, 90–93
Klassen, Janina, 74–76, 179n.58
Koegler, Horst, 115–17
Koerner, David, 183, 185
Kohlhase, Hans, 21–22, 55, 90–93, 120
Kottman, Pieter, 116, 134
Krebs, Harald, 14–15, 94–96, 99

Lecerf, F. A., 2–3
Lester, Joel, 14–15
Leipzig, 1–2, 3–4, 11–13, 22, 83–84, 142–43
Liszt, Franz, 1, 22, 26n.54, 57, 74–76, 142–43, 171–72, 180n.94, 185–87

London, 21, 77–78, 80–82, 142–75
London Royal Ballet, 107–8, 134–35
Lott, Marie Sumner, 8–9, 10–11, 47
Löwenskiold, Hermann von, 87–88
Loya, Shay, 34–35, 57
Lunn, Henry C., 167, 170–71

Macfarren, George, 175, 177n.35
Mackendrick, Karmen, 132
Manns, August, 150–51, 157–58, 159–60, 169, 174–75
Marschner, Heinrich, 70–76, 79–80
Mayer, Carl, 29
medieval references, 70, 71–76, 83–86
Mendelssohn, Fanny. *See* Hensel, Fanny Mendelssohn
Mendelssohn, Felix
  allusions to his music, 16–18, 79–80
  compared to/contrasted with Schumann, 11–13, 17–18, 19–21, 22, 142–44, 145–46, 147–50, 153–54, 163, 170–71, 173–74, 175, 177n.26
  as dedicatee, 4–6, 147
  elfin style, 19–20, 76–80
  English travels/reception, 21, 77–78, 142–43, 145–46, 147–50, 153–54, 155–56, 163–64, 165, 166, 169, 170–71, 172, 173–74, 175
  Die erste Walpurgisnacht, Op. 60, 85–87
  historical consciousness of, 2–3, 11–13, 22, 142–44, 148, 163
  influence of Goethe, 19–20, 77–78, 80–82, 85–87
  Die Lorelei, 149–50
  Octet in E-flat Major, Op. 20, 17–18, 77–82, 85
  Overture to *A Midsummer Night's Dream*, Op. 21, 77, 78–80
  Piano Concerto in D Minor, Op. 40, 151–52
  piano sonatas, 2–3, 16–17
  piano trios, 10–11
  response to Schubert's *Divertissement à l'hongroise*, 35–36
  string quartets, 8, 145, 147, 165, 166
  symphonies, 77–78, 80–82, 177n.26
  Variations sérieuse, Op. 54, 151–52
  Wagnerian view of, 11–13, 142–43, 148–50, 172–73
Meyerbeer, Giacomo, 22, 172–73
Monday Popular Concerts. *See* Popular Concerts
Moscheles, Ignaz, 2–3
Mozart, Wolfgang Amadeus, 1–2, 8, 9–11, 16–17, 69, 145

Müller, Christian, 16–17
Musgrave, Michael, 150–51
"music visualization," 108–10
Musical Union (London). *See* Ella, John
Musical World. *See* Davison, John

Native American Composer Apprentice Project (NACAP), 183–84
Néruda, Wilma, 162–63
Neue Zeitschrift für Musik, 2–3, 11–13, 70, 142. *See also* Schumann, Robert, writings of
New German School, 1, 11–13, 21, 22–23, 142–43, 148–50, 153–54, 163, 171–72
New Philharmonic (London), 155–56
Newcomb, Anthony, 6, 14–15, 97
Noack, Hunter, 185
Nureyev, Rudolf, 108, 134

Paganini, Nicolò, 74–76
paganism, 83–87
Pauer, Ernst, 153–55, 163–64
People's Concert Society (London), 177n.35
Philharmonic Society (London), 150–51, 152, 155, 159
Piatti, Carlo Alfredo, 160–61, 162–63, 179n.65
Pixis, Johann, 10–11
Plantinga, Leon, 6–7, 8, 23n.9
Pohl, Richard, 13
Popular Concerts, 143–44, 151–55, 157–58, 159–69, 174–75. *See also* Chappell, Arthur
Powell, John Wesley, 183–84
Premsela, Benno, 114
Pressley, Hannah, 183
Publishers of music (19th-century), 4–6, 8–11, 102n.4, 151–52

Quartet Association (London), 147, 150–51, 153

Reed, Trevor, 183–84
Reich, Nancy, 74–77, 160–61
Reiman, Erika, 80–82, 97–98
Reissiger, Carl, 9, 10–11, 16–17
Re-Union des Arts society (London), 164–65
Richter, Johann Paul Friedrich. *See* Jean Paul
Ritterman, Janet, 142–43, 155–57
river-rafting trips (music themed), 183–87
Roberts, Kate, 163–64
Röckel, Edward, 144–45, 163–64
Roma. *See verbunkos* idiom
rondo form rethought. *See* Schumann, Robert.
Roy, Sanjoy, 110

scherzo form rethought. *See* Schumann, Robert

Schloesser, Adolph, 164–65
Schmidt, Jochen, 108
Schubert, Franz
    allusions to his music, 16–17, 18, 57–58
    Divertissement à l'Hongroise, Op. 54, 18, 35–36, 57–58
    other piano music, 2–3, 68n.33, 97
    piano trios, 10–11
    use of *verbunkos* idiom, 18, 34–36
Schumann, Clara Wieck
    1842 Bohemian trip, 61–63, 185–87
    as dedicatee, 4–6, 160–61
    English tours and reception, 21, 142, 143–44, 146–47, 148, 154–55, 165, 166–69, 174–75
    on Hungarian-Roma music, 34–35
    influence on other disciplines, 106–7
    and Joseph Joachim, 157–58, 160–61, 162–64, 174–75, 179n.57, 179n.65, 180–81n.104
    performances of Robert's chamber works with piano, 10–11, 21, 155–58, 160–65, 166–69, 174–75
    Quatre pièces caractéristiques, Op. 5 (including "Hexen-Tanz," Op. 5a), 74–77, 79–80
    in relation to piano trio genre (including her own Op. 17), 10–11, 70–71, 160–61
    Variations on a Theme of Robert Schumann, Op. 20, 178n.47
Schumann, Robert
    ambiguous tonality, 16, 18–19, 33–64 (Leipzig chamber works) 18–19, 29–33, 67n.30 (other works)
    bait-and-switch techniques, 17–18, 90–97
    ballets/dances set to his music, 20, 106–7
    blurring of structural seams, 20, 58–59, 99–100, 121–25, 127–32
    compared to/contrasted with Mendelssohn, 11–13, 17–18, 19–21, 142–44, 145–46, 147–50, 153–54, 163, 170–71, 173–74, 175, 177n.26
    compared to/contrasted with Wagner, 11–13, 21, 142–44, 148–50, 163, 171–73
    compositional histories, premieres, and first publications of Leipzig repertory, 3–6
    confusion of principal/secondary materials, 18–20, 80–82, 89–90, 96–98, 100
    contrapuntal writing, 11, 46–47, 55–57, 59–61, 82–83
    digressive effects, 18–20, 80–83, 87–88, 89–90, 97–98
    early chamber music attempts, 4–6
    early output and influence on Leipzig chamber works, 3–4, 6, 18–20, 29–34, 52–55, 69, 80–82, 89–90, 96–98, 133, 185–87
    English reception, 21, 142–75
    fade-out effects, 55, 99–100
    fantastic style/influences, 17–18, 69–89
    formal cyclicism, 55, 59–61
    formal hybridity, 16, 18–19, 20, 50–61, 90–100, 120–21, 133
    honorary doctorate, 2–3, 142
    influence on other disciplines, 20, 106–7
    intermezzo usage, 70, 80–85, 87–90
    literary influences, 3–4, 19–20 (general); 69–70, 74–76, 80–82, 87, 105n.62 (Goethe); 19–20, 69, 80–82, 89–93, 97–100 (Jean Paul)
    medieval references/influences, 70, 71–76, 83–86
    mental illness, 24n.14, 106
    metrical innovations, 14–15, 93–96
    mountain imagery, 61–64, 185–87
    musical allusions, 18–19, 71–74, 96–97 (to his own works); 16344749–18, 57–58, 70–80, 90–93, 100, 101–2 (to other composers); 9–10, 16–17 (generally)
    "parallel" forms, 18–19, 50–55
    Phrygian movement, 45, 46–47, 58–59
    plagal inflections, 55–61, 129–32
    rondo form innovations, 16, 33–34, 50–55, 57–59, 120–21, 123–24, 127–28
    sacred influences, 70, 82–87
    scherzo forms in overall output, 88–89
    scherzo-trio form rethought, 16, 17–19, 69–90
    slow introduction rethought, 36–40, 46–47, 90–102, 117–33
    sonata-form innovations, 16, 33–34, 36–37, 40–46, 67n.30, 89–90
    string quartet study, 7–8, 9–10
    structurally significant codas, 55–57, 59–61, 128–32
    stylistic change of early 1840s, 4–8
    symmetrical key structures, 45, 54–55, 56–57
    undermined or misplaced cadences, 18–19, 29–33, 36–37, 46–47, 58–59, 99–100, 124–25
    variation form/principles rethought, 16, 17–18, 69, 90–102, 117–21, 123–24, 127–28, 129–32
    verbunkos idiom recognition and usage, 18, 35–36, 44–46, 49, 52–54, 55–61, 63–64
    views on his stylistic development, 6, 11–20, 22

Schumann, Robert, musical works:
 Albumblätter, Op. 124, 96–97
 Andante und Variationen, Op. 46, 23–24n.13
 Arabeske, Op. 18, 175n.3
 Bunte Blätter, Op. 99, 106–7
 Carnaval, Op. 9, 29, 80–82, 97, 106–7, 140n.39, 140n.42, 148, 155–56
 Concert Etudes after Paganini, Op. 10, 28n.75
 Davidsbündlertänze, Op. 6, 29–33, 106–7, 140n.40
 Dichterliebe, Op. 48, 71–74
 Drei Romanzen, Op. 94, 160–61
 Etudes after Paganini, Op. 3, 28n.75
 Etudes symphoniques, Op. 13, 157–58
 Fantasie, Op. 17, 80–82, 89–90, 133, 140n.39, 140n.40
 Fantasiestücke, Op. 12, 29–33, 155–56
 Fantasiestücke, Op. 73, 67n.30, 157–58
 Faschingsschwank aus Wien, Op. 26, 80–82
 Frauenliebe und Leben, Op. 42, 106–7
 Fünf Stücke im Volkston, Op. 102, 160–61
 "Hirtenknabe" (1828 song), 29–33
 Humoreske, Op. 20, 80–82
 Impromptus, Op. 5, 97
 Intermezzi, Op. 4, 29–33, 80–82, 140n.41
 Introduction and Concert Allegro, Op. 134, 106–7
 Kinderszenen, Op. 15, 106–7
 Kreisleriana, Op. 16, 29, 80–82
 Lieder und Gesänge, Op. 127, 71–74
 Liederkreis, Op. 39, 103n.23
 Nachtstücke, Op. 23, 175n.3
 Novelletten, Op. 21, 68n.34, 80–82, 97, 140n.39, 140n.40
 overtures, 150–51
 Overture, Scherzo, and Finale, Op. 52, 104n.48, 149–50
 Papillons, Op. 2, 29, 97, 106–7, 140n.39
 Das Paradies und die Peri, Op. 50, 6, 103n.29, 150, 169–71, 172–73, 181–82n.122, 182n.127
 Phantasie for Violin and Orchestra, Op. 131, 65n.10
 Phantasiestücke, Op. 88, 23–24n.13, 160–61
 Piano Concerto in A Minor, Op. 54, 67n.30, 103n.23, 106–7, 150–51, 155–56, 157–58, 159–60, 170–71
 Piano Quartet in C Minor (incomplete), 4–6
 Piano Quartet in E-flat Major, Op. 47, 3–6, 11–13, 18–19, 21, 68n.33, 89–90, 142, 143–45, 157–58, 160–61, 164–68, 173–74
 Piano Quintet in E-flat Major, Op. 44, 3–6, 11–13, 18–19, 21, 22, 33–35, 36, 50–64, 106–7, 143–44, 153–54, 160–64, 168–69, 170–72, 173–74, 185–87
 Piano Sonata in F Minor, Op. 14, 104n.48
 Piano Sonata in F-sharp Minor, Op. 11, 52–54, 88–89, 133, 140n.39
 Piano Sonata in G Minor, Op. 22, 104n.48
 Piano Trio in D Minor, Op. 63, 104n.48, 160–61
 Piano Trio in F Major, Op. 80, 104n.48
 Piano Trio in G Minor, Op. 110, 88–89
 Spanisches Liederspiel, Op. 74, 103n.23
 Spanisches Liederspiel, Op. 138, 103n.23
 String Quartets, Op. 41 (general), 7–8, 9–10, 11–13, 143–44
 String Quartet in A Minor, Op. 41, No. 1, 3–6, 18–20, 33–35, 36–49, 63–64, 69–93, 97, 143–44, 147, 153, 157–58, 167, 173–74
 String Quartet in F Major, Op. 41, No. 2, 3–6, 67n.30, 69, 90–102, 104n.48, 173–74
 String Quartet in A Major, Op. 41, No. 3, 3–6, 18–19, 20, 52–54, 57, 107–12, 117–33, 152–53, 173–74, 182n.132, 183, 185–87
 Symphony No. 1 in B-flat Major, Op. 38, 6, 88–89, 150–51
 Symphony No. 2 in C Major, Op. 61, 88–89, 106–7, 150–51
 Symphony No. 3 in E-flat Major, Op. 97, 150–51
 Symphony No. 4 in D Minor, Op. 120, 6, 104n.48, 150–51
 Szenen aus Goethes Faust, WoO 3, 22, 74–76, 104n.46
 Variations on the *Sehnsuchtswalzer* by Franz Schubert, F24, 97
 Violin Sonata in A Minor, Op. 105, 67n.30, 104n.48
 Violin Sonata in A Minor, WoO 2, 103n.23
 Violin Sonata in D Minor, Op. 121, 88–89
 Waldszenen, Op. 82, 147
 "Zigeunerleben," from *Drei Gedichte*, Op. 29, No. 3, 65n.10, 65n.12
Schumann, Robert, writings of:
 1842 Bohemian trip, 61–63, 185–87
 1849 letter to Liszt, 22–23, 185–87
 Beethoven, 2–3, 7–8, 9–10, 13, 16–17, 90, 101
 chamber music with piano, 10–11
 domestic chamber music, 9–11
 English translations of, 142
 external influences in his music, 22
 fantastic style/composers of, 70–71, 74–76, 78–79
 frustration with subjective/objective binary, 13

Schumann, Robert, writings of (*cont.*)
  Goethe, 74–76, 87
  historical legacies, 1, 2–3, 7–8, 9–11, 13, 16–17, 22, 69
  importance of innovation, 1–3, 8, 9–10, 16–17, 22–23, 63–64, 69, 89–90, 100–2, 185–87
  Mendelssohn, 2–3, 8, 16–17, 35–36, 78–79, 87
  merits of score format, 4–6
  mountain imagery, 61–63, 185–87
  musical allusions, 16–17
  satisfaction with Leipzig repertory, 4–6, 9–10
  scherzos and slow movements, 69, 70, 87–89
  Schubert, 2–3, 35–36
  string quartet genre and history, 7–8, 9–10, 90
  tonal ambiguity, 29
  transitioning from small- to large-scale works, 6–7
  value of chamber composition, 4–7, 9–10
  value/limits of small-scale composition, 6–7
  variation form, 100–2
  verbunkos idiom/poetic qualities of, 35–36
  Walpurgisnacht, 74–76
Sheeley, Tom, 183–85
Sobolewski, Eduard, 172–73
sonata form rethought. *See* Schumann, Robert.
Spitta, Philipp, 70–71
Spohr, Louis, 8–9, 16–17, 74–76
St. Boniface. *See* Boniface
St. James's Hall. *See* Popular Concerts; *see also* Chappell, Arthur
St. Walpurgis. *See* Walpurgis
Stanford, Charles, 170–71
Stefaniak, Alexander, 1–2, 10–11, 14–15, 155
Stravinsky, Igor, 108–12
string quartet genre and history. *See* chamber music (general)
style hongrois. *See verbunkos* idiom

Taubert, Wilhelm, 74–76
Taylor, Benedict, 14–15, 104n.35
Taylor, Franklin, 163–64, 181–82n.122
Tetley, Glen, 115–16
Thym, Jürgen, 11–13
Todd, R. Larry, 77–78, 79–80, 85

Uhlig, Theodor, 142–43

Van Manen, Hans
  aesthetic principles, 108–10, 114–17
  and Anthony Dowell, 107–10, 134–35
  choreographic preservation, 134
  Four Schumann Pieces, 20, 107–14, 115, 116–35, 185–87

Grosse Fuge, 108, 114–15
influence of Balanchine/formalism, 20, 107, 108–12
and London Royal Ballet, 107–8, 134–35
Metaforen, 115–16
and Rudolf Nureyev, 108, 134
on Schumann's A-major quartet, 108, 133
Situation, 115–16
views on gender/sexuality and disruption of gender protocols in dance, 108, 110–17, 121–24, 125–27, 128–29, 132
Van Schaik, Eva, 112–14
variation form/principles rethought. *See* Schumann, Robert.
Veit, Wenzel Heinrich (Václav Jindřich), 8–9
verbunkos idiom (*style hongrois*)
  extra-musical associations, including Gypsy stereotypes, 18, 34–36, 52–54, 63–64, 185–87
  linked to formal experimentation, 18, 36, 44–46, 52–54, 58–59
  origins and associated genres, 34–35
  plagal motions in, 55–61
  traits of, 44, 52–54, 57, 58, 64–65n.5
Verhulst, Johann, 9, 16–17
Vroom, Jean Paul, 108–10

Wagner, Richard
  acolytes of, 11–13, 22–23, 142–43
  and England, 21, 142–44, 148–50, 171–73, 180n.94
  on Mendelssohn and Schumann, 11–13
Waldura, Markus, 14–15
Walpurgis, St., 84–85
Walpurgisnacht, 19–20, 74–76, 77–78, 79–82, 83–87
wanderer trope, 35–36, 44–45, 49, 52–54, 55–56, 61–64, 185–87
Wasielewski, Wilhelm Joseph von, 61, 63–64
water imagery, 2–4, 183–87
Weber, Carl Maria von, 2–3, 34–35
Weber, William, 1–2, 65n.11
Weichlein, Siegfried, 83–84
Weingartner, Felix, 13–15
Wieck, Clara. *See* Schumann, Clara Wieck
Wieck, Friedrich, 74–76
Witz. *See* Jean Paul

Young, Percy, 13–14

Zelter, Karl Friedrich, 86–87
Zimmermann, Agnes, 163–64